MW00941399

THE NARROW ROAD BETWEEN RELIGION AND THE RIVER

THE NARROW ROAD BETWEEN RELIGION AND THE RIVER

JAMES PATTERSON

To my beautiful
wife, Kim, my
traveling companion on
the narrow road.

PROLOGUE

Are you ready to take a journey? If your answer is yes, then I welcome you to join me on the adventure found within the pages of this book. No hiking boots, no walking stick, no backpack, no tent, no beef jerky, no sleeping bag, no bug repellant and no canteen are required. You will not get bug bites on this journey, nor sunburn, poison ivy, blisters, hypothermia, shin splints, heat stroke or even muddy. If you have never hiked a day in your life, have no fear. On this journey, the only thing you need to bring is an open mind and an open heart. So if you are ready, let's take the first step on what I hope will be a life-changing experience for you.

Using the culmination of my life experiences, I have attempted to write a book that will serve as the following:

* a life preserver for those fighting to stay afloat
* a road map for those who seem to have lost their direction
* a drink of water for those who are thirsty
* a light for those wandering in the dark
* a rope for those who find themselves trapped in a hole
* a can of food for those who are hungry
* a winter coat for those stranded in the cold
* a bandage for those who have been hurt
* a friend for those who find themselves alone

These experiences include

* growing up in New Cumberland, West Virginia, with a love of the outdoors;
* accepting the Lord's offer of salvation at the age of five;
* being coached in various sports throughout my school years;
* joining the navy at the age of seventeen and serving for five years;
* working two years aboard an aircraft carrier and two years in a naval hospital as a hospital corpsman;
* working three years as a nurse in several geriatric facilities;
* working fourteen-plus years as a physical therapist assistant in various fields, mainly geriatric facilities;
* serving for several years as an adult Sunday-school teacher at a church;
* helping to lead a young-adult ministry at a church;
* receiving several opportunities to speak at various churches;
* serving for several years as a youth director at a church; and
* serving as an elder for several years at a church.

The best way I can explain this book is that it is a series of analogies within an analogy. The basic story follows the incredible journey of Garrett, who at times is representative of me. This story line in itself is meant to be an analogy of a Christian's walk through the trials and tribulations of everyday life. As Garrett travels along the narrow road, he encounters a variety of experiences that one would encounter while hiking, yet each is an analogy used to demonstrate a biblical teaching.

In addition to the ongoing story of Garrett, throughout the book I use my experience teaching the Bible and interject commentary as well as Bible verses to elaborate on the analogies. My main purpose in this is twofold: first, to have readers begin to look at the events, big and small, in their own lives and find what valuable lessons can be extracted from them that will help them grow in their spiritual walk with the Lord; and, second, to begin to teach readers how to apply Bible verses to the experiences taking place in their lives, enabling the Holy Spirit to breathe wisdom into the reader through God's holy Word.

In writing this book, I am in no way trying to imply that I have figured it all out or that I have all the answers. Nothing could be further from the truth. But I have found that, at least for myself, I seem to gain a better understanding of biblical truths when analogies are applied to situations. This must be why Jesus, time and time again, used parables in His teachings. Something so profound is found within their simplicity. I therefore took this love of parables and began to reflect on my life experiences, trying to find a way that I could help others through the lessons I have learned over the years.

My idea to use the narrow road as an analogy came mainly through a passion for hiking shared by my wife and me. We often feel closer to God as we walk through the woods, surrounded by the beauty of His creativity. As we would travel up and down the hills, I began to think about how this act paralleled the Christian walk we were on with its own ups and downs—thus the initial idea for my book.

The next phase came from a class I had once taught as an adult Sunday-school teacher. As I prepared to discuss the narrow road spoken of in the Bible, I developed an analogy of the road that focused on there being two sides to a road. Most people tend to think of Christians being on the narrow road and non-Christians off it. It was then that I thought about another group of people. If Christians are on the road and those not professing to be Christians are off it, where does that leave the people who claim to be Christians but do not live what they profess? I am referring to the "whitewashed tombs" that Jesus spoke of—those who He said will hear the following words from Him: "Depart from me, for I never knew you!" With this I came up with the concept of having two distinct groups flanking the narrow road, each distinct from the other but both facing the same destiny. As a Christian walks down the narrow road, he or she can be led off the path by Satan in two ways: he or she can be drawn off to the right of the path by the temptation of the world, or he or she can be drawn off to the left of the path by the allure of hollow religion. Either way, they are off the path.

If you log on to www.narrowroadbetween.com, you will find a free PDF available for download that provides study questions that correspond to the pages of this book. These questions dissect passages from Garrett's journal, asking you to analyze and process the lines of the book. The questions range from interpreting the thoughts and motives of Garrett and the other characters to deciphering the hidden analogies within the Northern Lands and the Southern Lands to comparing the characters' journeys to your own Christian walk:

* Have you faced similar trials?
* Which character do you have more in common with?
* Do you currently reside in the Northern Lands or the Southern Lands?
* Have you ever become discouraged while traveling the narrow road?
* What are the reasons for our various experiences on this journey?

The challenge stems from not only reading about the narrow road but also putting yourself on it and elaborating on the various analogies and situations faced by Garrett.

The main reason I wrote this book is to take you to a deeper level spiritually by posing challenging questions and points for you to consider about the content of the book. Some questions are theological, some questions are debatable and some are personal, forcing you as the reader to walk down paths and travel around bends you may find uncomfortable, although this is not my initial intention. The main reason I pose these questions is to challenge you as a Christian to step out of your comfort zone, to look at your journey thus far and to ask yourself, "Am I on the right track? Are there areas I can improve in? Am I focused on reaching my destination? What does my Christian walk look like to those around me?"

Just as it's easier to sit back in a chair compared to hiking down a trail, so too is it easier to avoid asking ourselves the tough questions that need to be asked in order for us to find our areas of weakness and then address them so that we may become stronger and more effective witnesses for Christ. The chair may be easy, but it will never get us to where we want to be. And at the end of the day, spiritual growth will only come when we allow ourselves to become vulnerable by testing our faith and our character against the truth of God's word. This will bring to light our areas of strength as well as our areas of weakness.

This brings us back to the questions. As was mentioned, they were designed to bring forth such a challenge. I would ask that you as the reader be as honest and transparent as possible when answering, in order to gain a better understanding of who you are as a born-again believer. I also strongly encourage that this book be used within group settings in order to facilitate an interactive discussion about the various subjects and promote a higher level of spiritual growth. As each and every Christian has had his or her own unique set of circumstances, unique set of hurdles and unique path, there is much to be gained from sharing our experiences within a small group setting of fellow believers who can be trusted to listen to us with understanding and respond in God's love.

Thus, we have *The Narrow Road between Religion and the River*. My prayer is that through the reading of this book, you will be able to gain a new perspective on life and a closer walk with Jesus. Pay close attention to all that is around you, make sure your shoes are tied, grab some beef jerky, stretch your legs, fill your canteen and roll up your sleeping bag. We're going hiking!

So without further ado, let's hit the road!

James Patterson
2013

Day 1

Through closed eyes, I feel the warm tears streaming down my face. I feel the wetness from the morning dew on my knees as I kneel on the ground. I tremble as I weep uncontrollably from my brokenness. I hear running water before me as of a raging river, my senses flooded by these new and unfamiliar sensations. Slowly, I open my watery eyes, look out before me and see a sight that makes me both tremble and leap with excitement. As I kneel at the banks of this mighty river, spanning this great divide is a bridge.

PREVIOUS TO THIS...

I've always been aware of the existence of the great river. I was even aware of the fact that bridges that crossed the river existed, despite having never seen one. The truth is that I had never had a reason to venture close enough to the river to see if they really existed. Yet here I am kneeling before the entrance of one. What made today so different?

Up to this point, I had lived my entire life on this side of the river. The majority of my friends and family resided here as well. For years, I had been content living here as I always had. The going was easy, for the most part. I went where I wanted to go and when I wanted to go. Life here was enjoyable and carefree. "Live for today" had been my favorite motto to live by. I tried to find enjoyment as often as I could, through whatever means I could. We can't live forever, so I figured I might as well enjoy life while I could.

I had always considered myself a good person overall. Compared to those who live farther away from the river, I saw myself as a saint. I had never murdered anyone. I had never robbed a bank. I had never even stolen as much as a piece of gum. I worked forty hours a week. I paid my taxes. I had even been a Boy Scout. I believed that after I passed on from this life, I should at least fall into the top third of the reward list for good behavior. Life was rolling along just fine, and then came the day when I met the man across the river.

Maybe I should explain the geography of my surroundings a little better. The land in which I reside is a vast expanse. All along its entire northern border runs a huge, raging river, flowing from west to east, thus giving us the obvious name of the Southern Lands. The river lies deep within a vast canyon with sheer walls on either side. In addition to the sheer walls, the river itself is a raging beast, pulling anyone and anything that should fall into its grip to a watery death. Most people in the land reside generally near the river. The terrain is flat and easygoing, making for easy traveling along its paths. The people living closest to the river generally tend to be like myself. They don't break any serious laws, and they don't try to cause any trouble.

For the most part, they are good people and good citizens. We consider ourselves to be moral, although we kind of leave the definition of morality up to each person to determine, not wanting to be judgmental of each other. Some areas of morality are enforced by law, those that over the years we have by consensus agreed on. Earlier I mentioned a few of these, such as murder and stealing. Other laws exist, such as destruction of property, assault, fraud and various others. We in the northern region of the Southern Lands generally accept these limitations, as we consider that most unlawful offenses pertain to acts that harm others. Those of us who abide by the laws are considered as good and righteous people. We live our lives believing that as long as we don't break the rules and behave as good people overall, we will surely have some kind of reward waiting for us after this life.

As one travels south, away from the river, it is not surprising to find the enforcement of the laws less common and the view of morality a more liberal one. The farther south one travels, the greater the chance of seeing such things as drug use, prostitution, alcohol abuse, robbery, sexual perversions and numerous other self-gratifying behaviors. Those of us in the northern part of the Southern Lands do frequent this region often, but we tend to not stay there permanently, not so much out of conviction but rather to protect our image as good citizens. Because the line between views of morality is so vague, it is difficult to judge anyone's behavior without being labeled hypocritical. Somehow, visiting the southern region and partaking in its pleasures rather than living there permanently gives us a sense of moral justification. The general thought is that at the end of the day, as long as we have more good deeds than bad deeds stacked up, we will be rewarded.

As to the other direction, as I mentioned earlier, there is a great river along the north. But on the other side of the river is another land that is also inhabited by people and generally referred to as, obviously, the Northern Lands. In fact, the people living on that side all began their lives in the Southern Lands. It seems perplexing at first as to how they reached that side, given the vast expanse and raging river as a barrier. But the general knowledge is that there are bridges at various locations that allow them to cross the river. I've never seen one of these bridges myself, but it's obvious that they exist. The truth is that I've never really looked for one because I've never had a reason to. I'm content living on this side of the river. The lay of the land across the river is not very accommodating. There are hills and valleys the people have to walk, unlike the level plains of this side. In addition, winding throughout the land is a narrow road they must travel. But the biggest reason that those from this side do not generally desire to visit the other side is because of the people who live there.

First, they find it necessary to strap themselves with an unrealistic view of morality. They live with extremely high expectations of self-discipline. They deprive themselves of the most basic physical pleasures, such as refraining from sex until marriage. They deny themselves the use of alcohol and recreational drugs. They frown on cursing and coarse language. They are the living definition of the term killjoy.

Second, they choose to travel such difficult terrain needlessly. They leave the comfort of the Southern Lands and spend the remainder of their days walking a narrow and difficult road. It is beyond my understanding as to why any sane and competent person would willingly choose to endure such suffering needlessly.

Finally, and most irritating of all, they spend their lives trying to draw people from this side to their side. They try to convict us for our behavior and tell us that we need to follow the narrow path on their side of the river. They claim to possess the road map to the true way through life. They even go so far as to say that if we do not cross to their side, we will face eternal punishment once we die. In my opinion, their minds are about as narrow as the roads they walk.

This was my point of view until recently. As I mentioned earlier, several days ago I had an experience that forced me for the first time in my life to reassess everything that I held true with regard to my beliefs and human understanding. For the past seven years, I have been employed by a great company. I enjoyed the people I worked with, the hours were great, I had my own company car, I recently received promotion, and I even went on the occasional business trip, which always ended up being more like a paid vacation. Life was good. Then one Monday morning, I arrived to work as usual, and instead of my morning cup of coffee waiting for me on my desk, I found a pink slip. It seems that the economy had taken a turn for the worse, and the company felt that the first place to trim the fat was from the executive office. I spent the rest of the day in a fog, my mind racing in a million directions. My mood drifted between despair, anger, hopelessness, anxiousness and numbness. At one point, I finally turned my attention to God and not in a very favorable way. I thought, "Why would God do this to me? Why would God allow this to happen to me? I am a good person; things like this aren't supposed to happen to people like me. Why is He picking on me?" It was not as though I spoke to God on any kind of regular basis. We just kind of had an understanding, I guess: I would live my life being aware that He existed, and He would make sure that everything went the way I wanted. It always seemed to work for me when things flowed smoothly. But when faced with situations like losing my job, He then got the full brunt of my wrath.

As my emotions wreaked havoc inside my mind, I found myself wandering farther and farther from my normal paths. I had tuned out the sights and sounds of the world around me as I engaged in a mental battle with God. Suddenly, I became aware of an unusual sound, which brought me out of my trancelike state. It was the sound of rushing water from the great northern river. I was standing at its banks. For the first time in my life, I was close to the great and mighty waterway.

As I stood at the edge of the high cliff, I looked down at the roaring river. Its awesome power was enough to make me temporarily forget my inner struggle with God. Gazing on it was both beautiful and terrifying.

Soon the events of earlier that day came flowing back into my mind once again. I began to wonder what I had left to live for. My lifestyle had grown to match my salary, and now I could no longer maintain it. For several minutes, I envisioned leaping into this mighty chasm and into the torrent below. At least it would be a quick death, I thought. I tried to think how life would go on without me, as I did not have my own personal "Clarence the angel" to play my life out for me to see. The waters below held me in a trance, and I found myself leaning farther and farther forward as I peered into it until the sound of a voice snapped me out of it and brought me back to reality.

At first I was shaken, asking myself, "Did God just audibly speak to me?" As I brought my gaze up and looked straight ahead, I saw standing on the land across the river a man staring at me. It was an unnerving sight because I had believed I was alone up to that point. He looked to be a slightly older gentleman, dressed in simple but definitely worn attire and leaning on a staff. He called out to me, "Hello there!" He had to speak loud enough for me to hear over the sound of the water, but other than that he didn't seem too far away from me compared to the average distance between our two lands.

"Yes," I answered. "Can I help you?" I was somewhat frustrated at the interruption of my private moment of self-pity.

"I don't remember seeing you here before," he called out. "Was there something you were looking for that I can help you with?"

Several seconds passed as the reality of the situation sank in and I could focus my thoughts again. I blurted out to the gentleman, "Not unless you have seen a job lying around; if not, then I guess there's nothing for you to help me with." After speaking the words, I realized their callousness, but my bitterness overrode any chance of my apologizing for my tone. In spite of my rudeness, he appeared more saddened by my statement than offended.

"I'm sorry, my friend," he replied. "I have not seen a job lying along these banks, but I do sympathize with you, if it is any consolation. I have been in your situation myself, and I can remember the pain and frustration associated with it."

A small part of me felt a twinge of comfort from his words, but the rest of me was still fueled by the newness of the hurt and did not want to let it go yet. Besides, this person was from across the river. Like I have any interest in what he has to say. Deep down, he was probably gloating at the fact that I was hurting, feeling like he was better than me anyway. Why was he even wasting his time talking to me? Why was I even wasting my time talking to him?

"You have been in my situation, you say? My friend, you don't know a thing about my situation! I'm sorry—were you an executive once who got thrown out in the cold? Were you making a six-digit salary and then had the carpet pulled out from under your feet? Unless you have experienced either of those situations, you have never been in my situation, and I would appreciate it if you would keep your self-righteous sympathies to yourself!" I stood, trembling after releasing my verbal assault on the man. In a way, I felt better after releasing some of my frustrations through the words that came out of my mouth. To be honest, I was a little shocked and embarrassed for having the audacity to speak to a total stranger in that fashion. I looked across at the man, expecting him to be turning red in anger for the way I had just spoken to him. But to my surprise, his demeanor had not changed at all. If anything, he looked more sympathetic than he had before I shouted at him.

Suddenly, he started speaking, as if the tantrum I had just thrown did not even happen. "When I said I have been where you have been, I should have been a little more specific. You are correct in saying that I have never been an executive or had a high-paying salary. In fact, I was just an average blue-collar worker, living across the river as you do now. Despite my modest income, I was a relatively happy man. I had a wife and a daughter who were my reason for waking up every morning and going to work. No matter how bad of a day I had, I knew that I could come home to the two ladies of my life, and my trivial stressors from work would soon melt away. I was a good father and a good husband, providing for my family's needs and most of their wants. Yet my one vice that I couldn't seem to shake was my desire for alcohol. I was what you would consider a 'social drinker.' I never staggered in the door at two o'clock in the morning, drunk from an all-night binge. I never went to work intoxicated or had it interfere with my job. In fact, I was the life of the party at any social gathering. I had a pretty decent tolerance for drinking, so I never showed any effects of the alcohol when around other people.

"One night, the three of us were returning home from a cookout at a co-worker's house. It had been a great party, with plenty of food, fun and alcohol. The evening was finally brought to an end by a sudden rainstorm of all things. With the bad weather, everyone decided to call it a night. As I drove the three of us home that night, the main thing I can remember is the torrential sheets of rain that hammered the windshield, making visibility nearly impossible. But we only lived four miles away, and I had driven this road a thousand times before. Besides, we were all wet and anxious to get out of our damp clothes, and our daughter was asleep in the backseat. I had the heater on full blast to warm us from our run-in with the rain. When we were about two miles from our house, all I could think about was getting dry and crawling into a warm bed for the night. The only problem was, my body decided to fall asleep before I got into my bed.

"From what I have pieced together from witnesses, I drove straight into an intersection through a red light and into oncoming traffic. My car plowed straight into the side of a small truck, driven by a teenage boy who was coming home from his part-time job. He was killed immediately on impact from what the coroner stated. My life was spared, oddly enough, by my steering wheel. Even though I had serious chest injuries from the impact with it, it kept me from flying through my windshield and most likely saved my life. My wife was not so lucky. Since neither one of us were wearing seatbelts and she did not have a steering wheel on her side as I did, she did fly through the windshield and was pronounced dead at the scene. My daughter had been sleeping on the backseat and was not buckled in either. She was rushed to the hospital but died just six hours later from severe internal injuries. I awoke ten hours after the accident and found myself in a hospital bed. When I learned what had taken place and what I had done, they had to sedate me to keep me from destroying my room and taking my own life.

"A week later, I was out of the hospital with no significant injuries, a bruised chest and no reason to live. Not only did I have to carry the shame of killing somebody's teenage son, but I also had to live with the fact that I had killed my own wife of eight years and my five-year-old daughter. With all the negative publicity from the accident, the company I worked for found a convenient excuse to let me go so as to not be the employer of a vehicular butcher. In one week's time, I had lost my job, my wife, my daughter and any reason to continue living.

"One night, the pressure was more than I could bear, and I found myself returning to an old and reliable friend, the one who lived inside a bottle. With about two-thirds of a bottle of whiskey in my stomach, I started walking aimlessly into the evening and found myself, as I assume you did, at the same river's edge. Gazing down into the dark valley and the raging rapids below, I had concluded that one last flying leap would be my penance to pay for all the destruction I had done.

"Just as I started to take a step toward the edge, I heard a voice, as you did, from this side of the river. I looked across to see a man, as you did, calling out to me. It was comforting to hear a voice at that moment, one that didn't have an undertone of disdain for me. Obviously, he must not have heard about what I had done because he lived across the river. He began speaking to me ever so gently, and his kindness brought tears to my eyes. Before long, I was pouring my heart out to him, explaining everything I had done and what I was planning on doing. But rather than judge me and look at me with disgust, he spoke to me about finding true peace and meaning for my life, even with everything I had done. I was skeptical at first, wanting to believe it but afraid it was too good to be true. After talking for quite a while, he finally convinced me that what he spoke of was true. I felt a peace in my soul that I had never experienced up to that point, even before the accident. He told me that I could leave my old life behind and find peace along the narrow road on the opposite shore. All that was required was for me to recognize my helpless state as a sinner, which I had no problem doing at that point, and ask Jesus to come into my life and save me from my sins. I fell to my face and wept as I had never done before. The mountain of shame and guilt that I was carrying seemed to be released from me through my tears.

"I stood up and faced the river. I grabbed the bottle and threw it into the valley before me. As I watched it fall on its downward journey, my peripheral vision caught sight of something out of the corner of my eye. I turned to the right and spanning across the river was a bridge that had not been there before. I wondered at first if this was a product of my drinking, but the man across the river motioned for me to walk across. As I stepped to the opening of the bridge, I turned to look behind me one last time and knew from that point on, I no longer belonged to that world. That was my old life, and it no longer had anything to offer me. I turned back toward the bridge and took a step of faith, followed by another and then another. Before I knew it, I was standing on the opposite shore, looking across at where I had previously been standing. Strangely, it looked so much different from this side of the river. I wasn't sure where I was going next; all I knew was that wherever it was, God was going to be in control of it, and that was enough for me. And let me tell you, it still is."

If a leaf had fallen out of the tree above me at that point, I think I would have been knocked to the ground. I stood speechless, staring at the man, tears streaming down my face. Suddenly, my life-shattering crisis seemed like a puddle of spilled milk in comparison to the tsunami this man had been drowning in all these years. My demeanor had changed from one of arrogance and self-pity to one of brokenness and shame. I dropped my head into my hands and openly wept as I had never wept before. All the hurts and frustrations I had been allowing to smolder within me were extinguished as when water is dumped on a flame. I said to the man, "I want to know this peace you talk about, but I don't know how to get it."

"That is fine," he said. "I will explain it to you. The world in which you live now is the world directed by your sinful nature. We are all placed in that world once we come to an age of accountability because we are born with a sinful nature from birth. From that point, we must make a decision and choose to continue being led by our sinful nature and live on the side of the river that you stand on now or repent from our sins and give our lives over to Jesus. He is the only way we can have true salvation and an eternal hope for our soul after this life. Jesus paid the price for our sin when He died for us on the cross after living a perfect life as a man here on earth. He paid the price so we wouldn't have to, not out of obligation, but because He loves us that much, not just the 'good' people but also any who call on His name, including drunks who commit vehicular homicide. It seems hard to understand that kind of love, but then again, we are not God. We are only commanded to trust in Him and His word, and we will be born again, adopted as heirs into His kingdom.

"I had trouble at first accepting it myself because I didn't feel worthy. But over time, He worked on my heart and reassured me that His promise was for me as well. You are only one prayer away from handing over your hurts to the Creator of the universe and being adopted as a child of God. I'm not going to try to sugarcoat *it for you. Life on this side of the river is not an easy one. As you can see, we follow a narrow road, and there are many hills and valleys to cover. It will not be like the easy paths you are used to. But you will be able to walk knowing that you have a future in store for you whenever your path finally ends.*

"The world you live in may offer pleasures for a season, but its paths all end in the same place, a place that was not initially designed for humans to reside in. But through our stubbornness and pride, as we reject Christ's sacrifice for us, we ultimately condemn ourselves to the same eternal punishment that's awaiting Satan and his demons, the lake of fire. But to those of us who choose to accept Jesus's gift of salvation, we have heaven to look forward to for eternity. We will be reunited with those who have gone before us, like my wife and daughter, and never again have to shed a single tear and never again be separated by death. You mentioned earlier that you were used to making a large salary and had obtained a high position. You obviously have acquired a taste for the good things in life. I'd like to ask you one question if I could. If you were to go back to your old lifestyle again and everything from this point on went as you hoped, what would you profit if you gained the whole world and forfeited your soul?"

Everything he said hit me in a void that I wasn't even aware that I had. I had tried for so long to not think beyond the moment that looking into my future from my present life, I was as fearful as I was looking into the deep, dark valley that lay before me. My heart pounded as if it were coming out of my chest. I didn't have all the answers, but I did know one thing: I needed Jesus to come into my life and give my life meaning. I was tired of taking the easy road. I knew I wanted more for my life, a sense of purpose beyond my job and my simple pleasures. Things had always come easy, but I found no satisfaction or fulfillment in them. They were only shallow victories that left me feeling hollow. All my happiness and self-worth had been wrapped up in them. As soon as the material things were taken away, so was my fulfillment. Deep down, I knew I wanted my contentment to be, not placed in possessions or positions but, rather, in something bigger than me, or the world for that matter. I wanted to find contentment in the peace that the man described, that comes from trusting in Jesus.

I collapsed to my knees and cried out to God, this time in humbleness and brokenness rather than in pride and arrogance as I had earlier. I asked Jesus to forgive me for all the foolish things I had said and done. I told Him that I didn't think I had anything to offer Him but that I would be honored to serve Him if He would have me. I prayed that He would come into my life and direct me from that day forward. I was not sure how long I knelt there, but once again I was brought back to reality by the sound of the rushing waves from below. I opened my eyes.

Day 1 (Continued)

I open my eyes and look before me to see, for the first time, a bridge spanning to the other side. I stare at it in amazement for several minutes. And then I look across at the far end of the bridge, only to see the gentleman motioning with his hand for me to come to the other side. As I stand and start to walk toward the bridge, like the old man had described doing himself, I look back one final time over my shoulder. I realize everything that I will be giving up from my old way of life. But I sense a feeling of contentment at my decision. The land behind me for the first time seems cold and dark. I have no desire to go back, only to cross the bridge.

As I turn back to the bridge, I approach the opening and look across to see the gentleman still there. Halfway across, I happen to look ahead and, sitting on one of the ropes of the bridge is a white dove that had not been there before. It is as if it is waiting for me. When I am almost near it, it spreads its wings and flies back toward the old man and rests in a tree, gently cooing as if it is pleased that I am coming toward it. I take the final step across the bridge and plant my foot on the path for the first time. It is the first step of many that I will be taking on that narrow road. And even though I know that the way is not going to be easy, for the first time in my life, I know that I am heading in the right direction.

To make a general breakdown of the preceding analogy, the Southern Lands represents the world or, more specifically, non-Christians. In the story, the land south of the river is described as flat and plain. This is meant to represent the lack of discipline and moral character found in the world. The land north of the river is described as hilly and containing a narrow road that runs through it. The narrow road obviously refers to the narrow way mentioned in *Matthew 7:13–14* that Christians are called to follow. The hills are meant to represent the spiritual discipline associated with living as a true Christian. The uphill walking is symbolic of the call for Christians to carry their crosses, as mentioned in *Luke 9:23* and *Hebrews 12:11–12.* The wide valley between the Northern and Southern Lands represents the spiritual gulf that lies between God and humankind. First, we are all born with a sinful nature, as shown in *Romans 3:23.* Second, God is holy and must punish sin, as mentioned in *Romans 6:23.* Third, we cannot enter heaven as sinners, as shown in *1 Corinthians 6:9.* Fourth, there is no forgiveness of sin without the shedding of blood, as seen in *Hebrews 9:22.*

So here we see our crisis. Everyone has sinned, God is holy and must punish sin, sin cannot enter into heaven and without the shedding of blood God cannot forgive sin. In this scenario, every man and woman born would have no chance of entering into heaven because of our sinful nature. But God is not only a "just" God; He is also a "loving" God. Because He is a loving God, He made a way for us to be with Him for all eternity. Unfortunately, this solution meant that He would have to send His one and only Son to die in our place. This would allow Him to remain a just God by punishing sin, even though He would have to punish His own Son in our place, who knew no sin, as seen in *2 Corinthians 5:21.*

Thus, through the crisis described, we see the symbolism for the great chasm of the river representative of humankind's spiritual separation from God because of our sinful nature. We also see how the bridge is symbolic of Christ and His sacrifice as the only way to connect sinful man to God and eternity in heaven. Without the bridge, we could not get to the Northern Lands, just as without Jesus, we could not be pure enough to get to heaven. This is also why only Christians will get to heaven, even though many in the world look on that statement as narrow-minded. But as we just saw, it took Jesus dying on the cross for us to be able to get to heaven. If there were any other way, then Jesus would have died for nothing. But the reality is, there was no other way, which is what makes His sacrifice all the more worthy to be praised, as we see in *John 3:3, 14–15.*

The bridge was not visible to Garrett at first. This is because he had initially approached the river as a member of the world. He was looking through human eyes at the river. It was only when he was brought to a state of brokenness and repentance and opened his heart to the Holy Spirit's calling that he was able to see the true way to salvation through godly wisdom. We are able to find this demonstrated in *1 Corinthians 2:10–14.*

The great river in the analogy represents perspective. As we draw close to the river, we are drawing closer to God's influence through those of us who are born again. We find that in times of crisis, many who do not have an ongoing relationship with God seem to find themselves in a position similar to those at the river's edge. They tune out God when all is going well, but when in a time of need, such as an illness or financial difficulty, they are put in a place where they have to change their way of looking at issues from the common worldly perspective to a spiritual perspective. For most people, as long as things are going smoothly, they have no real need to look to God for any guidance or relationship.

But when troubles arise that they can't control, they seem to run back to God, expecting Him to answer like a twenty-four hour on-call fix-it man. I believe God often allows adversity to settle on us when we become distracted by this world and tune out His calling in order to draw us and force us to look into the river of perspective. The fast-flowing river reminds us of how quickly life is passing by and how little time we really have in the great scheme of things.

From the banks of the riversides, Christians are given opportunities to witness to non-Christians. As those of us who are born again find non-Christians at the river's edge during times of struggle in their lives, we must make the most of these opportunities to witness to them and share the good news of salvation through Christ to them. This is when they are most open to what we have to say. This is where the Holy Spirit draws them through conviction of the heart. Many times they are not even sure why they are at the river's edge, but God has them there for a reason, and often that reason involves an opportunity to preach the gospel to a heart that the Holy Spirit has prepared for us. When we ignore these opportunities, we are not guaranteed a return visit by the person to the river. We may only get one chance sometimes before a person hardens his or her heart and tunes out the Holy Spirit's call to the river.

In the analogy, the description of the Southern Lands getting more sinful the farther south one travels represents the destructive nature of sin and the slippery slope sin takes you on the farther away you run from the Holy Spirit's calling. It represents the downward spiral of a person's moral compass as they fall deeper and deeper into sin's clutches. As illustrated in the story, God does not send people back across the river to witness to the Southern Lands. He brings those from the Southern Lands to the river, where the witnessing can occur. This is representative of the Christian staying on the narrow path and still being in a position to witness to those in the world as God directs; crossing back to the Southern Lands would be symbolic of a Christian leaving the narrow road and returning to "the world," which the scripture does not support. We obviously are still connected to people in the world, but the distinction the analogy tries to make is that one can witness to non-Christians from the narrow road (those seen across the river), but they are never called to compromise their religious convictions as an excuse to partake in the acts of those who do not know Christ (those in the southern regions of the Southern Lands). This would be the equivalent of going against the Holy Spirit's direction and relying on our human wisdom to try to accomplish a task for Christ in our own power.

The dove, obviously, represents the Holy Spirit, as we find in *Matthew 3:16.* As we will find throughout the story, the dove will guide the writer along the narrow road. The writer will soon discover that it is easy to lose sight of the dove because there are many distractions even along the narrow road. The old man across the river represents a fellow Christian traveler whose path has placed him in a position to witness to the writer at a time when it is most needed by him. That he was standing across the river at that exact moment is no coincidence. The dove led him there at that specific time and place. The old man could have chosen a different path that day because he is given free will as all do to choose his own course. But he was obedient to the Holy Spirit's calling and was able to be used by Him to win another soul for Christ's kingdom.

Day 2

I open my eyes this morning and wonder for the first waking moments if every-thing that had transpired yesterday was just a dream. This doubt is soon laid to rest as I look out and see before me a narrow road that winds on until it eventu-ally is hidden behind a bend. In my mind, I play back everything that was spoken yesterday, my words of bitterness, the old man's words of humility and hope and my final words of remorse and brokenness that brought me to where I am right now, standing on the opposite shore of the great river. I look out across the valley and see the land where I have lived my entire life up to this point. Everyone and everything I know lies across this great divide.

I start to question my decision briefly: "Did I make the right decision? I don't even really understand anything about Christianity and this way of life. How am I supposed to start a brand new life? Besides, why would God even want me? It's not like I have anything to really offer Him. What am I going to say to the people over here? They are probably going to wonder themselves why I am even here." I really hope I didn't bite off more than I can chew.

I look out across the river again. As I scan the distant landscape, I'm amazed at how a place I spent my entire life in can look so different from a changed point of view. For the first time in my life, I can look out and see the whole of my old stomping grounds in one glance. Before today, I had never had such an opportu-nity. As I mentioned earlier, the Southern Lands are generally flat, so I have never been able to see things from a perspective as I have now, separated and elevated from the entire area. My view on things had always been limited to what was right in front of me, which makes me wonder in hindsight if that is why I had never tried to look too far ahead when making decisions, thus my previous motto, "Live for today." But now from where I stand, my previous residence somehow has lost its luster. The places that I used to look on as impressive and inspiring now look small and unimpressive to me from the hillside I'm standing on.

Suddenly, a voice breaks my focus on the distant land and brings me back to reality. "Good morning, young man," I hear from beside me. I turn to see the old man from last night standing along the road. "It's quite a view from here, isn't it?" he asks.

"Yes, it is," I reply. "I have never viewed the Southern Lands from this angle. From here, they seem so much smaller, so disappointing to be honest."

"Very true," he replies. "I believe introductions are in order, as last night did not give much of an opportunity. When you came across the bridge yesterday, you were pretty emotionally spent. As you probably remember, after I sat and prayed with you, you went to rest beside the road and wept until you fell asleep. But now that you are awake, you seem like a new man, refreshed and much less burdened than when I saw you across the river last night. Let me introduce myself. My name is Clarence."

I chuckle before I catch myself. I may not know a lot about God, but at least He has a good sense of humor, I guess. He sent me my very own Clarence the angel. "Nice to meet you, Clarence; my name is Garrett. I never got a chance to say it last night, but thank you for everything you did. Your story moved me more than words can tell. I came to the river feeling sorry for myself, and my troubles ended up looking like a hill of beans compared to what you had to endure. Now thanks to you, for the first time in my life, I feel like I have a definite game plan."

"You are most welcome," Clarence says, "and I'm glad that God put me in a position to be able to help you in your time of need. As to your problem compared to mine, that is the beauty of standing before the river of perspective. Typically, our carnal nature forces us to see and experience life through self-gratifying lenses. It has us focus on our own wants and needs rather than on those of others. This produces a very selfish and shallow view of the world. But when the Holy Spirit leads us to the river, we are forced to look at our lives in a more meaningful way.

"The constant flowing of the river reminds us of the steady and uninterrupted movement of time and of how little of it a lifetime actually contains. The awesome force of the raging rapids reminds us of how small we are in the big scheme of things and how big God's power truly is. The great divide from one side of the river to the other reminds us how hopeless our situation is as humans without God's influence in our lives. We look across to the distant shore and see the path that God desires for us to travel. The river brings believers and nonbelievers alike to a place where they are forced to snap out of their day-to-day tunnel vision regarding what are most often trivial concerns and worries and look at the world from a godly perspective.

"Those from the Southern Lands come to the river as you and I did, which allows those of us who are born again to witness to them. Usually, it is not by choice that they come. Most, as in our case, are lead here during a time of crisis by the Holy Spirit. Some wander here after finding their life in the Southern Lands unfulfilling and lacking. They are not exactly sure what is missing in their life, but they recognize that something is. This is not a guarantee that the person will always make a decision for Christ. Unfortunately, even though many who stand here momentarily are able to see their lives from a true perspective for the first time, they lack the discipline to make the decision to cross as you did.

"As for those of us on this side, the river also provides an opportunity to share the message of salvation to a lost and dying world. It reminds us of where we came from and helps keep us from losing sight of our mission as we travel the narrow road, which is to bring as many to salvation as possible. One of the benefits of being on this side of the river is that we are given a perspective of the world through the power of the Holy Spirit that the world is not privy to. This is not because we are superior to those in the Southern Lands by any means because we ourselves once came from there as well. It is because the very geography of our land allows us to look out to the south from an elevated standpoint and see 'the big picture.' It's no different from the view an astronaut has of the Earth from outer space. From above, removed from the chaos and commotion of the activity taking place below, they can witness the entire planet as one large, revolving sphere. But from our standpoint on Earth, we are only able to see a small fraction of the same Earth the astronaut is observing, our view being limited because of our position on the

Earth's surface. The gift of this perspective is an additional blessing that comes with walking the narrow road."

The perspective that Clarence speaks of refers to spiritual wisdom that comes from being filled with the Holy Spirit. The reference to the geography being more elevated than that of the southern region first has to do with the fact that worldly wisdom pales in comparison to godly wisdom. We find this expanded on in *1 Corinthians 3:18–20* and *1 Corinthians 1:18–30.* As is demonstrated in the verses, worldly wisdom falls short of godly wisdom. Worldly wisdom could not even recognize Jesus as He came to earth and walked among men. But to those who believe on His name, the Holy Spirit fills and gives godly wisdom rather than worldly wisdom. The world sees godly wisdom as foolishness, thus we correlate those on the narrow road with standing on higher ground as in the story. The Bible further speaks of godly wisdom in *1 Corinthians 2:10–16.*

As Christians, we are given a "moral high ground" from which to observe the world and use godly discernment. This is not a gift that is given to Christians for the use of judging the world but that those in the world might be saved through it. As Christians, we may still live *in* the world, but we are called to separate ourselves *from* the world, as seen in *John 15:18–19* and *Romans 12:2.* We find in the story that the world can be seen from the narrow road, especially near the river. But we also see that even though those on the narrow road are able to speak to those on the southern shore, they are still separated by the great river. This is representative of the verse's description of not belonging to the world. So in summary, we are set apart from the world spiritually, but we are still connected to the world through our obligation to draw the lost to Christ.

After listening to Clarence's analogy of the river, I'm able to comprehend the difference between how I used to look at life and how I now see things. In my old

lifestyle, I would judge my worth by the things I did or did not do. I had relied on worldly wisdom. It is clear to me now in hindsight that the underlying motive for all my actions stemmed from my desire to satisfy my wants and needs first and foremost. My limited view on this life led me to spend all my time and energy focusing on temporal and self-gratifying ambitions. This allows me to understand the lack of fulfillment I felt from my worldly pursuits.

"I think I understand," I state to Clarence. "Without being on the narrow road, one cannot put life into a proper perspective as God would have us do. When we look across the river, the things of the world are put into context against the 'big picture' and lose their influence over us."

"Yes, that is precisely it," he responds. "If you don't mind me suggesting, what say we begin our walk down the road today? I can explain more as we go."

"To be honest, I'm not sure where I'm supposed to go from here. I feel I made the right decision in walking across the bridge, but now that I'm here, I'm not sure where I'm supposed to go. I greatly appreciate everything you have done for me up to this point, but I don't want to slow you down from where you need to go. You see, I'm not used to walking such difficult terrain, as you probably remember from your days living across the river. My legs are accustomed to the flat, open terrain of the south, not the hilly, winding roads over here. I'm afraid my lack of endurance is going to be more than obvious compared to your walking ability. I can tell by looking at you and your well-worn walking stick that you have covered many a hard mile in this land."

Clarence simply smiled at me. "Every journey must start sometime and somehow. Your crossing of the bridge yesterday started with one step, which led to another and then another. It eventually brought you to where you are right now. Whether you know it or not, that first step you took yesterday was the toughest step you will ever take. And as far as endurance, that will come with practice, just like anything else does. God does not expect us to cross over here and start sprinting down the trail as if we are running in a race. He knows that we come here weak and out of shape, which is why He expects those of us who have experience on the road to come alongside people new to this area and mentor them and show them the way. Just take it one day at a time, and before you know it, you'll be miles down the path and growing in strength every day. Eventually, you will be at a point in your walk where you will be able to be a mentor yourself to a newcomer. But let's begin with that first step."

☙

As new Christians, we are as "born again" as any other Christian is, but we lack the spiritual maturity that can only come with time as we walk and grow in the Lord, as we read in **Hebrews 5:13–14.** Garrett mentions that he is not accustomed to walking the rough terrain. This is symbolic of a new Christian lacking spiritual strength because they have never been disciplined by the Holy Spirit. As these verses mention, they are the equivalent of a baby spiritually when compared to a mature Christian. Just as a baby is not fed solid food, a new Christian is not expected to handle Bible teachings in the same way as a more mature Christian. But as they grow more and more in the Lord, more and more is expected of them by the Holy Spirit, just as a baby progresses from milk to solid food.

☙

"Before we begin, there's something I need to give you."

I watch Clarence reach into his coat and pull out a book.

"This is the guide to the narrow road. You won't get very far without it."

He hands it to me, and I start to flip through it.

"That will be the most important possession you will ever own. With this book, you will be able to navigate the narrow road and stay on course. You can spend your entire life studying it, and you will still learn something new from it every day. It may look unimpressive, but as you will soon learn, there's more to it than meets the eye. The words on the pages are not just mere instructions written by men, they are God breathed and God inspired. Not only will they guide you; they will also shape you as you journey. Yes, there is much to learn about this book but more than you know. For not only can it be used to give direction, it can also be used to get you where you need to go."

He reaches out and takes the book from my hand, opens it up and closes his eyes. After several seconds, the book begins to glow. I stand in utter amazement at what I'm seeing happen right before me. Suddenly, not only does it glow, it begins to change shape. The glowing finally fades away and in his hand is another staff, not too unlike the one he carries himself.

I turn to him in amazement. "How did you do that? Is this some kind of magic trick? I know you said this book is special, but honestly?"

"Yes," he replies. "It is a special book; it is, in fact, called the Guide Book. *But like I said, it not only guides you where you need to go, it also helps you get where you need to go. Because it is God inspired and God breathed, it is designed to serve many different functions because there are many needs along the road. As a book, it guides the traveler with regard to direction and destination. As a staff, it is used as an aid to assist the traveler as they encounter some difficult terrain. But there will be times that you need more than just help in walking, for there are many dangers and enemies that will target you as you journey. For times like these, you will need more than just a staff to protect yourself."*

The staff began to glow once again and then dimmed, revealing an intimidating sight, a shiny, silver, double-edged sword. "Do not be nervous at the thought of using such an object. Over time, with practice, you will be more than prepared to attack the enemy or defend yourself as the occasions arise. But there is yet another use for this gift."

Once again, he holds the sword up and the glowing transformation takes place. This time, after the glowing fades away, he is left holding a lantern. I stand staring at him, speechless.

"The lamp is also needed often along the way. It provides the light of truth when a traveler gets lost in the dark and needs to find the way back to the path. Another additional benefit with the lantern is the fact that when travelers use it to help themselves, many times others who are also lost will be aided in finding their way back to the path by seeing the light."

⳼

The *Guide Book* described in the story obviously refers to the Holy Bible. The description of the *Guide Book* being able to take various other shapes symbolically reflects how God's word is more than just a mere book. It has the power to breathe life into the reader. In regards to the Bible being described as a guidebook, we find examples of this in **2 Timothy 3:16–17.** In **Proverbs 4:10–13,** we find godly wisdom and instruction being promoted by a father to his son in hopes that it will help him along life's road. This is symbolized in the story through the transformation of the book into a staff. The sword can be used as a weapon along the road. The description of the Bible as an offensive and defensive weapon can be found in **Hebrews 4:12.** The transforming of the *Guide Book* symbolizes the Bible being living and active. As to the transformation of the book into a lantern, we find this parallel in **Psalm 119:105.**

♄

"I never realized that one would need so much assistance just to get from one place to another on this side of the river. I just assumed that everyone knew where to go," I say to Clarence.

"Actually, as you begin your journey, you will notice that there are many narrow roads that sometimes overlap one another. This is because even though everyone on this side is traveling toward the same destination, God has a unique path planned for each person to take on their journey. Sometimes you will find that your path will parallel another's for a time, as ours happen to be doing at this moment, but then at some point they will separate once again. The most difficult thing you will find as you travel is trying to stay on the narrow path. Even though we are on the opposite side of the river from the world, plenty of sin still abounds throughout this realm. It may help if I explain the layout of the terrain in a little more detail.

"If you will look ahead of us at the path we are standing on, you will notice first and foremost that the path is narrow and winding. The path follows an easterly direction and runs to the left of the great river. At some points the path draws very close to the river's edge; other times, there are trees and foliage that lay between the two, blocking our view of the river. If you look closely, you will notice that the path has an uneven angle to it. There is a slight slanting of the path with the lower side being to the right, the side closest to the river. This is not just a random happening.

"As I mentioned, sin abounds even on this side of the river. The land between the path and the river is controlled by Satan. When one travels down the path, he or she must be observant to where he or she is walking. The lay of the path, if one is not focusing, will gradually draw them to the right and off the path. This is because of our carnal nature that still exists within us. It is constantly at war with the Holy Spirit that also resides within us. The carnal nature will take the path of least resistance any chance it gets, whereas the Holy Spirit will try and keep us on the path. When we become fatigued from walking and lose our focus on where we are heading, we will find ourselves gently drifting to the right and into sin's grip. Satan has many traps that lie between the path and the river.

"Sometimes we wander off for a short period of time and come right back to the path with little negative consequence. But other times, we can find ourselves entangled in situations that leave permanent consequences that will follow us to the end of our days. This is why we must follow the path above all else. If the path takes us near the river, then we should make the most of the opportunity while we are there, but we should never try to get to the river by wandering off the path and finding it on our own. This will only result in leaving ourselves vulnerable to Satan's attacks. We are protected from such evils when we hold true to the narrow road."

The reference to there being many narrow roads refers to the fact that each Christian has a unique and individual plan and course for their life as directed by God. We find in *1 Corinthians 12:4–6* that the various gifts from the Spirit are analogous to the narrow path assigned to each Christian. The eastern course taken by the travelers represents the hope we have as Christians in the return of Jesus, as noted in *Matthew 24:24.* The description of the road being slanted slightly toward the river is symbolic of how our fallen human nature is constantly drawing us toward the world and its wide, easy road. It always requires inner strength to go against one's fleshly desires and remain obedient to the path that God has laid out for us. When we take our eyes off the narrow road, we soon find ourselves drifting to the right and the temptations offered there. We see this conflict between the sinful nature and the Holy Spirit presented in **Galatians 5:16–17** and **Romans 7:14–25.** In reference to the danger that exists to the right of the path, we see in **1 Peter 5:8** the comparison of Satan to a roaring lion, a threat that would commonly exist along some wilderness paths.

It is mentioned that wandering off the path and returning can sometimes leave us unscathed but other times with permanent scars. This reminds us of the fact that even though God will forgive us of our sins (bringing us back on the path), sometimes we return and are forced to live with the consequences of our wrongdoings. This can be seen in the case of Adam and Eve not being allowed back into Eden or Samson losing his eyesight after being captured by the Philistines. It can also be seen in today's world, for example, with those who perform criminal acts becoming born again after they commit their crime but still being required to serve a sentence for their wrongdoing.

♋

"Now, as you may notice, there's not just a right side to the path, there's also a left side to the path," Clarence states as he points to the left. "I know it sounds like I'm stating the obvious, but most people are so focused on avoiding the right side of the road that before they know it, they find themselves off the path and to the left of the road. You might think at first that it's not a big deal, but they call it the narrow road for a reason. God intends for us to stay on the road because we are surrounded by sin on either side. And as bad as things can be on the right side of the road, it is actually worse to drift off to the left. It might seem to not make sense at first because going to the right draws one closer to the world, but those who get drawn to the left usually end up worse off.

"Satan leads Christians to the right of the path using temptations that appeal to the old sinful nature. To the right, you will find such snares as adultery, fornication, murder, lust, theft and other such sins that appeal to the flesh. But to the left of the path, Satan uses a different tactic. He taps into one of humankind's worst shortcomings: pride.

"To the left you will find Christians being drawn to false religions, idol worship and other forms of godliness that lack any spiritual truth. Satan realized long ago that even though many could be led away from the path by simply appealing to their sinful nature, many others had the strength to not fall as easily for these devices. So he made his strategy a two-pronged attack on humankind. He went to the left of the path and appealed to people's pride, knowing that he could offer an alternative path to the narrow road that made people appear to be righteous without having to be obedient to the discipline of the Holy Spirit.

"These people present themselves as religious, but because they leave the Holy Spirit behind, they lack any true spiritual power. They are followers of rules rather than believers in a relationship with God. This is the most insulting behavior to the Father, primarily because it rejects the need for Jesus's sacrifice to gain our eternal reward. Second, it is pride that made Satan rebel against heaven in the first place and be cast out of it, ultimately forcing God to create hell and then the lake of fire as a punishment for him. And it is this very same punishment that Satan continues to lead humankind toward every chance he gets, as his ultimate revenge toward God."

⌘

We see those on the left side of the road representative of the Pharisees that Jesus spoke so bitterly against. In **Matthew 23:13–33,** we find Jesus describing such people.

Day 3

Clarence and I covered a lot of ground yesterday, both physically and spiritually. The farther down the path I go, the more I understand how true his words are and just how difficult this journey will be. But in spite of it all, I do not regret making the choice for Jesus. A satisfaction comes with going against the grain and doing what is right rather than what is convenient. I found it interesting that as we walked yesterday, every so often we would come upon a white dove sitting in a tree, always just ahead of us. As we would start to draw near to it, it would gently fly from its limb and out of sight farther up around the bend. I believe it is the same dove that I saw on the bridge two days ago, but I can't be sure. I was going to ask Clarence about it, but I didn't want him to think me odd, considering the seriousness of the material we were covering. I'm hoping we will run into it again today. There is something very comforting about seeing it. It's almost as if it is waiting for us when we come upon it. I'll just have to wait and see how today pans out. Clarence said that he had something to show me today that would help me understand things a little better. I'm so glad to have him at hand to help me understand this new land. The staff also comes in handy I find, especially as the terrain starts to go uphill. Takes some of the burden off when one has something to lean on during the rough spots.

We find, once again, the Holy Spirit being represented as a dove that seems to stay just out of reach from the travelers but always waiting for them to come to Him. This function of the Holy Spirit can be seen described in *John 16:13*. We can see another example of the Spirit functioning in this same capacity even with Jesus. In *Matthew 4:1,* we see the very Son of God following the Spirit's lead.

ഏ

"Good morning!" Clarence says as he walks up to me. "Are you ready for some more words of wisdom from an old man?"

"I don't see any old men here, but I'll take the words of wisdom," I tell him.

"We better get you some glasses then, son." He chuckles. "Let's get going then. There's something I want to show you, about a mile down the road. It will help me put things into perspective for you. Have you ever heard of an analogy?"

"I believe so. You are referring to using two similar things to make a comparison, such as comparing the players of a football team to the workers of a company. We used that one quite a bit at my previous place of employment."

"Exactly, I plan on using the same technique today to help you get a better grasp on the core principles of Christianity. It only takes a second to become born again, but a lifetime to process all the nuances of the Spirit's impact in our lives. Even at my age, after walking more than thirty-seven years on this path, there isn't a day that goes by that God doesn't reveal something new to me pertaining to my walk with Him."

After walking for a short time, Clarence suddenly stops and points across the road to my right. There, standing just off the path, is an old, abandoned house. It's obvious that at one time, it had been a beautiful house, but now the effects of time and weather are clearly seen. "This is what you wanted to show me?" I ask him.

"Yes, this is the subject of our analogy," he states.

"And can I ask what this is supposed to represent?"

"Why, you, of course," he says with a sheepish grin. I look at him in bewilderment. Finally, he lets out a huge laugh, which makes me laugh as well. "Maybe I should explain a little better. The analogy I'm referring to deals not so much with

*the external appearance of the house but the actual design of the house. The build-
ing blocks of a Christian can be compared to a house's layout. Let me start at the
beginning. If you were to rebuild this house from scratch, what would be the first
thing you would do to start construction?"*

⤧

In *1 Corinthians 3:16,* we find an analogy that describes Christians as temples that hold the Holy Spirit.

⤧

*"Well, I would assume that the first thing would be to prepare the ground by mak-
ing a level spot for it to be built upon."*

*"Very good, that is exactly right. This would correlate to what the Holy Spirit
does in our hearts. Before we can become born again, He convicts us and brings us
to a state of repentance, which allows Him to be able to establish a residence in our
hearts. So what comes next in your plan?"*

⤧

We see this principle discussed by Jesus in *Matthew 7:24–27.*

⤧

"They would have to lay a foundation on which the house would rest," I say.

*"Correct. The foundation is the most important aspect of the house's makeup.
And why would that be?"*

*"Because if the foundation is not solid, the house will shift as it settles from its
weight over the years. I've seen this firsthand with the first house I owned. One
corner of the house began to settle and it became very noticeable," I reply.*

*"This is why we must not only lay a foundation but also build it using the proper
materials. Inferior materials will compromise the integrity of the entire house. If we*

were to use this analogy on those across the river, we would find foundation stones composed of such things as money, fame, titles, possessions, human relationships, positions of power and many other worldly passions. What people soon find though, as time goes on, is that these materials cannot hold up under the pressures of life and soon crumble under the weight. And just as with your first house, it becomes visibly noticeable to those around them that something is off balance in their lives. They are left with two choices: abandon their worldly house and rebuild one using God's design plan or stay in their collapsing house out of denial that anything is wrong. Unfortunately we see the latter happen more times than not, as demonstrated in those who will not admit they have addictions, have a love of money above all else or strive for positions of authority at the cost of others. Yet we as Christians build with a plan that is designed by God, which allows our house to have structural stability that will weather the storms of life."

⚭

We see in **1 Corinthians 3:11–17** this concept laid out from God's perspective.

⚭

"The first stone we lay is the cornerstone. This has always been considered the most important of the foundation stones. What do you think would represent the cornerstone in a Christian's body?"

"I would have to say that God would be the obvious answer to that one. Am I right?"

"Correct once again. More precisely for this analogy, the Holy Spirit. When a person is born again, the Holy Spirit comes in and takes residence. So, ultimately, God is the correct answer, but if we are speaking about the cornerstone of a person, we will say the Holy Spirit more specifically."

⚭

If we go back to the Old Testament, we find in **Isaiah 28:16** a reference to God being described as a cornerstone. The Bible primarily recognizes Jesus as the true cornerstone of a Christian's foundation, as seen in **Matthew 21:42.** But as we see in **Ephesians 2:19–22,** Jesus lives in this temple through His Spirit.

⚜

"So now we have the first stone in place. What would be the next foundation stone that would be placed diagonally from the cornerstone? Think of it kind of like a seesaw. What would be the only thing that could hold enough weight to balance out the house as the opposite stone from the Holy Spirit?"

Leaning on my staff, I ponder this for a second. Suddenly, I look at the staff and shout to him, "His Guide *Book! If God's Spirit represents the cornerstone, then His word must represent the opposite corner."*

"Correct, that's very impressive." He nods. "We not only have God's Spirit to guide us; we also have His word. He speaks to us through both of them. So when I mentioned a seesaw earlier, this is what I was referring to. If we communicate with the Holy Spirit but ignore God's word or read God's word but never communicate with the Holy Spirit, we will have a house that settles in one of the corners. We must pray daily for the Holy Spirit's guidance as well as read God's word daily in order for Him to speak to us through it. It's an ongoing balancing act we must maintain."

⚜

In **John 1:1–2,** we find Jesus referenced to as "the Word." In **2 Timothy 3:15–17,** we see that the scriptures of the Bible come directly from God. And in **Hebrews 4:12,** we find that not only is the Bible God breathed, its words are living and able to play an active role in spiritually shaping us.

⚜

"That leaves us with two other corners to define. Being that this analogy is meant to depict a Christian's makeup, and the first two corners reflect God reaching to

us, the other two corners reflect us reaching to God. They would represent zeal and discipline."

"Aren't the definitions of those two terms basically the same?" I ask.

"They may appear to be at first, but there are definite differences with them. Let's look at it this way. Say you were obsessed with weight lifting. You read every book on the subject, bought workout clothes to dress the part, showed up at the gym every day for a year and even became friends with the weight lifters. This would demonstrate that you have zeal for weight lifting. But let's assume that for the entire year, you did not lift a single weight. You may have zeal for the sport, but you lack any discipline, leaving you looking no different compared to the beginning of the year.

"Now let's say the opposite happens. You have discipline to go to the gym and lift weights. When you do go to the gym, you go through the motions and perform the routines, but are easily distracted from going to the gym by other interests, often finding yourself not even going. This would show that you are disciplined to perform what you feel obligated to do, but you lack any zeal to push yourself above and beyond, therefore showing little growth after a year. In either situation, muscle growth is inhibited because zeal and discipline are not utilized in conjunction with each other. This combination is what produces Olympic athletes, great musicians, motivating speakers and any other person who rises to the top of their talent or trade.

"In Christianity, it works the same. We have to have zeal and discipline as God's people if we are to influence the lost that they need Jesus in their lives. What kind of witness would we be if we were not disciplined enough to go out and live the gospel or not zealous enough to speak passionately to the unsaved around us? Therefore, just as the Holy Spirit and God's word balance each other, so do zeal and discipline. When all four of these are balanced in our lives, our house's corners are on a solid foundation."

❧

To begin with, we must accompany our zeal for Christ with spiritual wisdom in order for it to be productive. This is pointed out in **Proverbs 19:2.** We see

God's view on zeal as we read **Revelation 3:15–16.** We realize that God does not want us to be wishy-washy people riding the spiritual fence. Zeal is an important factor if we are to be effective witnesses for Christ. If we cannot be passionate about our salvation, what can we be passionate about? On the other hand, the Bible makes numerous references to discipline, with one example being found in **Hebrews 12:11.**

❧

"Now that we have laid the four corners, we have to lay the remaining foundation stones. These are represented as eight large foundation stones, each one signifying a fruit of the Spirit. The fruits of the Spirit are love, joy, peace, patience, kindness, goodness, faithfulness, gentleness and self-control. These according to God are traits that those who are born again and filled with the Holy Spirit should exhibit on a regular basis. Thus, because they are expressions of the Holy Spirit's impact on our lives, they are worthy of being used as foundation material." (See **Galatians 5:22–23**)

"Wait a minute; I think you made a mistake," I say to Clarence. "You said that there would be eight large foundation stones, but you mentioned nine fruits of the spirit."

"Very observant of you, young grasshopper; I'm glad to see you are paying attention. You are right in that I said there were eight stones and listed nine fruits of the Spirit. This is because I did not include love as one of the eight stones. It's not because it is not as important; it's because it's more important. In fact, for the purpose of this analogy, love represents the mortar that goes around all the foundation stones. It is the cement that binds everything together and gives stability to the stones. No matter how strong the stones are individually, if there were no mortar to hold them together, they would eventually shift out of place. The same is true with love. Each fruit of the Spirit is very strong individually. But without love to accompany each one, they will not be effective in providing strength to our lives."

❧

We see this matter referenced in the Bible in *1 Corinthians 13:1–3*. Jesus personally defends this point in *Matthew 22:35–40*. If we look at the Ten Commandments, we see a list of spiritual dos and don'ts given to us by God. Many people see these merely as a list of rules that they are obligated to obey to avoid the wrath of God. But if we live our lives with godly love, obeying the commandments will come as second nature to us. For example, if we have true love for those around us, we will not steal because we will not want to hurt another person by doing something so selfish. We will not worship any other God, not because we are told not to but because our love for God will keep us from wanting to do anything that would hurt our relationship with Him. This is why love is the fulfillment of the law, as explained in the verse.

One of the greatest conflicts found among Christians today is the ability to differentiate religion from relationship. Both have an appearance of righteousness, but there is a stark difference. Religion does not require love; relationship does; and love is the key that separates the two. Religion is a concept that promotes the enforcement of rules. Rules are present in relationship but are not followed out of fear of punishment. They are generally followed out of the desire to please the other in the relationship.

An example of this would be a comparison of two scenarios. One regards a driver pulled over by a police officer due to speeding. The other regards a husband who breaks his marriage vow by cheating on his wife. With the first scenario, the driver is aware that he broke the law and remedies this by paying the fine. He does not worry that the police officer thinks less of him for breaking the law. He merely pays his fine and moves on with his life. But with the second scenario, the husband broke a law the same as the driver did, but his situation is further complicated because of the relationship he has with his wife. He not only broke a rule, he emotionally hurt his wife. This is because of the relationship between the two of them. This relationship does not exist between the driver and the police officer. The husband is not only sorrowful because he broke a rule and, thus, faces a consequence; in addition, he has damaged his relationship with his wife.

Love separates these two scenarios. The husband's love for his wife causes him pain because he realizes that by breaking a vow of his marriage, he not only has to face a personal consequence; he also has to face the fact that he hurt his relationship with his wife. This is the same principle we find with religion and relationship. Too many people today find it easier to live a religious life of following rules than to live with a personal relationship with Jesus Christ, thus having to deal with the consequence of knowing that they bring emotional pain to Him when they sin.

But the Bible is clear: Jesus does not want a bunch of followers who follow rules, because we can never be good enough to get to heaven anyway by following rules alone. He wants believers who follow Him and strive to be obedient to Him because they love Him. He wants to have a relationship with us, not just rule over us. This is why we find in *Galatians 4:4–7, 1 John 4:16* and *1 Corinthians 13:4–8* that God demonstrates love to us by not only providing us with an opportunity for eternal salvation but also by adopting those who accept His offer as sons and daughters.

❧

"Now that we have the foundation established," Clarence continued, "we can lay the floor over it. The floor will represent grace. Grace can be defined as unearned merit. God shows His grace to us by offering us eternal salvation, even though Jesus is the one who had to pay the price for it. We receive merit that we did not earn, so just as a floor covers the foundation of a house, grace covers our sin and gives us access to God that would not be available without it."

❧

This concept is further explained in *Ephesians 2:8–9. Romans 3:23–24* explains that we are all sinners, deserving God's punishment. In spite of our fallen nature, God continues to love us and wishes for us to join Him in heaven one day. We see this described in *2 Peter 3:9.* Grace from God covers our sin, but it's not a justification for us to keep on sinning, as many like to believe. To continue sinning would not only be an attempt to take advantage of God's mercies, it would demonstrate a lack of love for Christ. As Christians, everything we do should be based on our love for God.

❦

"Now that the floor is in place, we are able to start working on building the walls of the house. Within the walls of a house, we find studs spaced out; the purpose of these being to reinforce their strength. In many homes, large sheets of drywall are used for the walls. If studs are not placed behind the drywall, it would be very easy for a person to bust through the material with the slightest amount of weight applied to it. But by spacing studs behind the drywall, the walls can withstand increased external pressure without damage.

"The symbolic representation of the studs in a Christian would be the ability to articulate the defense of the gospel of Christ to others effectively, also referred to as apologetics. When those in the world try to argue against Christianity, the first thing they will do is to try to punch holes in our doctrine. If we cannot defend our beliefs against spiritual attack, not only will we not win others to Christ; we may also be in jeopardy of falling for false doctrines ourselves, resulting in holes being punched through our spiritual drywall. Some common arguments used against Christians are

* *How do we know there is a God?*
* *How did the universe begin?*
* *How can we believe in something we can't see?*
* *Can we choose to not believe in God?*
* *If there is a God, why is there evil in the world?*
* *How do we know that Jesus is who He says He is?*
* *Why is Jesus the only way to heaven?*
* *Why would God send anyone to hell? and*
* *Why should we believe in the Bible?*

These questions that a non-Christian should be asking Christians about their faith are legitimate. If you will recall, before the Holy Spirit gives us godly wisdom, we are forced to rely on worldly wisdom, resulting in a worldly perspective on such questions. The world attempts to give a variety of alternative solutions to Christianity, but if researched, it soon becomes apparent that none are able to measure up to its authenticity. We as Christians should encourage questions from skeptics. One should not follow a set of beliefs blindly, even if it is Christianity. We are not going to be successful witnesses for Christ if the best defense we can muster is that we are Christians simply because our parents were Christians or because that was just how we were raised. We need to be able to articulate scripture and give sound arguments for the justification of our beliefs. As we are presented with questions that we don't have a strong answer for, it is our duty to research the question and have a valid answer ready for future encounters. Over time, this will continually increase our walls' integrity and make us more effective witnesses for Christ.

"Once we have the walls constructed, the next thing we must do is run the wiring throughout the house. The wiring represents prayer. As a house without electricity has no power, so does a Christian without prayer. Prayer is our way of tapping into the 'heavenly power company,' or the throne room of God, to function as an effective Christian. Electricity is what allows lights to operate inside of a house. The same is true within a Christian. Prayer is what allows a Christian to be a 'light to the world.'"

ॐ

Prayer is the act of communicating with our heavenly Father. Because we, as Christians, are adopted as sons and daughters by God, we should not wonder why we are expected to pray to God on a regular basis. Communicating with God should be as routine an act as communicating with our spouse or parents. In addition, we see in *1 Thessalonians 5:16–18* that God calls us to pray. Even Jesus, as He walked this earth, spoke with God the Father through prayer daily. We find in *Deuteronomy 4:7* that praying draws us closer to God, as should be the goal in any relationship.

ॐ

"We have an open line of communication with the Creator of the universe, who also happens to be our adopted Father. He wishes to bless us, just as an earthly father wishes to bless his own child."

"Answer me this then," I ask Clarence. "Why did God not answer my prayer to Him when I lost my job?"

"A very valid question, Garrett; let me see if I can explain. Just as an earthly father would not grant his young child's request for a loaded gun to play with, so God has the same discretion when dealing with us. Just because we ask God for something does not mean He is obligated to grant our request like a genie in a bottle. Some things we ask for do not match up with God's plan for our lives. Some things may be appropriate requests but do not fall into God's timing for us. And some things only come to us when we pray for them. We do not know which of these three categories our prayer requests fall into when we ask God for something. All we can do is ask and then have faith that God will answer as He deems appropriate for our lives."

❦

Regarding things that do not match up with God's plan for our lives, in **2 Corinthians 12:7–10** we find Paul praying for God to take away what he refers to as a "thorn" in his side. We see that God does not answer Paul's prayer as Paul wishes. Paul then realizes that the "thorn in his side" is serving a purpose that he did not initially understand. It is keeping him humble, forcing him to rely on God. With regard to appropriate prayers that depend on God's timing, an example is Job. Even though Job prayed to God throughout his trials, it seemed to him that God was not answering his prayers. In fact, the testing was part of God's plan to demonstrate Job's character and prove Satan wrong, and Job was eventually rewarded with twice what he started with. And some things merely depend on persistent prayer to be answered. In **Luke 18:1–8,** we find Jesus giving a parable about the reward of persistence.

❦

"We can learn from Jesus, as He prayed to God regarding the crucifixion. He asked God to 'take the cup from Him' but only if it was God's will. This is the prayer model we should imitate when sending requests to our Father, if it is your will."

❧

Jesus further reinforces the need for prayer, as He Himself prayed to God while on earth, as seen in **Luke 22:39–42. 1 John 5:14–15** further speaks of seeking His will. We also have the Holy Spirit to assist us in bringing our prayers to God and seeking His will, as seen in **Romans 8:25–27.**

❧

"In addition to praying with persistence and seeking His will, we also have to pray in faith. Prayer is not just a recitation of words. It is a drawing of confidence on our relationship with our Father that He will assist us in our time of need. We must believe that He will hear our prayers and either fulfill our requests or give us peace and understanding as to why He chose not to."

❧

In **James 5:13–16, Mark 11:24** and **Philippians 4:6,** we find instruction regarding praying in faith.

❧

"The next aspect of our house involves the heating and cooling of it. For our purposes, we will design our house with a central air furnace, which is able to heat and cool. The furnace is going to symbolize character in a Christian. To understand this concept, let's first look at the function of the central air furnace. The goal of any homeowner is to reside in a home that can provide a comfortable temperature. When the sun is blazing during a hot and humid summer day, the

homeowner will run his or her central air to cool down the interior of the home. And when the winter winds bring snow and cold temperatures, the homeowner will run his furnace to provide warmth for the interior of the home. So basically, the goal of the machine is to provide consistent comfortable temperatures in the home regardless of the external factors outside of the home.

"To go back to our analogy, the goal of one's character is the same as the central air furnace: to maintain consistency within ourselves despite external conditions. The best definition for character I ever heard: who we are when no one is looking. That is why as Christians, we should have the same character whether we are with Christians or with non-Christians. If we allow external factors to dictate who we are inside, we will change our character to match those around us. We will be like a house with no heating or cooling capability. In the winter, we will freeze and in the summer, we will swelter. To be effective witnesses to the lost around us, we need to maintain our character at peak performance, whether faced with the heat of peer pressure or the cold shoulders of the world around us.

"In most homes, the central air furnace is not something that is normally seen by visitors, but they have no doubt of its presence when they feel its effects. The same should be said of Christians. We don't need to wear a T-shirt saying we have character, but those around us should have no doubt of its presence when they experience it from being around us. The world lacks this quality, leaving them to be at the mercy of the conditions surrounding them. Thus, when they come in contact with a Christian, they should experience a feeling of comfort that is inviting, no different than when walking into a warm house in the winter or a cool house in the summer. We should be a positive influence on the lost through the demonstration of our character."

The Bible implies that a person's character can be found in the heart, as seen in **Proverbs 27:19.** God emphasizes the importance of character for the same reason a house needs heating and cooling. God wants the best for His children, so He does not want us to live in uncomfortable living conditions, described in **Jeremiah 17:9–10.** Once a unit is installed in a home, it must be maintained properly. We cannot take it for granted, or else we will forget how miserable we were before it was installed. Similarly, we cannot take our character for granted. We must remember how miserable we were before the Holy Spirit came into our lives, as demonstrated in *Ezekiel 36:26–27, 31.*

If we use cheap fuel to operate our unit, we will soon find ourselves with a nonfunctioning system. The same goes for our character. The fuel the world offers us is cheap and tempting, but over time, it will destroy our character. God's fuel does come at a higher cost, but it is well worth it to keep our character operating at peak performance. The cost is taking up our cross daily and being obedient to what His word says. This view is reflected in *Matthew 12:33–37.* Buying fuel is an ongoing process for a central air furnace. If at some point we stop paying for the fuel, we will be cut off from receiving it. The same bodes true for Christians. We must be held accountable to the debt owed to Christ. If we neglect this debt, we will be cut off from receiving the benefits that the Holy Spirit provides, as shown in *Luke 16:10–15.*

༂

"Another component that works along with a central air furnace to maintain the internal temperature is insulation. A house that is well insulated within its walls will require less effort from the unit to fight off external forces. Insulation in a Christian would represent his or her priorities. When our priorities match those that God expects from us, it becomes easier for us to be men and women of character. Just like insulation, the good stays in; the bad stays out."

༂

This principle is described in *Matthew 6:19–21.*

༂

"The last section of our house to discuss is the roof. This will be representing faith. Along the base of the roof we find the gutters, which drain into one main pipe that empties into a rain barrel. This gutter system will represent hope."

"Excuse me for interrupting, but I have a stupid question to ask."

"There are no stupid questions," Clarence says, "so please, ask away."

"OK. Maybe I'm just confused, but I thought that faith and hope would basically be the same thing? Yet you have them as two completely separate parts of your analogy. Can you clarify this?"

"Absolutely, my friend, and a very keen observation you have made. Yes, in many ways, the two are very similar, and they are easy to confuse. But I'll explain the difference. The definition of faith is a belief in, trust in and loyalty to an idea. The definition of hope is a combination of faith along with an optimistic and confident anticipation for the outcome. In the case of God's return, faith demonstrates our confidence that it will take place, yet hope demonstrates not only our belief but also our longing for the return to happen. This is the difference between the two.

"In reference to the analogy, faith signifies the roof of our house. Just as the roof protects the interior of a house from adverse weather, so too does our faith in Christ protect us from the severe storms of a sinful world that rain down upon us daily, attempting to dampen our spirits and flood our bodies in despair. Yet when the rains do come down upon us, we understand that God will use all things for His good. This is why hope is represented by the gutter system. The faith of our spiritual roof protects us from the storm; the hope of our gutters and spouts is that as the rains pound down on us, the very water that would attempt to flood our house is channeled to the downspout and into the rain barrel, providing water for us to use as needed.

"Our anticipation of the blessings of God is manifested by creating a system that turns something initially seen as harmful into a blessing from God to be used for our benefit. The unsaved of this world hope for temporary, worldly things that will perish. Things such as wealth, fame, success and possessions bring temporary happiness but soon leave one feeling empty. At some point comes the realization that death is inevitable, and no matter how successful we are in this life, we cannot take it with us when we die. The only things that will matter when we die are the treasures we have stored up in heaven."

1 Corinthians 15:19 puts this into perspective. *1 Thessalonians 4:13–18* reminds us that our hope is not found in anything the world offers, but in the returning of our Lord Jesus.

⚭

"If we keep our thoughts on heaven and the reward that God has promised us, there should not be anything that this world can offer that would tempt us to trade our salvation for the sinful, temporary things of this world. Our hope should be to be with Jesus, whether it is after we die or in our lifetime when He chooses to return. We hope to be united with Him above all else. So whether God gives us another day to live or calls us home to be with Him, we have something to look forward to."

⚭

Titus 2:11–14 and *Hebrews 11:1–2* encourage us to avoid putting hope in the world.

⚭

"Well, does the analogy help you understand things any better now?"

"Actually, it does," I tell Clarence. *"As a new Christian, all the concepts you mentioned in the analogy are confusing at first. But when you put them into a symbolic context, I can almost see them visually as I picture the house. The only concern I have is building my house and having it look like that one!"* I jokingly say as I point to the abandoned house.

"Maybe once you get to be my age, then you can worry. I've lost a shutter or two over the years, but then again time catches up to the best of us."

We turn and walk down the road. I look over my shoulder at the old house, just in time to see a white dove fly out of an upstairs window and head past us down the road, out of sight.

Day 4

"Any more abandoned houses to check out today?" I ask Clarence as he strolls up to meet me, sporting his walking staff as usual.

"Not exactly," he says and chuckles a little. "But strangely, in a way, I guess you could kind of say yes. When we spoke yesterday, using the analogy of a house to describe our spiritual makeup, I detailed the fact that the Guide Book *describes our bodies as 'temples of God' and that we are called to treat them as such. Today I want to continue along the same premise. Instead of using an abandoned house to describe our spiritual body, I want to use the physical body as an analogy for our spiritual body. You see, I've spent most of my life working in the healthcare field, so I've had plenty of time to consider the workings of the body and the amazing design of our anatomy. So if you are ready for another ear beating from me, just let me know."*

"I'm all ears," I tell him, "so let the beating begin."

"Great. Let's discuss it as we walk."

We begin our hike down the path, and I am anxious to gain more nuggets of wisdom from him.

"I've always been amazed by the human body, even before I came to walk on this side of the river, thus explaining my career choice, I guess. But since I've come to walk the narrow path, I believe I have an even greater appreciation for it,

most likely due to the fact that I've come to have a personal relationship with its Creator. The body truly is a living miracle in every way."

I could tell Clarence was passionate about this subject. That's not to say that he did not speak passionately about everything else to this point, but this topic seemed to put a gleam in his eyes and a spring in his step. "I guess you're right, but I never really thought about it that way," I stated.

"Most definitely a fascinating piece of work," he replied. "It's astounding that anyone can actually look at the body, especially from a scientific point of view, and continue to say that there is no God. I have to wonder if they are blind or just close-minded. Let me begin with this point. I'm sure you have taken biology before in school, correct?"

"Yes, unfortunately, I have. Science was never my strong suit I must say. I was more of a numbers man, math and accounting, which probably helps to explain my choice of career. But science, no. I actually faint at the sight of blood, even my own."

Clarence seems to find this tidbit of information humorous. After he finishes his hearty laugh at my expense and wipes the tears from his eyes, he continues. "As I was saying, the body's design simply screams God at every turn. This is one of the things that hit me most when I became a Christian. I had spent years helping people physically on a daily basis in a healthcare format, but I had never fully appreciated the awe and wonder of the body's makeup. After becoming saved and turning my life over to God, I returned to my line of work with new eyes.

"Let me explain a little further. First, if we simply look at the body in a structural standpoint at the surface level, we notice symmetry—our first clue of an organized, functional design. We have two eyes, two ears, two arms, two legs, two hands and two feet working together under the control of one brain. It always reminds me of God's will for marriage, two people coming together to form one couple, guided by one God. Two people to hear, two people to see, two people to reach out to others, two people to walk through this world and yet come together as one body, under obedience of one higher power, one flesh from two souls united by God. (See **Mark 10:7–9**.)

"Internally, we witness the same symmetry, two lungs breathing in unison, working hand in hand with one heart, the provider of life to the body. Once again, *we see the marriage design, two people breathing as one, sharing one heart, which enables them to continue. (See **Ephesians 5:25–30.**)*

"As unfortunately happens from time to time, life sometimes delivers a painful blow. When injury occurs and one of the two body parts becomes damaged, the other part assumes the responsibility and performs the deed for the whole body. This is not the optimal plan for us, but at times it is the reality. If a body loses sight in one eye, the other eye assumes full responsibility and does the best it can. Even though it can perform successfully, it will never have the full range of peripheral vision as when both eyes are working in unison.

"The same applies with the ears. If one ear loses hearing, the body relies on the other completely. As hard as it may try, it will never have the full range of hearing capabilities as two ears working together. Losing an arm is a most traumatic situation. There are so many day-to-day tasks that we take for granted that would either be extremely difficult or virtually impossible to perform with the loss of said appendage. Driving a car, opening a jar of pickles, typing, changing a diaper and countless other menial tasks would be agonizing undertakings should such a crisis present itself.

"The same dynamic applies with a couple. When one spouse is not capable of reaching out to help the other physically, spiritually, emotionally or in any other capacity, an extreme burden falls on the functioning spouse. This can often lead to burnout on the part of the working spouse, affecting the body as a whole. With the loss of a leg, the remaining leg shares the limitations of the affected leg with regard to not being able to move about as desired. Regarding a couple, the failure of one partner to move forward in growing the relationship results in the other partner being restrained as well. As with a person positioned with one leg, they may try to achieve walking by relying solely on the remaining leg, but they soon find that fatigue and muscle pain are the result because one leg was not designed to carry the weight of an entire body by itself. Each leg's muscle design was created with the expectation of an opposing leg providing equal assistance in accomplishing its tasks.

"Last, should people find themselves having to rely on one lung, they will soon realize that with each breath taken, they are drawing in less oxygen to the body than normal, resulting in dizziness, increased labor of the working lung and muscle weakness due to the lack of oxygen reaching them. As I stated earlier, the

body works best when each symmetrical part performs its designed function to the best of its ability. Likewise, a couple remains healthier when each partner performs their role to the best of their ability, becoming more functional and more productive to themselves and those around them.

"Next, in addition to symmetry, the body holds the mystery of a Creator. The union of a man and a woman provides the capacity of creating a life through the passing of genetic material from each parent. Through God's design, the joining of a man's and a woman's reproductive products results in the creation of a single cell, a single cell that begins a dividing process that occurs time and time again over a course of nine months, resulting in a living, breathing, brand-new life, composed of genes from each parent, on this earth. Physical traits, personality, genetic predispositions, all passed on from both parents to the child, contained in their DNA at a cellular level. But the creation is much more than just an anatomical concoction made up of passed-on material; the creation is a person. (See **Jeremiah 1:5.**)

"In addition, the creation contains something that did not come from the parents but rather directly from God, a soul and a spirit. Animals contain a soul—that is, the force that brings life to it—but what separates us from the animals is the fact that in addition to a soul, we also contain a spirit. When an animal dies, they simply cease to exist, but a person contains a spirit that lives on after the physical death of the body." (See **Hebrews 4:12** and **John 19:30.**)

"The spirit is eternal by God's design, intended by God to join Him in heaven on our death, but unfortunately most end up in hell because of their lack of accepting Jesus's sacrifice on the cross for their sins. The union of body, soul and spirit is truly an astounding feat that makes each person a living vessel for God's Holy Spirit should he or she accept Him.

"In addition to all this, the physical body is also a perfect analogy for the spiritual body. Our bodies function on so many different levels that it would take numerous books to cover everything completely. The same can be said for our spiritual bodies. They are just as complex as our physical makeup. First off, our bodies are equipped with a powerful immune system. Its function is to fight off harmful germs that attempt to compromise our systems. As efficient as it is, however, its ability to protect us can be reduced through actions of our own. Poor nutrition, *lack of sleep, stress, overworking—all these can lower our immune defenses and leave us in jeopardy of infection, disease and numerous other maladies.*

"Similarly, our spiritual life works in generally the same way. When we stop taking in our recommended daily reading of the word" (see **1 Timothy 4:13**) *"allow our prayer life to fade away"* (see **1 Thessalonians 5:16–18**) *"and distance ourselves from the support of fellow Christians"* (see **Hebrews 10:25**) *"our spiritual immune system begins to weaken, leaving us vulnerable to Satan's attacks. Just as flu viruses wreak havoc on our bodies, so too can Satan influence our spiritual health.*

"As mentioned earlier, this is why nutrition plays such an important role in keeping our bodies healthy. When we choose to deprive ourselves of food, our bodies become weak from a lack of fuel. Likewise, when we do not feed our spirit from the word of God on a regular basis, we also become spiritually weak, making it difficult for us to stand up against Satan. Oftentimes we are drawn to the sight and smell of cakes, pies, pastries, candies and other delectable items because of their visual stimulation, their enticing smell and their sensual taste.

"Yet, unfortunately, should we decide to live on a diet based solely on such empty calories, our bodies would soon feel the effects of such a diet by becoming sluggish and less functional because of the lack of protein and other important vitamins and minerals found in healthy foods. Our spirit works in the same way. When we decide to solely take in the visually stimulating, aromatic and mouthwatering temptations that the world offers to us, we deprive ourselves of the 'fruits of the spirit' that truly enhance our spiritual well-being and energize us for the tasks God has appointed for us. We are filled with 'empty spiritual calories' and leave no room for 'nutritional spiritual calories.' (See **1 Corinthians 10:13**.)

"Speaking of immune systems, another great analogy exists. When we look to a human body, we find two common ways that it can fall prey to disease. The first route would be through harmful bacteria. Bacteria are foreign substances that invade the body and wreak havoc on its systems. Initially, we have outer defenses that prevent entry into our bodies, such as skin. If these systems become compromised, the body uses a secondary system to combat these invaders, by means of proteins

and white blood cells, which carry antibodies. The antibodies are microscopic killing cells that seek out anything they don't recognize as being part of the body.

"The second route in which disease can be brought to the body is through a virus. A virus differs from bacteria in that rather than attack the body independently, it chooses to invade our very cells, corrupt them and then reproduce more corrupt cells. Unlike bacteria, the body is not able to distinguish between a healthy cell and a cell that has been occupied by a virus, thus making its attack similar to a Trojan horse.

"As we go back to the analogy, if we correlate the human body to the symbolic body of Christian believers, the cells of our body would be representative of individual believers. In the case of bacteria, a symbolic representation would be false religions, cults, atheists and other non-Christian groups who profess a doctrine contrary to Christ. As with bacteria, they are easily identifiable as being in contrast with Christian doctrine, thus easier to keep away from the body of believers.

"But in the case of a virus, the symbolic representation would be those professing to be Christian believers but corrupted by the world, having a watered down and counterfeit version of Christianity. As with the human body, they often go undetected and are given ample space to corrupt other healthy believers within the church body. An attack from within is much more difficult to combat and much more destructive than an attack from without.

"With regard to our health, sometimes the issue is not eating too little but eating too much. Over time, this situation becomes just as critical, if not more so, than starvation. We allow our appetites to dictate our eating habits, becoming undisciplined and taking in more than is needed. This generally creates a chain effect that bodes negatively for the person, given the fact that each of us has a prescribed amount of calories that we are recommended to take in daily to maintain a healthy, functional body. As a person continues to take in too many calories, the body is not able to burn them off entirely, thus forcing it to store the excess as fat deposits throughout the body. Over time, the increase of fat, which also means an increase of weight, puts additional strain on the body to perform its routine functions. The body must work extra hard to perform tasks that came easy before the change. The increase in weight also affects the person's energy levels negatively, leaving him or her more sluggish with less energy, ultimately resulting in a sedentary lifestyle that only further exacerbates the spiraling problem.

"We can see the same scenario played out before us regarding our spirit life. When we become focused on the things of the world, taking in the 'empty spiritual calories' in excess, we bog down our spirit with the carnal baggage we allow to accumulate in our lives, thus affecting our drive as Christians and making us more ineffective witnesses for Christ. The two major factors that determine our physical health are not only food intake but also exercise. Cardiovascular activities and strength training are critical to a person's health and well-being. As one participates in these activities, metabolism is increased, excess fat is burned, muscle fibers grow in strength, reaction time is improved, circulation becomes more efficient and energy levels skyrocket. (See **Proverbs 23:20–21** and **1 Corinthians 6:12.**)

"We should not be surprised, then, that the same theory would apply to our spirit. As we challenge ourselves spiritually, we will note the same type of improvements in our lives. Just as improved metabolism helps to burn fat and calories in a person, improved spiritual metabolism helps to burn off the hold that weighty, worldly baggage has on us. Just as muscle fibers grow when tasked with resistance training, so too the spirit grows in strength as it encounters resistance from Satan and the world. (See **1 Peter 5:8–10.**)

"Athletes know that in order to grow muscle size and strength, they must basically perform exercises that in a sense 'tear down' the muscle fibers in order for them to regrow stronger. The same applies to our spirit. When we face challenges and hurdles spiritually, we are forced to work through them and, in the process, improve our strength against such obstacles. And just as reaction time is improved through exercise, so too is our spirit when we routinely discipline ourselves by facing the warfare brought on by the world and our enemies. God does not call us to be spiritual 'couch potatoes' or 'armchair quarterbacks,' sitting on the sidelines and watching the world go by. He expects every born-again believer to be in the game, growing daily and disciplining themselves. (See **Proverbs 1:7** and **Revelation 3:19.**)

"Speaking of muscles, God designed a peculiar arrangement for some of those in the body. This arrangement of muscles is called antagonistic pairs. The purpose for this setup is to have certain sets of muscles working in opposition to each other. For example, take the biceps and triceps muscles. The biceps muscle is responsible for bending the arm at the elbow; the triceps muscle is responsible for straightening *the arm at the elbow. They have completely opposite functions. The result of this is that when the biceps muscle contracts and shortens to flex the arm at the elbow, the triceps muscle must relax in order to allow this movement to occur. Similarly, when the triceps muscle contracts and shortens to extend the arm at the elbow, the biceps muscle must relax to allow this movement to occur. If the triceps were to work at the same time as the biceps, or vice versa, there would be no movement of the arm, rendering it nonfunctional.*

"In addition to this, the muscles help each other out in the sense that the muscles can only contract and shorten. Once the biceps muscle contracts and flexes the arm, it cannot extend the arm. It needs the triceps muscle to contract to straighten the arm out again. The opposite is true for the triceps. So in a sense, these muscles are dependent on each other to make the arm functional. What I find interesting in this relationship is that each muscle must share periods of taking the lead as well as being submissive to the other muscle in order to accomplish a task.

"Symbolically, we can find this same principle at work in the body of believers. In the church, there are times when a person is called to take the lead, and there are times when a person is called to submit to accomplish certain tasks. Just as seen with the muscles, if both believers work against each other rather than in harmony, the church body becomes nonfunctional. This doesn't make one person better than another; it simply means that each believer must identify what his or her calling is and serve the Lord within that capacity without trying to compete against other believers with regard to what his or her calling is. The biceps will never be able to straighten an arm out, just as the triceps will never be able to flex the arm. This doesn't make one better than the other; it simply means that they need each other to balance out their shortcomings. Working together, they produce an arm that can reach out to those in need, fulfilling God's calling.

"We cannot fulfill His calling on our lives when we are spiritually out of shape and gasping for breath over the least little task. You can be assured that Satan and the world are gearing up to compete against us. Therefore, we must do our part to stand against such resistance.

"One sad reality that comes with this world is the fact that we are plagued with countless diseases and illnesses on a daily basis. Some cripple, some impair and some simply take our lives. One of these that I want to mention specifically is

cancer. It is one of the most predominant blights to ever face our world. It presents itself in many different forms, attacking various parts of our bodies. But the one basic fact that all occurrences share in common is its modus operandi; it exists through out-of-control cell replication. This is what makes it such a difficult disease to cure. It is not a foreign virus or bacteria infecting our bodies; a malfunctioning at the cellular level continues the overproduction of cells, which ultimately destroys us if it is not stopped. Much progress has been made in the treatment of this disease, but there is still a long way to go.

"The reason I bring up this disease is the fact that we have a parallel condition that affects us at the spiritual level: addiction. Addiction works much the same way as cancer. It becomes an act or a behavior that rapidly grows out of control, eventually crowding over to affect our spirit and potentially resulting in physical and spiritual death. There are many types of addictions, such as alcohol, drugs, pornography, sex, gambling or even something as simple as food. Some things that turn into addictions are not inherently bad in themselves. We are required to eat food to stay alive; God designed us that way. He blessed us with an endless variety of tasty foods, as well as taste buds for us to appreciate them in moderation. But when we begin to eat compulsively and in excess, beyond what our metabolism can handle, we face the physical consequences of an eating addiction, including increased body fat levels, obesity, high blood pressure, diabetes, compromised cardiovascular capacity and decreased physical function. Usually at some point, the person doesn't even enjoy the eating anymore but has become powerless to stop because of a lack of discipline, depression and low self-esteem. The person realizes his or her condition but often feels helpless to change his or her habits, thus continuing the downward spiral.

"Sex is another act that God created for us to enjoy in the context of marriage. He even gave us the command to be fruitful and multiply. But as Satan is famous for doing, he takes something ordained by God and perverts it in order to make it sinful and destructive to us. With regard to sex, Satan plays on the natural desires that God blessed us with and leads us into temptation by enticing us to act on these urges outside of God's will, which would be sex outside of marriage, or fornication; sex while married with another, or adultery; and even sex with those of our same gender, or homosexuality. Once experienced, men and women often find themselves being drawn into a lifestyle of sexual addiction because the sinful act feeds an unquenchable hunger from our carnal nature.

"Those involved in such a lifestyle find themselves on a perpetual 'slippery slope,' that is, beginning with a single step outside God's will and soon finding that they cannot regain their footing as they continue a downward spiral into addiction. This is because over time, our bodies experience desensitization; that is, they become accustomed to stimulation and over time must experience higher and higher levels to accomplish the same affect. Addicts wake up one morning only to find themselves in a place they never thought they were capable of reaching. Sometimes this place is an ongoing affair. Sometimes it is a lifestyle of one-night stands. Sometimes it is an unnatural same-sex relationship, all of which are far away from the course that God intended for us to follow. They become aware of their condition and may even recognize that their life is spiraling out of control, but as with the eating, they resign themselves to continue in the lifestyle because of a lack of discipline and will power. Unfortunately, the consequences to such choices can often include broken marriages and relationships, sexually transmitted diseases, fractured families, unplanned pregnancies, financial ruin and countless other hardships. (See **1 Thessalonians 4:3–5, 1 John 2:15–17** and **Leviticus 18:22**.)

"Another addiction that commonly stems from sexual addiction is pornography. In this age of having Internet technology at our fingertips, pornography is all the more readily available and easily accessed to the curious observer on the other side of the screen. This addiction works very much like a true physical sexual addiction in that the same slippery-slope principle applies. The person who begins by simply giving into temptation for the first time never thinks in a million years that he or she could ever end up so far away from where he or she began before encountering pornography for the first time. These people find what begins as observing nude photos eventually progresses to watching pornographic videos. They find what begins as ten or fifteen minutes a day browsing the web for sexual gratification progresses to an hour a day, then two, and then into the wee hours of the night and even into the workplace. They find what begins as chatting on the Internet to another while married cascades into phone calls and ultimately into actual meetings with the new love affair. This is because, as with the sexual addiction described earlier, desensitization takes place in the addict, resulting in a need to increase the level of activity to obtain the same level of gratification from the stimuli.

"A common analogy used to describe this condition is the frog in the pot. If we were to drop a frog into a boiling pot of water, the frog would instantly jump out of the pot because of the high temperature. But if we were to place a frog in a pot of water that is room temperature and then slowly bring the pot to boil, the frog would stay in the water until he boiled to death. This is because the transition of the water temperature happens slowly, allowing the frog to become desensitized without realizing what is taking place. The same concept applies to the sex addict. If prior to any addictive nature people were to be exposed to hard-core pornography, offers of prostitution or enticements for physical adultery, they would, as the frog, jump away from the 'boiling pot of sin' because of the sensitivity of their moral compass. But if they began as most do, with very basic levels of exposure to such material, gradually increasing in frequency over time, they, too, will suffer the same fate as the frog on a spiritual level. They will ultimately 'boil to death' in their own sin. (See **Colossians 3:5–8.**)

"As I mentioned earlier, food and sex are not inherently bad in themselves. They were created by God as blessings for us to enjoy when used in moderation and within the boundaries He designed. But there are other addictions that are not crucial to our lives but still used by Satan to destroy us physically and spiritually. The main ones that I am referring to are drugs and alcohol. One could write books on books detailing the social ills and the damage done by these two alone. I could not hope to cover adequately all the death and destruction brought about by these weapons of the enemy. But I will briefly summarize some basic generalizations about them.

"Alcohol and drug addiction begin no differently than any other addictions do. The person who takes his or her first drink never thinks that he or she may someday become an alcoholic hitting rock bottom. Just as the person who smokes his or her first joint, pops his or her first pill or smokes his or her first pipe would scoff at the proposition that he or she may one day become a drug addict. Yet the facts are all around us, and they are all too real.

"The damages wrought on society over the years from these tools of the evil one include broken homes, broken marriages, ruined careers, flooding of our jails, *millions of dollars spent by our legal system and our health care system, rampant crime, the spread of disease, an increase in rape, prostitution, unwanted pregnancies, poverty, downfalls of communities, depression, child and domestic abuse, creation of dangerous cartels, ruined lives, ruined health and death to the abusers and innocent alike. I don't believe that Satan could come up with a more powerful and effective means to destroy generation after generation even if he searched within the deepest pits of hell. It is the gift that keeps on giving for him.*

*"Once again, Satan uses the perpetual 'carrot on a string' technique to draw unwitting people to their demise through opportune times, such as in cases of depression, peer pressure, grieving, generational influences, tragedy, stress or any other factor that leaves the person spiritually vulnerable to experimentation. Some people dabble and miraculously come out unscathed, but for many, this is just the first step in a hellish downward spiral they soon experience. It also takes on the nature of a spiritual cancer, spreading out of control and metastasizing into every aspect of a person's life, leaving only death and destruction in its wake. (See **Isaiah 5:11, Proverbs 23:29–35** and **Luke 21:34**.)*

"Gambling is another tool hanging from the tool belt of Satan. It often goes hand in hand with some of the other addictions, as some addictive personalities find themselves becoming consumed by more than one addiction. Gambling may not have left behind the amount of carnage that drugs and alcohol have, but it is a powerful tool all the same. The prospect of making fast, easy money is a huge temptation to most. To the poor, it plays on dreams of finding a shortcut out of poverty. To the rich, it plays on their pride in regards to showing off their excess money they are able to squander. To the middle class, it appears to be a train ticket to reach the same financial level as the rich without having to work for it. Regardless of the motivation, gambling ultimately becomes a destructive siren sitting on jagged rocks, singing a hypnotizing tune that draws in lost sailors afloat upon the waters of the world, sending them to a watery grave.

"As with the previous addictions, it appears harmless at first. One may even experience some strokes of luck from time to time. But ultimately, it catches up with the person. It is no coincidence that casinos are so large, so lavish and so opulent and enticing; they have a steady stream of revenue flowing into them, which means they must take in more money than they put out. This should make

it clear to anyone who thinks he or she can make a long-term success story from such a lifestyle.

*"Sadly, the progression usually trends from occasional playing for fun to becoming hooked on the adrenaline of the game to winning some and losing some and then, ultimately, to losing more; playing more to win the money back; reaching desperate measures to continue playing; sacrificing homes, careers and relationships to fund the addiction; and finally hitting rock bottom after losing everything of value in one's life. The addict is left feeling ashamed, angry with him- or herself, depressed, hopeless and worthless. By this time, addicts may have lost their homes, their cars, their families, their life savings and their careers, not to mention their dignity. Satan scratches another notch on his bedpost as he achieves another victory. (See **Proverbs 13:11, Matthew 6:24, Proverbs 16:33** and **Luke 12:15**.)*

"Even something as basic as television can be used to draw us away from God's plan for our lives; it's not that it is inherently evil, but just as with anything, when used in excess, it can become an addiction. I do not wish to make this a legalistic argument, only to have each person perform some soul-searching before God and assess where he or she stands with regard to this topic. Television perfectly depicts desensitization at work. If someone were to jump into a time machine and travel back to the fifties, when television first became widespread, that person would note a huge difference in television standards compared to this day and age.

*"Likewise, if we were to take someone from the fifties, bring the person to this day and age and allow him or her to observe modern television programming, he or she would look very similar to the frog jumping out of the water. They would experience such a response from their moral compass that they would be left appalled by what they witnessed. This would be due to the fact that they did not go through the slow desensitization process the rest of the country's population has. If we follow television programming from one decade to the next, we will witness a slow and steady progression of moral decay injected into the themes and broadcasting material fed to us. We have unfortunately reached the point where we can watch some of the vilest, most offensive sights on television and yet not have a flag raised from our moral compasses. This is because we have grown accustomed to such material. We have become 'boiled in our own sin.' (See **Psalm 119:133, Psalm 139:23–24**.)*

"And regarding the time spent watching television, someone once said that we can tell a lot about people's priorities by looking at how they spend their time. This is very true with regard to our walk with Jesus. If we spend more time watching television or partaking in any other recreational activity than we do with God, then we have a misdirected set of priorities. (See **Matthew 6:21**.)

"We should be able to substitute God for our spouse in order to help us put this into perspective. If we spend more time watching television or engaging in any other form of entertainment than we do with our spouse, how healthy will that marriage be? The same should apply to our heavenly Father. (See **Revelation 19:7** and **Ephesians 5:25–27**.)

"We are not merely following a bunch of rules; we are in a committed relationship with the Creator of the universe, adopted as children of God, coheirs with Christ in His reward. Don't we owe Him at least a fair amount of our time? (See **Romans 8:15–17**.)

"But this is ultimately where addiction's purpose is revealed, it is meant to take our focus away from God and His plan for our lives, playing right into Satan's ultimate goal: to destroy as many lives as possible in order to prevent them from choosing Christ's offer of salvation, resulting in eternal punishment to be shared alongside him for all eternity. He knows the destruction that is in store for him, and he also remembers losing his place of honor in heaven, through his pride and rebellion against God. (See **Isaiah 14:12–15** and **Luke 10:18**.)

"This is why he and his minions strive so hard to keep us from becoming saved; it is his way of getting back at God, as he knows that God does not wish for any to be lost. He will stop at no end and will leave no prisoners behind. He knows that time is short and that he is running out of opportunities to accomplish this task, which is why we cannot afford to squander such a precious gift from God; and that being the gift of time. (See **Matthew 25:41, 46**.)

"This is why we cannot allow anything to keep us from the will of our Father, as we will all have to one day stand before the throne and give account of how we used our time. Let us therefore live a life free of addictions, disciplining ourselves to follow His command, so that we may one day hear Him speak these words: 'Well done, good and faithful servant.' (See **Matthew 25:21**.)

"By the way, I have another gift to give you before we move on."

Clarence reaches out his hand and offers me what appears to be a pile of folded material. I take the object and hold it up to reveal a plain canvas backpack. "Let me guess, this turns into a parachute!" I jokingly say.

"Unfortunately not," he replies. "Unlike the Guide Book, *with this gift, what you see is what you get. Its use should be obvious, I guess. As you walk the road, you will find many souvenirs that you will want to hold on to. But choose wisely because the more you pick up, the more you have to carry. And it doesn't take long for the pack to get rather heavy."*

❀

The backpack represents the heart and the mind of a Christian, two places in which God's word, wisdom, hurts, character, grudges and various other things we pick up along our journey in life can be stored. Some things stored within them are good, such as God's word, as is described in **Psalm 119:11, Proverbs 4:20–22, Matthew 6:20–21, 2 Corinthians 3:3** and **Hebrews 10:16.** Other things stored in them are evil, such as hurts, bitterness, hatred and unforgiving of wrongs, as seen in **1 Chronicles 28:9, Revelation 2:23, Proverbs 27:19** and **Matthew 12:34–35.**

❀

I look and notice for the first time that he too carries a backpack. I had never really paid much attention before, as I was more focused on what he was telling me and showing me. From its appearance, it is obvious that it has seen many a mile. Oddly, however, it appears fairly empty. Thinking back to Clarence's words, I realize that he has been very selective as to the items he chooses to carry, thus providing him a lighter load. "I feel guilty taking so many gifts from you, as I have nothing to give you in return."

"Just pay it forward," he says. "Those were the words spoken by the man who gave me mine years ago. Are you ready to go?"

"You bet," I tell him. "Lead the way." I put the pack on, and we begin down the road, the morning sun just above the trees.

Day 5

For quite a while this morning, we just walk and do not speak, taking in the beauty of the surrounding scenery. As we round a corner, I notice to the left of the road that the trees come to an end, revealing rolling fields of grain that appear to flow as waves in a large golden ocean. I notice a man standing in the center of the field holding a large scythe. He is hard at work swinging the tool through the tall grain, appearing to barely make a dent in the vast expanse surrounding him. He appears fatigued, stopping occasionally to wipe the sweat from his brow. The grain eventually ends farther down in the direction we are heading, opening up to flat and empty ground that takes up as much space as the rolling grain does.

In this opening, I notice a woman with a large sack hanging across her. She is reaching in it, pulling out what appears to be seeds and casting them out onto the barren ground. Then I look past the man and notice a hillside rising up at the edge of the field. Resting upon the hillside, I see a large group of people. Some are talking to each other, some are reclined back on the hill with their eyes closed and some are simply sitting watching the man work in the field. "They are going to be there forever trying to finish those jobs," I tell Clarence. "Couldn't any of the people on that hill go and help them?"

Clarence sprouted another one of his smiles. "A very good question indeed; I was hoping you would ask it. Yes, they could benefit from some help, and as you can see, there is no shortage of people available who could help them. But this is the downfall *of those to the left of the road. First, they love to place themselves on higher ground in order to be seen by others. Second, they talk a mean storm. They have plenty of opinions about everything and don't hold back when it comes to giving them. They have general knowledge about religion, but they lack any spiritual wisdom. And third, as you can see, they are all talk and no action. They speak of their faith, but they do not demonstrate it by their works. They will be the first to stand and point to the ripe fields and speak of how they need to be harvested and to the barren ground and how it needs to be seeded, but you will never find them actually entering the fields and doing the work they speak of, as you are witness to right now. They prefer keeping their positions of comfort and elevation rather than going where they are really needed. They are a danger to those on the narrow road, luring many from here to the left because of their semblance of religion. This is why we must take heed to the paths before us and rely on the Holy Spirit to guide us along the true path."*

We see in **Matthew 9:37–38** Jesus speaking about the ready harvest and lack of workers. We as Christians are called to be doers, not just speakers. The reference in the story of sowing refers to spreading the message of salvation to the unsaved. The reference to harvesting refers to saving those who have had seeds planted in a fertile heart that was prepared by the Holy Spirit and are in a position to make a decision for Christ. Again, Jesus further explains this situation in **John 4:31–38.** As Christians, we are called by God to sow seeds that will produce spiritual fruit, not seeds that only produce worldly fruit, as mentioned in **Galatians 6:7–10.** There are times we are called to sow, and there are times we are called to reap what others have sown. This concept is reiterated in **Ecclesiastes 3:1–2.** The description of those on the left side of the road being "all talk and no action" is clarified further in **James 2:14–18, 26.**

We have been walking for about an hour since we saw the fields. I've noticed over the last couple of minutes that the road has started to incline more. Clarence does

not seem to be phased by the transition, but it is taking its toll on me. Slowly I start to fall behind, and soon Clarence turns to see me quite a distance from him. He stops and waits until I finally catch up. I tell him, "I'm sorry for the slow pace. I guess I'm just not used to walking the hills yet."

"No problem. It does take time to adjust to them. I remember it all too well. But you do have something on you that can make the hills a little easier to climb, your Guide Book.*"*

At first I look at him, puzzled, but then I remember what he is talking about. "Oh the staff, that's right! I had forgotten all about that. To be totally honest though, I'm not sure how to make the transformation like you did." I pull the Guide Book *out of my jacket.*

"That can be fixed," he says. "Let me see the book for a second."

I hand it to him and watch as he turns several pages. Then he hands the book to me and says, "Read this section here."

I take the book and look at the passage on the page. I begin to read aloud. **"Isaiah forty-one, ten, 'So do not fear, for I am with you; do not be dismayed, for I am your God, I will strengthen you and help you; I will uphold you with my righteous right hand.'"** *Suddenly, the book starts to glow and I feel a transformation take place in my hand. The glowing fades and there in my grasp is a staff. Even though I had seen it take place before, I'm still left speechless after experiencing it personally.*

"Not your average book, hmm?" he says. "Like I mentioned before, it is God inspired and God breathed, living and active. Many times it is used as a guide book to navigate the narrow road. But many times, such as now, it is used to strengthen us as we face the hard climbs of the road. It seems overwhelming at first, but over time, you will feel more and more comfortable in using it."

We begin walking down the road again. It's amazing what a difference it makes in getting over the hills with the use of the staff. I find traveling the road with it allows me to make better time and leaves me feeling less tired.

We have covered many miles today, and evening is drawing near. I look up ahead and notice something bright moving in a large tree. As we draw nearer, its white body stands out even more against the shadows of the tree. I take this opportunity to ask Clarence about this mysterious companion of ours. "I've been meaning to ask you, Clarence, can you tell me more about that?" I point up into the tree.

He turns his head and stares for some time. "See what?"

I say, "The white bird, right there on the limb, I've seen him several times since we met. Don't you see it?"

"I'm afraid I don't. But I have no doubt that you see it."

I look at Clarence perplexed. "I don't think I understand. How can you not see a white dove sitting in a limb right above us?"

He smiles. "Oh I've seen it quite often over the years in my travels. In fact, it is with you even when you don't see it, because it is in you. It is the Holy Spirit; just as the Guide Book *takes many forms, so can the Holy Spirit. Sometimes He comes to you as a still, small voice; sometimes He goes before you and helps to guide the way. The reason you can see Him now and I can't is because He reveals Himself to each person individually in His own time. We each have our own course in life. Many times our paths overlap, as ours have these past couple of days. Other times you will be on a path by yourself. These can be the discouraging times tempting you to go off the path. But it is often during these times that God reveals the most to you and also strengthens you. You may not see Him every second, but He will never leave you, that is, as long as you stay on the narrow road. There will be times that you find yourself distracted by something to the left or the right of the road. You will take your eyes off the path and before you know it, you are off course. That is when you will hear the calling of the dove from the path. He will speak to your heart and try to draw you back on track. It's not a question of if you stray, but of when, for none of us are perfect, even here on the narrow road."*

ॐ

As mentioned earlier, the Holy Spirit is commonly depicted as a dove, as seen in **Matthew 3:16.** The Holy Spirit is part of the Trinity, as is the Father and Jesus. We see in **Genesis 1:2** that even before the creation of the earth, God's Spirit was present. Just as willingly choosing to walk off the path separates us from the dove in the story, **Isaiah 63:8–10** describes God's people walking away from the Holy Spirit in rebellion. The Holy Spirit speaks to us just as the dove calls out from the narrow road in the story. We see this referenced in **John 14:25–26.** Just as the dove flies ahead and guides in the story, so in **John 16:13** we see the Holy Spirit taking on the role of a guide. The Holy Spirit lives inside those who are born again, as explained in **Romans 8:9.**

✂

"You will find yourself off course from time to time, but the goal as you journey is to try and step off course less and less the longer you walk it. If you look at my clothes, you will notice little tears and rips in my shirt and pants. These are constant reminders of the times I wandered from the path, visual consequences of my disobedience, from such things as thorn bushes, cacti, briars and many other unfavorable things. Some consequences are temporary, like scratches on the arm that heal over time. Some consequences, like the tears in my clothing, are not painful but are permanent reminders of my missteps. But for some, unfortunately, the consequences can be dire and can ultimately cost them their lives. For there are dangers off the path, such as cliffs, quicksand, mountain lions, bears, snakes, loose rocks and many other perils that make leaving the path a sad and permanent fate. Your best bet is to spend time daily learning from the Guide Book *and listening to the calling of the Holy Spirit. These are your two greatest advantages in staying on course and reaching your destination."*

✂

Clarence's point is that, other than Jesus, no one who has ever walked this earth is perfect. We are born with a sinful nature, and even if we accept Jesus as our Lord and Savior, we continue to carry that same sinful nature. It is constantly at war with the Holy Spirit within us. So when Clarence tells Garrett that he will continue to walk off course from time to time, he is not in any way condoning sin or making excuses for it. He is simply stating the reality of it. Even Christians from time to time will step off the path, whether from being distracted and taking our eyes off our focus or from being tempted by Satan. As we mature as Christians, there should be a noticeable decrease in the number of times we stray, but all the same we will stray from time to time. The best we can do the minute we realize we are off course is to turn back to God, repent for the mistake we have made and let Him lead us back to the narrow road.

But as Clarence mentioned, just because we are brought back to the narrow road does not mean that we are exempt from any consequences of the sin we were involved in. Many who sin are left facing criminal charges, which could result in fines or even jail time. Some, like Clarence, are left with the burden of knowing that their sin cost others their lives. Some may experience ruined relationships that cannot be healed, such as a person involved in adultery. And others may face the results of compromising their character, such as losing a job or position through unethical and immoral behaviors. Again, this is not to say that God cannot redeem those who are caught up in such behaviors, but unfortunately, they may also have to live with the heavy weight of the consequences of their actions. Examples of this from the Bible would include David, Samson and Cain.

Day 6

After walking a short time this morning, I notice up ahead that the road branches into a Y. Just as we approach it, I see the white dove fly over our heads and go down the path to the right. I start walking to the right side of the path when I notice that Clarence is heading toward the left. I ask him, "Where are you going?"

He replies, "I'm following my white dove, and from the sound of your voice, I'm guessing that yours is leading you toward the opposite path. Am I right?"

"You are," I tell him. "But I'm not ready to be on the road by myself. I still have a lot to learn and there are plenty of dangers out there."

He looks at me with a sympathetic expression, the kind a father gives his child when the child is facing a hurdle that must be overcome for him or her to grow in some area of life but the child does not understand that it is for his or her own good. "I know it's scary, but you will not be alone. You will have the Lord on your side to guide you on your way. There are some lessons that He wants to teach you, but they will only come to you while being alone with Him on the road. You will have to learn to trust Him in this. Use this time to become familiar with the Guide Book. *There are many lessons you still need to learn from it. I'm sure we will cross paths again soon."*

"Thank you for all your help. I learned so much from you in just these few days. Hopefully we will be on the same path again soon." I shake his hand and then turn to walk down my path, hoping that he was right and that I will be fine.

In my heart, I know I have to do this, but it still doesn't change the fact that I'm petrified, not knowing what I'm going to come across. As I go around the bend, I look back just in time to see Clarence walk out of view. Now it's just me and God.

I close my eyes for several seconds and start to pray. "Lord, I'm not exactly sure how this prayer thing works, but I ask that you help me right now. I'm scared, as I'm sure you already know. If you can, please give me the strength to do what I'm supposed to do and go where I'm supposed to go. And please calm this fear inside of me. Thank you."

I'm not sure if I did it right, but I feel a little more at ease. I continue walking down the road, eagerly looking ahead to see what is coming next. The trees cover my head like a canopy, providing plenty of shade. Suddenly, I notice up ahead an opening in the canopy, with sunlight coming through. As I approach it, I look up and gasp at what I see arching above my path: the most vivid rainbow I have ever seen in my life. My heart flutters a little, as I feel that God has just confirmed to me that He heard my prayer. I continue walking, not being able to hold back my huge smile.

After walking for about an hour or so, I notice a small mossy section beside the path that looks extremely comfortable. I decide to stop and kick back on my temporary green bed and use the time to become more familiar with my Guide Book. *As I sit and place my back against a tree, I hold out my staff and focus. Soon, the staff begins to glow, and suddenly I'm holding the* Guide Book *once again. I open the book and start at the beginning, eager to see what it has to teach me.*

Day 14

One thing that comes from walking the narrow road is the need to be fed, as many calories are burned during one's journey. Food plays an important role in maintaining one's health and strength. As I've found from my travels on this road, God makes it possible to stay well fed without the need to stray off course in order to look for nutrition. According to the Guide Book, *all along the path, one can find fruit trees, berry patches, wild vegetables and small ponds and streams for fishing. But off the path, there are alternate food sources that exist that prove to be a great temptation to many. Honey is one of them. Many greatly crave its sweetness, leaving them unsatisfied with the harvest God provides on the path. The only problem with desiring honey is that one must leave the path in order to obtain it. This act, in itself, is riddled with danger. But in addition to this, in order to obtain the honey, one must go to the bee hive, which also means facing the wrath of the bees. Despite the pain that comes from multiple beestings, it never ceases to amaze me that so many people continue to go after the honey. As time goes on and their stings have healed, the craving for the honey overrides the memory of the pain of their previous attempts.*

The reference to straying off the path in order to reach the forbidden honey is an obvious analogy to the temptation of sin and how it draws us from our

Christian walk. Many types of sin can produce this effect; I believe the mention of honey is particularly symbolic of sexual sin. We find throughout the Bible many verses that back this statement up, including **Proverbs 5:1–6.** Godly wisdom is the solution mentioned in **Proverbs 2:16–19** and **Proverbs 7:4–5** to avoiding the allure of sexual sin.

Just as it was mentioned that there are sweet and pleasing things to eat along the path, God also designed sex to be a beautiful and pleasing gift to be enjoyed between a husband and a wife. But when we decide to partake of this gift outside the context in which God has designed it, by having sex prior to marriage or with another person while we are married, it is then that we put ourselves in spiritual danger. The honey off the path may be sweet, but as Christians, we must learn to be content with the treats provided on the path, else we face severe consequences. Just as the person going after the honey must contend with the bees, so the Christian lured off the path must contend with the judgment of a holy God. We see in **1 Corinthians 6:13, 18–20** that God commands us to not defile our bodies in such a way. As Christians, our bodies are considered temples of God. Taking part in sexual sin is the spiritual equivalent of defacing a church.

Continuing on with the Guide Book, *I find that another source of food that sits out of reach from the path is the grape harbor. All along the path, mixed occasionally with the other fruits and berries, are the occasional clusters of grapes. But away from the path, finding acres and acres of rolling grape vines calling out to the weary traveler is common. For those who venture away to indulge on the sweetness offered by the abundant delicacy, it is not unusual to find them consuming the grapes to a degree that leaves them physically incapacitated from their fermenting power. This is a dangerous situation, as they become vulnerable to the many pitfalls and entrapments that lay away from the safety of the path.*

Satan is a master at taking things created by God and defiling them, making them sinful. As we described earlier, Satan takes the beautiful gift of sex and perverts it to make it sinful and spiritually destructive to humankind. In the same way, he takes a simple creation such as grapes and produces from it a means to create physical and spiritual destruction. How many millions of lives have been destroyed from the abuse of alcohol? Whether from drunk driving, the loss of jobs, physical deterioration of the body, broken marriages, child abuse or a myriad of other calamities, alcohol abuse has been one of the most destructive forces in human history. As far back as the days of Noah, we see the dire consequences that alcohol has produced, as seen in *Genesis 9:20–27.* Other verses include *Ephesians 5:18* and *Proverbs 23:29–35.* As mentioned earlier, we are again called to rely on godly wisdom, as described in *Proverbs 20:1.* In fact, both sexual immorality and drunkenness are described as obstacles to entering heaven, as seen in *1 Corinthians 6:9–10.*

The Guide Book *also notes that as people stray from the path, they also come across huge, densely packed clusters of beautiful berries. The berries are the same as those found on the path, with the only difference being that to reach the off-road variety, one must push through thorny bush after thorny bush. The major problem with this is the fact that it becomes impossible to see where one is stepping when navigating through such thick brush. This provides an opportunity for danger to the traveler, as a common companion to the berry bushes is the snake. They are commonly found lurking under the foliage in order to find shade in the summer heat. As a person pushes forward to pick the berries, it is not uncommon for them to risk stepping on a snake, as the bushes provide poor visibility to the traveler.*

The obvious symbolism of the snake is in reference to Satan. As mentioned in *Genesis 3:1,* we see him depicted as such. As we go from the first book of the Bible to the last book, we again see him being related to a snake in *Revelation*

12:9. The reference to the snake under the berry bushes correlates to how Satan finds ways to tempt us and draw us from our Christian walk, only to strike us and harm us when we least expect it, resulting in pain and death. When we entertain sin, our feet tread where they should not go, leaving us vulnerable to sin and putting us within Satan's striking range.

Disturbingly, the Guide Book *points out that danger not only lies at our feet when we wander off the path; it also lies in wait from above. As we walk toward the object of our desire, we generally do so with a sort of "tunnel vision"—that is, focusing on that which is tempting us and being oblivious to the dangers surrounding us. There is a predator that takes advantage of this circumstance, the mountain lion. The mountain lion usually rests quietly on a tree limb, waits for a victim to approach and then pounces on its victim from above. A very strong animal, the mountain lion can easily overpower a grown man. Unfortunately, many of its victims are the wayward travelers who become prey to this hidden danger when they let their guard down while in pursuit of forbidden fruit.*

The use of the mountain lion is meant to describe, once again, Satan. The lion is another animal used to describe humankind's nemesis, as seen in *1 Peter 5:8*. Whether from a silent, stealthy attack as that from a snake or a violent, overwhelming attack as from a mountain lion, Satan will destroy us the same either way. Both ways are painful and potentially deadly. Stemming from our disobedience to God's word, by our pursuit of worldly desires, both beasts gain their advantage over us off the path. As we stay on the path, we are able to see where our feet are stepping as we walk. The snake does not have a hiding place in which to strike at us unseen. If he wanders into our path, we are able to see him and avoid him. The same pertains to the lion. The path allows us to see what lies ahead. If the lion lies in wait, we are far enough from the tree that he is not able to pounce upon us from above and catch us by surprise. We will have ample time to see him coming and be able to protect ourselves from the attack, using our sword against him, which is the word of God.

♋

The Guide Book *reveals yet another common threat that is connected to both the berry bushes and the honey found off the path: the bear. A very dangerous predator, it also shares a taste for the two treats. Many wayward travelers who have stepped off course, believing only temporarily, to obtain the forbidden fruit, find themselves face-to-face with hundreds of pounds of raging fur. For this reason, we are called to stay on the narrow road and avoid the temptations of the surrounding landscape.*

Another way to think of this scenario is to consider very hungry people walking to have a meal at a restaurant, which is quite a distance away. As they are walking toward it, they find themselves passing by exquisite bakeries and stores selling candies and chocolates. The wares are placed in the display windows to catch the eyes of those passing by. The smell of the goods carries out into the street, enticing the passersby, causing their mouths to water out of desire for the delicacies. The hungry people are constantly tempted at every step to hang a right and devour one of the many luscious treats. Should they decide to take this option, they would quench their hunger with the sugary treats and fill up on their goodness. But after doing so, despite the initial gratification that comes from filling their craving, they will be left with an empty, hollow feeling inside, as the dessert treats contain no significant nutritional value.

Next, consider another group of people who, rather than walking to the restaurant, are leaving the restaurant after polishing off a complete, well-balanced meal that leaves them very satisfied and with full stomachs. These people are walking toward the first group of people, heading for the same line of stores. Yet as these people pass the same storefronts, despite the appealing sights and smells that pervade the senses, they have no desire to partake of them because they are already full from their meal.

So considering the two groups of people mentioned, what are they supposed to represent? The first is representative of Christians who choose to not spend time in prayer and Bible reading, resulting in spiritual starvation. As they go throughout their day, their spirit is left hungering. But what they find is that, unlike the nutritional feast provided by God's word and prayer, the world only offers a sugary, empty-calorie substitute that is very appealing to the senses of the carnal nature but devoid of any spiritual nutrition. Spiritually hungry people, out of weakness, will end up filling their spirit with this junk-food diet, resulting in a brief and immediate gratification that ultimately leaves them feeling sluggish and unmotivated. The other people represent the Christian who partakes of God's word on a daily basis, as well as a healthy, well-balanced prayer life. They are left feeling spiritually satisfied. Thus, as they navigate through the world on their day-to-day business, they are able to withstand the temptations that they are bombarded with throughout the day because their spirit is already full. Because they are not hungry, they have no desire for the delights of the world that would leave them feeling empty.

This is why we, as Christians, must learn to fill ourselves with those things that will quench our spiritual hunger rather than with what merely appeals to our human senses. When we become content with the bounty provided along the path, we will eventually find it easier to avoid the desire to stray from its course.

⚘

In this example, the bear is analogous to the severe consequences that are possible from sin. As mentioned, the bear is encountered as one strays from the safety of the path after being enticed by forbidden pleasures. Usually, when one is attacked by a bear, the result is fatal. This is representative of the heavy drinker who dies in a car wreck, from alcohol poisoning or from cirrhosis of the liver. It is representative of the drug user who dies from overdosing, from a drug deal gone wrong or from an accident due to impaired judgment. It is representative of the adulterer or adulteress who dies at the hand of an angry spouse or from a sexually contracted disease. It is representative of the greedy person who dies at the hand of a storeowner as he attempts to rob him or a homeowner during a break in.

And just as some people occasionally survive a bear attack, they are almost always left with severe scars and deformities that they must bear for the rest of their lives as reminders of their dangerous encounter. The same reality applies with sin. Even if we are not killed, we are often left with horrible scars to bear for the rest of our lives, such as physical impairments, jail sentences, broken marriages, ruined careers, damaged relationships, financial debt, mental anguish or even death and injury to others stemming from our actions. As obvious as it is for most people to avoid contact with bears in the wild, the same attitude should exist in avoiding sin in one's life. Nothing can be gained, and everything can be lost.

Day 24

Many are the nights that I find myself resting beside the campfire, looking up into the dark sky and gazing at billions of stars roaming above me. And each time that I observe this, I am continually amazed at how majestic and vast the night sky is and how small I feel compared to it. In a world of constant change, knowing that I merely have to look up to the stars to be reminded of the one who is above all the chaos here on earth is comforting. I am also reminded that God is not only the God of all creation; He is the God of order as well. One only has to observe the night sky to realize this fact.

The multitude of stars were placed in the heavens and set in motion by our heavenly Father. As decades and centuries have passed, the rotation of the stars as seen from our planet has remained orderly and constant. Since the beginning of time, empires have been built and fallen to ruin; billions of people have come and gone and mountains have been raised, only to be brought low again; but the stars continue their course year after year, unaffected by the happenings that take place on this blue marble we live on. It has always reassured me to have an anchor present in a time of storm.

Just as the stars can be counted on to stay true to their course, the same can be said for the promises and commandments of God. They are as unfailing beacons of light set against the backdrop of a dark and sinful world, never changing in their course and reliable guides for each and every generation. Just as sailors used the positions of the stars to chart their courses for thousands of years, so humankind has looked to the word of God to navigate this dangerous world and guide it safely along its journey. The Ten Commandments are the spiritual equivalent of a beautiful constellation, made up of ten majestic stars that have shined before men century after century.

Each star in the night sky would represent a promise that God has given humankind, such as *"I will never leave you or forsake you"* or *"Where two or more are gathered, there I will be also."* The sun, being the greatest star in our sky, would represent the greatest commandment that Jesus gave to us, which is *"to love the Lord your God with all your heart, with all your soul and with all your might."* The moon, the second greatest light in our sky, would represent the second greatest commandment given to us by Jesus, which is *"to love your neighbor as yourself."*

These two commandments interact together in a way very similar to the sun and moon in fact. The sun, as mentioned, is our greatest source of light, followed next by the moon. The sun is self-sustaining, not requiring any outside influence to maintain its luminescence. The moon, on the other hand, produces no light on its own. The light that we see coming from it in the night sky is merely its surface reflecting the sun's light. When the moon is positioned in direct line of the sun, we are able to witness a full moon, or the moon reflecting light from its entire surface facing earth. But as the moon's orbit alters, slowly the earth begins to come between the moon and the sun. The more the earth blocks the moon, the less light it reflects to the earth, until we reach the new moon phase and the moon appears dark in the night sky. Then the cycle continues back to the full moon. In the same way, the first and greatest commandment is the true source of light in the lives of men, as found in *Matthew 22:37–40.*

Our love for God is the true source of light in this world. When we obey this commandment, the second one comes automatically. If we love God with all our heart, the natural result of this should be that we love our neighbor as ourselves. Just as the moon is a reflector of the sun's light, in the same way, we should be as the moon, reflecting our love for God to our neighbors. However, I find it curious that just as the earth can block the sun's light from reaching the moon and cast a shadow upon it, so too the worldly things of this earth can block out God's light and keep it from reaching us, resulting in a spiritual shadow and preventing us from reflecting the light of God to others.

Day 37

Today, as I was walking down the path, I happened to notice one of the most beautiful and unique flowers I had ever seen growing along the left side of the path. It was pinkish/purple in color and was shaped similar to a crown at the top. It lay just out of arm's reach of the path, which should have been my first warning, but I blocked out any wisdom from my judgment and took several steps off the path to reach this thing of beauty. As I approached it, I leaned forward and reached out to pluck it from the ground. But to my surprise, I was suddenly aware of a sharp and piercing pain in my hand! I released it from my grip and drew my hand back in agony. Looking down at my hand, I noticed little pinpricks of blood springing up. I knelt to get a closer look at what had caused me such discomfort. To my surprise, on inspection, the green stems that supported the crown were actually covered in cactus-like barbs. I was amazed at what I saw.

I opened up my Guide Book to see just what this deceptive piece of foliage was and was amazed to discover that I had stumbled on my first thistle. How a thing of such beauty could also produce so much pain left me astonished. I turned and walked back to the path, feeling foolish for leaving it in the first place and nursing a throbbing hand, as the sting of the thistle left me with hours of pain and discomfort. It was a life lesson I would carry with me throughout my journey, the knowledge that things are not always what they seem—or, to put it another way, watch out for wolves in sheep's clothing.

The thistle is used in the story to represent false prophets of God's word, which is why we find them growing along the left side of the path. Just as the thistle, they have an outward appearance of beauty or godliness. But as one puts their trust in them, they soon feel the spiritual sting of their deception. We see this analogy played out in *Matthew 7:15* and *2 Peter 2:1–3.* This is why we must not follow people blindly but rather must examine their actions and their words against the word of God. If the thistle had been studied thoroughly up close prior to reaching for it so quickly based solely on its deceptive appearance of beauty, the thorny barbs would have been noticed and the painful grasp would have been avoided. This point is spoken of in *1 John 4:1–3.* In the story, Garrett suffered only a sore hand for a couple of days because of his rush to judgment. In real life, the result of being spiritually deceived can mean an eternity in hell.

Day 52

Several days ago, I was walking down the path when I noticed an extremely at-tractive woman walking parallel to me to the right but well off the narrow road. I watched her for several moments, entranced by her beauty. Suddenly she caught my gaze and gave me a sheepish grin. I looked away in a hurry, embarrassed that she had caught me spying on her. She began to make small talk as she continued to walk parallel to me, so I returned the conversation, not wanting to be impolite. At first I kept looking back and forth between the path and her as I walked while continuing the conversation. Eventually, I found myself focusing more on her and her looks than where I was going. I was enraptured by our conversation, not to mention her attractiveness. She was playing the flirting game well, speaking more through her body language than verbally. Even though she was very appealing to me, part of me knew that I should not let myself get too drawn in by this girl because she was walking well off the path and was obviously trying to entice me to join her.

I was just about to give a witty retort to one of her flirtatious statements when suddenly I felt a vine brush across my face. The sensation snapped me back to real-ity, and as I suddenly looked around, I noticed that I was surrounded by weeds in all directions; I had walked into a clump of vines hanging down from a tree. I looked to my left and saw the path about fifty feet away and, perched on a limb along the path, sat the white dove. He looked in my direction, softly cooing as if beckoning me back to the path.

Then I realized that I had veered off the narrow road without even knowing it, as my focus had been fixed solely on the girl. Her seduction techniques had played on my human nature, arousing lustful passions within me that clouded my direction and took me off course. Realizing what I had done, I hurriedly made my way back to the path, stomping through high weeds to get there. As I stepped back onto the path, I turned to my right and found that the girl was nowhere in sight. Where she went, I was not sure, but what I did know was that she had brought me to a place where I did not wish to go, leaving me feeling rather foolish for straying from the path.

The next day, as I walked down the path, I continued to think about the girl I had seen, bringing all sorts of carnal feelings to the surface. Thoughts of her flooded my mind, shoving out any thoughts of spiritual discipline from focus. I also couldn't help but notice a general itching spring up on various parts of my body. I would scratch them, only to find that shortly after the itch would return, a little stronger each time. The next day, which happened to be yesterday, I continued reflecting on the girl as well as scratch my itchy body. Only this day, I noticed that the affected areas were not only red from scratching, but a rash had developed as well. I tried to block the thought of itching, as well as the girl, from my mind. I knew deep down that my thoughts about her were not pure, but each time they would surge back even stronger. My carnal nature was overpowering the Holy Spirit's influence on me. The only thing more powerful than my lusty thoughts was my itching body.

Today, I realize what has happened to me. When I strayed off course several days ago, I had walked into a patch of poison ivy. It didn't become apparent right away, but the initial seeds were planted. As my body began to itch and I would scratch it, I would temporarily feel a surge of relief. Then, within a short amount of time, the itching would be back but only more intense, resulting in a progressive growing and spreading of the rash in response to my scratching. Now as I stand on the trail, looking down at my various patches of rashes over my body and feeling an overwhelming desire to scratch them until my fingers fall off, I realize what I have to do. I have to make a conscious effort to ignore my basic instinct to scratch the rash in order to let it heal.

While searching through the Guide Book, I found a section on remedies for poison ivy. The prescribed treatment is leaving me a little unexcited. It involves taking the mud found under a certain type of plant that is common to the path and covering the rashes thoroughly with it. I only have to walk several hundred feet before I find a patch of these plants growing to the side. I kneel down and uproot a plant, digging my hand in the soil and grabbing a large scoop of the dirt from under it. The plant emits a rather pungent odor, which, of course, transfers to the soil underneath it. As I apply the smelly dirt to my body, I am initially disgusted by the fact of what I am putting on myself. Its putrid smell severely offends my nostrils. But then the odor soon takes second place on my disgust list, directly behind the fact that I brought this malady on myself by my wandering eye and lustful intentions.

As I begin walking down the path again, I am continuing to process this life lesson in my brain. I now see the correlation between the poison ivy and my transgression. Just as the temptation of the girl drew my focus away from the path and into the weeds, I spiritually wandered away from the Holy Spirit's guidance and walked right into Satan's realm. With regard to the poison ivy, I found the more I scratched it, despite the temporary relief, the more severe the itch returned and in larger quantities. Similarly, regarding my feelings for the girl, the more I glared at her lustfully, the more my passions grew within my mind and the more effect they had over me. Despite the initial gratification they brought to me, the sexual rash that was planted in my brain continued to spread and become more intense with each scratching.

Only when I made a conscious decision to stop entertaining the thoughts and deal with them was I able to start reversing the negative effects on myself spiritually. I realize now that the spiritual poison ivy will remain in my mind throughout my life, waiting for me to simply scratch it so it could restart its malignant spread throughout my soul. I have to discipline myself to steer clear of the temptation each time it arises in the future, to avoid the foul, wretched smell that sin leaves behind, which is symbolized by the humbling, offensive mud I had to apply to my body.

In this story, we see the result of dealing with any addiction, whether it be sexual, alcohol, drugs, gambling or any other vice. The sin takes root and then starts to grow and spread as more and more "scratching" takes place. This is because of our human nature and its constant craving for things that are not beneficial for us. We see this dilemma depicted in *Romans 7:17–25.* As we can see, the desire to sin, stemming from our sinful nature, can override the influence of the Holy Spirit in our thoughts and desires. They are at constant war with each other. The Holy Spirit's main objective is to produce spiritual fruit within us and to help us mature as Christians. The human nature that remains within us, even after we are born again, only desires to bring pleasure and self-gratification to our bodies, even at the cost of destroying it. It is blind to the consequences that stem from its actions. *Galatians 5:16–18* discusses this conflict.

This brings up another very important concept, that of the law. As mentioned, we, as Christians, are led by the Spirit and are not under the law. This does not mean that we, as Christians, do not have to follow the law. Rather, it means that as Christians follow the Spirit's influence, complying with the law should come naturally. Part of being led by the Spirit is the desire to please God through our relationship with Him. As we strive toward this goal, disobeying the law would be contrary to our efforts. This is further elaborated in *Romans 8:1–14.*

To use the example of the story, the law would represent the order to not go off the narrow road. The beautiful girl would represent sin and its seductiveness. The poison ivy would represent consequences put in place by God because of disobedience. As Garrett follows the Spirit, he will continue to walk on the path and avoid the poison ivy. But with every step, the temptation to sin exists and calls out to him. As long as his desires match with those of the Holy Spirit, he will not desire to stray from the path. But once he acts on a temptation and feeds the desires of his human nature, he will find himself off the path and susceptible to the consequences of the poison ivy. He can always return to the path and seek redemption from God, but he will have to suffer the effects of the poison ivy for a time.

Sadly, this analogy can be seen in everyday life with the person who turns from alcohol but carries an internal weakness to the vice, the drug addict who seeks treatment for his or her addiction but must battle the body's insatiable appetite for the drugs or the sex addict who admits his or her weakness and seeks help but always carries a vulnerability to the allure of pornography and sexual sin. Addiction is a horrible condition that originates under the radar and secretly grows until its destructive ways can no longer be concealed from those around the addict, much like the rash of poison ivy. And just as the person who has contracted poison ivy is contagious to those around him or her, so too can an addict's self-destructive ways cause collateral damage to friends and family who try to help him or her. If you are wondering how to best avoid going through this condition, stay out of the bushes.

Day 71

Early this morning, as I was preparing to start my journey, I sat with my back against a huge, old oak tree. Just as I was about to stand up, something hit me on top of my head. It wasn't anything big or heavy, just a light plop on my head. I looked to my side to see what the culprit was and found that it was only an acorn. As I reached down and picked it up, I had to laugh at the situation. I was about to toss it to the ground when a thought appeared that blew my mind. This little thing that fits between my two fingers has the potential to one day become as large as this very tree I'd been leaning against. Every great big oak once began as a tiny little acorn.

I turned to look at the huge tree and admire its beauty, when I spotted something on the branch that gave me another epiphany moment. Crawling up the trunk of the tree was a caterpillar. I watched for several moments as he journeyed, eventually reaching the base of a limb. On the limb, I spied several cocoons wrapped in silk. Then I made the connection; inside these cocoons are the very things that I am watching crawl up the tree. As I thought about this for a second, one of the cocoons began to wiggle and twitch. The movement snapped me out of my thought, and I gazed as a beautiful butterfly crawled out of the cocoon, opened its wings and flew away. I was so enamored by the sight that I watched for several minutes as it made its maiden flight up and down and forward and back and in all sorts of zigzag patterns. My focus then came back to what I was thinking of moments ago, the acorn. Suddenly, I realized the similarity in the two spectacles I had just observed. The acorn and the caterpillar both share an amazing capacity for transformation, one becoming an enormous tree and the other a beautiful winged creature. It would be easy to look at the two and not be very impressed with either of them at first glance. But once we comprehend the potential that lies in both of them, it radically changes our perspective.

As I continue walking again, I can't help but think how similar my situation is to theirs. Outwardly, most would not understand what I am referring to, but inwardly, I am as transformed spiritually as the acorn and the caterpillar. I started off living across the river as an unsaved, empty vessel, just like every other person living there. But on the day I crossed over the bridge and came to this side of the river, I received the gift of the Holy Spirit within me, transforming me from a lost soul to a child of God. I may not have a difference in physical size as an acorn does compared to a tree or wings like a butterfly to confirm my transformation, but my change will be most evident after this life, when my soul is admitted into heaven rather than facing an eternity in hell.

༉

It is an amazing concept when we consider the process of a born-again Christian. As Garrett describes, those around us don't see a physical metamorphic transformation take place when we become saved, but if they could see us in the spiritual context, they would be astounded at what they see. **John 3:3** reinforces the fact that a change takes place within us. A man of the Pharisees questioned Jesus when He made this statement, thinking He was referring to a physical manifestation, as we see in **John 3:4.** As described earlier in the book, a non-Christian is only able to judge things through worldly wisdom. They cannot comprehend spiritual wisdom or those things revealed through the Holy Spirit, resulting in such a question. Jesus responds to him in **John 3:5–6.**

For an acorn to begin the transformation process into an oak tree, it must first be buried underground. This is symbolic of the born-again process, as described in **1 Corinthians 15:35–38, 42–49.** When we look at all acorns, in general, they are relatively the same in appearance. Some are a little bigger than others, and they can be found in a variety of colors, but overall, their makeup is basically the same. The truth of the matter is not every acorn will become a tree. Some factors that prevent this process from occurring are

* being eaten by squirrels or other woodland creatures;
* insects burrowing into the acorn and destroying it; and
* being crushed as they lie aboveground.

But ultimately, the biggest factor that determines an acorn's success is whether they are able to be buried in the ground. As long as it resides aboveground, it stands no chance of becoming a tree. It is only when it is buried that the process can take place. Once it is underground, the hard outer shell surrounding it must be broken down in order for sprouting to begin. This is not unlike the non-Christian that finds him- or herself with a hardened heart from sin. This person must first allow this hardness to be shattered in order for God to begin the transformation within it. *Hebrews 3:15* speaks of this condition of the heart. The outer shell of the acorn must be sacrificed to achieve the goal strived for. In a sense, the acorn is dying so that the oak tree can be born and flourish. The same applies to humankind. We must be willing to sacrifice our love of self in order to achieve a higher goal. *2 Corinthians 5:1–5, 17* explains the process that takes place in our spiritual transformation.

Once the shell is broken and the sprouting begins, the small plant eventually finds its way to the surface and starts the growing process aboveground. At this stage, it is no longer an acorn; rather, it is an oak tree, though at a very immature period. During these early formative years, it is very susceptible to external influences, just as a new Christian who lacks spiritual maturity would be. Its roots start to grow, and it starts to gain height, but it still appears to be a lifetime away from a mature tree. We find Jesus giving a parable that speaks to this perspective in *Matthew 13:31–32.* The sprout over time grows to a sapling. What is curious to think about is that even at the sapling stage, the tree can be bent in various directions, allowing one to dictate the direction in which the tree will grow. But once it has reached a certain size, this becomes an impossible task. There is a parallel to this in bringing up a child. Children are like the sapling. They can be positioned to grow in a certain direction, for better or worse, by those around them. But once they reach a certain age, trying to change direction in their lives is similar to moving a tree. This is why it is so important for parents to take full advantage of children's formative years to teach them how to live godly lives. If parents wait too late, their job becomes a much more difficult one. *Proverbs 22:6* illustrates this point.

Regarding the caterpillar, we also share in its transition. Just as it spins itself into a cocoon for a period to reach its new form, we as Christians are called on to set ourselves apart spiritually from the rest of the world. We are in a sense asked to "cocoon our minds" in the word of God to prevent the world from polluting it, as described in *Romans 12:1–2.* To those of us who give our hearts to Jesus and accept His sacrifice, we can look forward to the same blessing as the caterpillar. Instead of being tied to our earthly bodies and a hopeless future, we can look forward to one day "spreading our spiritual wings" and rising above the sin that so easily entangles, as seen in *Isaiah 40:31.* God does not want us to be content to "crawl" around this world of sin. We were made for something better. He desires for us all to be transformed and to let our souls "take flight" in His loving grace. *Ephesians 4:22–24* speaks of His plan of making us new. The caterpillar represents our old life, one of letting our selfish passions and appetites dictate our actions and following our basic instincts. Just as the caterpillar is content to crawl around and eat, the butterfly takes advantage of its transformed body and soars to heights that the caterpillar could never dream of. We, too, were meant for something better. *Romans 6:6–8* demonstrates the transforming power of salvation.

Day 73

Today I was doing some research in the Guide Book, *reading about some of the vegetation that exists along the path. One specimen in particular seemed very curious to me, a particular type of pinecone that has an interesting aspect to it. The pinecone stores within it fertilized seeds that will one day become future pine trees. But the unique thing about this type of pinecone is that the seeds can only be released after going through a fire. The fire destroys the mature pine trees of the forest, but the fertilized seeds within the cone go on to replenish the forest. What struck me most about the process described is that it is only through a trial by fire that the seeds can be released and start the growing process.*

This made me think of my own life and how at times God has used the same technique to produce something in me that couldn't have come about without going through the fire. During a forest fire, just as with a devastating trial, there appears to only be total destruction. We don't understand the reasons why, and we focus on what has been lost. But as with the pinecone, we should be focusing on how God can use the experience to bring about something new in our lives, something that couldn't have been gained without the loss of something else.

This is a very basic principle used by God frequently throughout the Bible in order to achieve a higher purpose with His children. One of the best examples can be seen with Job. The forest fire in his life cost him his possessions, his family and his health. It would have been easy for him to only focus on the destruction and become angry with God. Instead, he trusted in God and was rewarded with new seeds, reaping a greater harvest of wealth than he had prior to the trial, a greater understanding of God's ways and the blessing of more children. For this reason, we must not doubt God's goodness and wisdom during times of chaos in our lives. Our perspective should be that of Job's, as seen in *Job 2:9–10* in how he answers his questioning wife.

But the greatest example by far would have to be the final days of Jesus. His trial by fire included being beaten, whipped, spat on, mocked, abandoned by His disciples, taking on the weight of our sins, nailed to a cross and pierced for our transgressions, ultimately leading to His death. Yet just as the pine-cone brings forth life out of annihilation, so too did Jesus bring forth salvation to humankind out of His death. The spiritual seeds released from His sacrifice have continued to flourish for more than two thousand years after His death. Thanks to Him, the blood spilled on one lone tree on Mount Calvary has produced a "forest" of Christians in heaven. Jesus understood the process well, as He was able to use spiritual wisdom to see the big picture rather than human wisdom as Peter used, depicted in the conversation between the two in *Matthew 16:21–23.*

Day 91

Earlier today, I ran into another traveler along the road. As we were talking, he informed me that later in the day we would have the rare opportunity to observe a solar eclipse. I had heard of them but had never seen one firsthand. I was very excited at the concept of seeing one for the first time and told the other traveler that I would definitely be watching for it. He warned me about looking directly into the eclipse, saying that if I were to do so, I could suffer permanent eye damage. I was stunned to hear this and asked him why that would be. He informed me that during a solar eclipse, the moon moves directly between the earth and the sun, blocking out nearly all of the light from the sun and bringing darkness to the earth temporarily. During the phase when the moon is directly in front of the sun, the earth experiences the most darkness, and it happens to cause the pupils in our eyes to dilate to see better. But as the moon moves past the sun, a sudden resurgence of sunlight suddenly appears. Because our pupils had opened during the darkness to allow more light in, it is traumatically barraged by the unexpected dose of sunlight striking it.

Later, as I was walking, I thought about what he had said and it made me think of how that whole process is very symbolic of something. If we think of the sun, the giver of light as Jesus, the moon, the reflector of the sun's light as Christians and the earth as those unsaved in "the world," as often referred to in the Guide Book, *the makings of an analogy exist.*

As Christians, when we are faced with attacks from the world, if we position ourselves directly in line with God's word, those attacking us will be blinded by the light of God's truth, as we see described in *John 3:19–21* and *John 1:4–5.* Jesus confirms this analogy in *John 8:12.* We are called to use the light of Jesus when dealing with those in the world, as is mentioned in *Ephesians 5:8–11.*

Day 130

I have recently made an observation regarding my journey along the road. Many times I have come across obstacles that serve more or less as road blocks, such as rock slides or fallen trees. As I stand before them, I am forced to make a choice of either working my way over them and continuing on the narrow road or bypassing them altogether, which would require me to go off the narrow road and take an easier route to the right or left of the obstacle. As I reflect back on my early days on the road, I realize that many times I chose to skirt the hurdle rather than go over it.

At the time, it seemed to make more sense to take the path of least resistance, but now I'm beginning to realize that I was looking at the situation using human wisdom rather than spiritual wisdom. What my human eyes saw as an inconvenience was actually something that God put in my path to make me stronger. By taking the easy way around, I deprived myself the opportunity to grow stronger by overcoming what was placed before me. Even though I knew that I was called to stay on the narrow road, I was able to rationalize going off the path to myself, thereby compromising my spiritual integrity. At times, I would find out that what appeared to be the easy way around usually resulted in me facing hidden dangers that laid in wait off the path. I have come to learn through spiritual maturity that even roadblocks play a part in God's plan for my life. By overcoming the hurdles rather than avoiding them, I find myself better prepared when facing challenges in my life. I also find that I am better able to help others overcome obstacles in their own lives, as I have experienced them in mine as well.

From my personal experience as a wrestler throughout my school years, I have always found the development process of a wrestler to be analogous to the development process in a Christian's spiritual life. The following are examples to demonstrate the relationship between the two:

* In both wrestling and Christianity, one must make a conscious decision to commit. Either a person is on the wrestling team, or they are not. Likewise, either a person is born again, or they are not.

* In wrestling, once someone chooses to join the team, they are just as much a member of the team whether they are a first-year wrestler or a ninth-year wrestler. The only thing that separates them from the other wrestlers is maturity and experience. These traits only come with time and effort. The same applies with Christianity. A person newly born again is just as much a Christian as someone with decades under his or her belt, but the latter person is only differentiated by maturity and experience that, as mentioned, comes only with time and effort. We see this principle described in *1 Corinthians 3:1–2* and *Hebrews 5:13–14.*

* As a wrestler gains years of experience under his belt, more is expected from him with regard to his abilities and performance. The same applies to Christians. God expects spiritual growth and maturity from each of us, as demonstrated in *Hebrews 6:1–3.*

* Wrestling is an individual sport as well as a team sport. During a wrestling match between two schools, each wrestler faces an opponent one-on-one to win an individual match, but the result of the match also determines the amount of points a team receives or doesn't receive. Similarly, as Christians, we are called to come together as a team, as described in *Hebrews 10:24–25.* Yet, even though we are

called to come together to strengthen each other, we will ultimately be judged individually before God, as mentioned in *2 Corinthians 5:10.*

* In wrestling, the only way wrestlers improve their abilities is to have a partner who will push them mentally and physically during practice on a consistent basis. If a wrestler chooses to continually spar against a weak opponent, he or she will stunt his or her growth in the sport. The same applies in regards to Christianity. We are called to sharpen each other spiritually or, as mentioned earlier, "spur one another on toward love and good deeds." If we are never challenged to grow spiritually by our brothers and sisters in Christ, how are we going to be able to stand against the enemy outside of the church when the attack comes? We see the Bible's call for this in *Hebrews 3:13.*

* A wrestling team is composed of various weight classes, ranging from a lightweight to a heavyweight. Each wrestler falls to a specific weight class, depending on his or her physical makeup. No one weight class is more important than another. Each one affects the team's score positively or negatively in the same manner. But what is important for a team is that they have a wrestler for each weight class who can meet the opposing school's wrestler for that weight class. Basically, a heavyweight cannot wrestle an opposing school's lightweight, or a lightweight cannot wrestle an opposing school's heavyweight. Each wrestler has an individualized task presented to him or her: making weight for the specific weight class. Likewise, within a church family, each Christian is given different spiritual gifts and talents by God to be used to promote the gospel of Christ. As with a wrestler's weight class, these talents are geared specifically for each Christian. The Bible further elaborates on this concept in *Romans 12:4–8.*

To be a successful team, each person must be content with the position he or she is given. They cannot be envious of each other because of differing gifts or talents. The lightweight cannot be jealous of the heavyweight or vice versa. It would be counterproductive for the team if this mind-set were to exist. The same applies within a church. Each Christian must seek God's individualized calling for his or her life and then strive to grow in that specific calling, as expanded upon in *1 Corinthians 12:12–27.* As wrestlers, we carry the responsibility of knowing that the results of our matches affect not only us individually but also the team as a whole. The difference between a team winning or losing a match can often come down to an individual win or loss. The same applies within the church. Some battles can be won or loss by an individual's actions. An example of this would be the impact of a sexual scandal with a person who is in a position of leadership in the church. The loss from such an act would not only hurt the individual involved but the church as a whole.

* To be a good wrestler, one must not only have strong knowledge of the sport and its techniques but also be physically capable of putting the skills into action against his or her opponent. A wrestler may study and be familiar with every possible move and technique, but if he or she never physically trains him- or herself to do the moves, this knowledge will be useless when facing another opponent who is proficient in technique. The same applies to Christians. In this day and age, we have no shortage of information that is available to us. Unfortunately, I also believe that as technology makes learning easier, there is an inverse correlation to how this knowledge is utilized. We are fast becoming a generation of armchair Christians, obtaining knowledge but failing to train ourselves to be effective in using it.

This is where discipline comes in. As mentioned during the foundation analogy, discipline was described as one of the four cornerstones of our spiritual temple. Without discipline, there is no growth. From my experience in wrestling, I was fortunate to have a coach who understood the importance of balancing knowledge with discipline. Each season, during the first week of training, we would go through the ordeal of reorienting our bodies to the brutal demands of our coach. He would push us physically and mentally beyond what we thought was humanly possible, leaving us dehydrated, nauseous and exhausted. During this period, rookie teammates usually made their decisions to either continue or quit the team. Some would quit and return to their normal lives, no longer facing the demands of wrestling.

But by taking the easy way out, they unknowingly deprived themselves a level of self-respect and self-discipline that would have shaped their lives beyond the wrestling mat. For those who stuck it out through the initial pain, they soon were amazed to learn that their bodies gradually started to acclimate to the grueling demands of the practices. Endurance started to develop, making it easier each day to perform the drills. Our technique improved as we practiced wrestling against each other. As unpleasant as the training was, a part of us knew it was the only way for us to reach the level of skill that we desired. Even though the coach pushed us beyond our comfort zone, we trusted him and respected him for helping us to grow as athletes. Day by day, we were beginning to comprehend the true definition of discipline. Discipline is the act of striving toward a goal without ceasing in spite of pain and hardships. We see this definition spoken of in *Hebrews 12:11–12.*

As Christians, we are faced with the same expectation of discipline. Just as a wrestler must deprive him- or herself the luxury of kicking back and hanging out with friends whenever he or she wants, abstain from eating what he or she wants when he or she wants and not take part in the pleasures that a person choosing not to wrestle enjoys, so too are Christians faced with the daily challenge to discipline themselves on a spiritual level. They cannot follow the crowd and do what comes easy or what feels good at the time; they must make choices daily that will help them mature spiritually and become more effective Christians.

* As Christians, we are engaged in a spiritual war daily. The Bible makes this fact clear in *2 Corinthians 10:3–5.*

As wrestlers, the battlefield is found on the wrestling mat and their war is composed of a series of battles referred to as wrestling matches. Some battles are won; some battles are lost. Victory or defeat is determined by a combination of factors, such as experience, physical conditioning, technique and personal drive. The well-rounded wrestler generally holds the advantage. I've seen from experience wrestlers who appear intimidating because of their physique but fall short during the match because they lack either experience or technique. I've seen wrestlers who are well trained in technique but fall short during the match because they lack the physical stamina of their opponents.

The same theory applies to Christians. When facing spiritual warfare against the enemy, one specific factor does not win battles but rather a well-rounded approach gives the advantage. The skill set needed to be an effective Christian would be strong character, an active prayer life, time spent in God's word and putting our faith into action. Rather than facing an opponent on a wrestling mat, Christians meet their opponents daily in the real world. It may be a coworker who professes being an atheist and challenges our faith in front of others. It may be an unbelieving spouse who mocks us for our stand. It may be classmates who rejoice in singling us out from the crowd and tormenting us for not giving in to peer pressure. It may be times of trial in our life, such as financial hardships or health issues. It may be the culture as a whole trying to draw our children away from our teachings and into an amoral abyss. Each of these situations describes a real spiritual battle that Christians face on a daily basis. The outcome of the battles usually depends upon the state of readiness of the Christian. A strong prayer life will provide strength and guidance. Being knowledgeable in God's word will act as both an offensive and a defensive weapon. Working daily on practicing our faith will be the equivalent of possessing physical endurance for an athlete. But the most decisive factor of each battle will often be our level of character at the time of attack.

We, as humans, even after we are born again, continue to fall short at times. We do not reach a level of maturity and simply turn on autopilot. Every day brings new troubles and new circumstances that affect our readiness as a witness for Christ. This is why each battle is unique in its own circumstances. We cannot assume that just because we have been a Christian for many years we can coast through future struggles. Satan will work tirelessly to bring us down. Regardless of how long we have walked with Christ, he will study our weaknesses and bring forth a new attack daily. This is why we must reassess ourselves each and every day and make sure that nothing in our lives will weaken our character. Each battle we face must be given our full attention and our full effort.

From my wrestling career, I can remember two specific matches in which my level of character determined my outcome; one for the better, one not. The match that resulted in me paying the price for my shortcoming was during my high-school state wrestling tournament. Having lost my first match of the tournament, I was fortunate enough to win the next several matches afterward. I found myself facing this scenario for the upcoming match: if I won, I would go on to wrestle for third or fourth place, if I lost, for fifth or sixth place. The opponent for the next match had a reputation as a very good wrestler. I started the match in the right frame of mind. I wanted to win the match more than anything. I was giving 110 percent.

By the halfway point in the third period, I was ecstatic to find myself winning the match by one point. All I had to do was keep him from scoring any more points and I would win the match. I was in the top position and was holding him at bay underneath. Suddenly, with less than thirty seconds left in the match, the referee blew the whistle and stopped the match. My heart sank when I saw him charge me with stalling and give my opponent one penalty point. The term *stalling* is used when a wrestler does not show offensive movement when it is possible. Basically, I had been charged with resting on my laurels before the match was won, resulting in a tied score at the end of the third period. This forced us into overtime, which resulted in my opponent achieving an escape and scoring one point, the point needed for him to win the match.

To this day, I reflect often on that match. It's not so much that I'm consumed with my ranking in the tournament. I live with the regret of not giving my all those last seconds of the match. Being so close to victory and then losing, not because I was outwrestled but because I lost my drive, is a hard pill for me to swallow. As a Christian, I have to wonder how many times I've experienced the spiritual equivalent to that match. How many times have I been close to winning a lost soul to Christ only to quit too early? How many designs did God have planned that were never accomplished merely because I failed to be persistent in prayer?

The other match I spoke of came during an ordinary dual meet with another school. I found myself in the third period of the match one point behind my opponent and in the bottom position. As the whistle blew, I shot up to my feet with my opponent controlling me from behind. I repeatedly attempted to break away and gain one point for an escape, which would have tied the match. But I found that each time I got to my feet and attempted to escape, he would drive me out of bounds, forcing me to start over from the bottom position. After several repeat attempts of escape all resulting in failure, I found myself once again coming back to the bottom position with only ten seconds left to go in the match and still one point behind. I was so frustrated that I was not able to escape each time that I stood.

As I got into position at the center of the mat, rather than panicking, I suddenly felt a sense of calm and a focus that I didn't expect. My opponent slowly positioned himself over me, and then the referee blew the whistle. This time, rather than coming to my feet as I had done every previous time, as soon as the whistle blew, I broke my arm from his grip and threw myself to the side, performing a switch and scoring two points for a reversal. I no sooner completed the move when the buzzer sounded, ending the match and giving me the win by one point.

In hindsight, it was just another match, but the part of it that encourages me to this day is the fact that for that one battle, I didn't give up even when things seemed hopeless. I found the strength to persevere and was blessed with a victory for the effort. Spiritually, I strive now for that same experience. When I am faced with an attack from the enemy and I'm down to the last ten seconds of the fight, I want to be disciplined enough to go full steam until the very end. It doesn't mean that I will be successful with every battle, but I will be able to be content knowing that I gave everything I had, leaving me with no regrets.

* The last major similarity between wrestling and Christianity is the anticipation of eventual reward. At the end of the wrestling season, a

banquet would be held to honor the wrestlers. Family members would attend and trophies would be passed out to the members of the team. I can remember how excited each of us was to receive a trophy, which represented the completion of an entire season. Now that I'm older and years away from those days, I have to laugh at how my perspective has changed with regard to the significance of the trophies.

As important as they were to me at that time, I can honestly say they now reside inside an old trunk that hasn't seen the light of day for more than twenty years. How symbolic of our lives in general. How much time and energy do we spend chasing "trophies" year after year, only to find that once we obtain them, their importance soon fades away? The dream home, the new car, that position at work, that degree, fame and the large bank account, these are all common things strived for, but when we lie on our death bed, they will hold the same amount of importance to us as the trophies in the trunk. But in Christianity, the reward strived for is not temporary and will not end up hidden away. The reward is eternity in heaven, where there will be no more tears, no more night and no more death! That certainly is worth more than any material possession this world can give us. And the wrestling banquet will pale in comparison to the reception we will receive after this life, when we will be reunited with friends and loved ones who have gone before us. Therefore, let us keep our focus on the true prize and not grow weary in facing the enemy on a daily basis. We must be ready to wrestle with the evil forces that come against us until we face our last match with the devil and are called home to our reward!

Day 166

Today started out as any other day. I began my journey as usual, taking in the sights and sounds around me, strolling pleasantly down the path. As I rounded a corner, I noticed something peculiar that caught my attention. The path I was walking on came to a Y ahead of me. As I neared the Y, the path to the right continued unimpeded, but the path to the left was blocked by a rockslide starting about two hundred feet from the Y. The left path, about seven feet wide, ran alongside a sheer hillside that was completely vertical for over a hundred feet. On the other side of the rockslide, the narrow path ran about fifty or sixty feet until it came to the mouth of a small cave entrance, about six or seven feet high.

Between the path to the right where I stood and the small section of the left path that remained was a deep chasm, whose bottom could not be seen. The chasm's width between the two paths was about thirty feet. But as peculiar as all this was, this was not the most fascinating thing. For sitting in the middle of the path between the rock slide and the cave entrance, leaning against the hillside with his head hung down, was an elderly man. His clothes were tattered and rather dirty. He didn't seem to be in pain but rather asleep. I gazed at him for several moments, my mind trying to take in the whole scene and process what I was looking at.

After about a minute, I was about to yell to get his attention, when suddenly he slowly lifted his head up and looked at me, a grin appearing on his weathered face. It took me a second to figure it out, but I finally realized who I was looking at, it was Clarence! I barely recognized him with his disheveled appearance and head down. "Clarence!" I yelled over to him. "I can't believe it's you! What happened?"

He was silent for several seconds, as if building up the energy to answer back. Then suddenly he yelled back, "Great to see you again, my friend! Although I would have preferred it was under better circumstances. But all the same, it is great to see you!"

"Are you hurt?" I frantically asked him.

"Well, yes and no," he replied. "I was not injured by the landslide, but you could say that I am hurt though."

"I'm afraid I don't understand what you mean, Clarence. Did you hit your head or something?"

He began to chuckle slightly. "No, I didn't hit my head, although it's probably been years since that thing has worked properly to tell you the truth. What I meant was that I'm hurt, but unfortunately, it's nothing you can do to help me. I'm simply dying."

The weight of his words hung in the air like a fog on a windless day. I just stood and stared at him in utter disbelief. I don't know if I was more shocked by his words or his nonchalant manner when saying them. Suddenly, a panic came over me. "Don't move, Clarence. I'm going to find a way to get over to you, don't you worry."

He held out his hands with his palms facing me. "Please. There's nothing you can do now. It's OK."

I became indignant. "What do you mean it's OK? I have to help you. I'm not going to let you die!" My mind raced as I frantically looked for a way to get over to him.

"You don't understand," he said. "It's my time. It's nothing that needs fixed or tended to; it's just my time. Just like every single person who ever lived on this earth, God has a day accorded to each of us. When it's our time, it's our time. And there's nothing wrong with that. We weren't meant to walk this earth forever. I know it might seem like a very foreign concept to someone of your age, but I have traveled many, many, many miles on this earth. I've had a lifetime of experiences, and I was fortunate enough to make a decision to serve God for most of my life.

"But to tell you the honest truth, I'm just plain tired. My body has served me well during my existence here, but unfortunately, it's a wear-and-tear item. My

muscles have grown weak, my joints sore, my bones frail and my eyes blurry. You may think me crazy, but I'm actually looking forward to this. I have nothing left down here to prove. I've run my race, now I want to go and trade in this tired, old body for a new one. I can no longer remember what it felt like to run and not grow weary. But I will, just as soon as I take my final couple of steps on this earth and enter that cave entrance. I'll finally be home."

Tears streamed down my face as I took in everything he told me. I understood what he was saying, but I didn't want to accept it. My mind and my heart were in conflict. Looking at his frail body, I completely understood what he was saying and had compassion for him. But as for my heart, I was thinking selfishly about my own wants and fears, not wanting him to go so soon. "There is so much I wanted to say to you when I saw you again. You don't understand how much you helped me and how much I have learned because of you. I was hoping for more lessons from you. I've learned a lot, but there is still so much more for me to learn."

"And you will. God will lead you to others just like He led you to me. I'm grateful that He sent you into my life and that I could play a part on your road to salvation. But there is one last lesson I would like to share with you before I go."

Choking back tears, I nodded. "Yes, I would like that."

"After all these years of traveling and serving the Lord, I've stumbled on a secret that most of humankind has spent time and treasure trying to discover but never seemed to have grasped. The funny thing is the answer has been right in front of their noses, the last place they would think to look. I've discovered the secret to happiness! And believe it or not, I can say it in one word."

I was stunned at what I was hearing. As much as I was hanging on to every word he was saying, I was still emotionally trying to process what was soon to come. I managed to muster a thought despite the situation and asked him, "God?"

He replied, "Obviously, but more specifically, let me ask you this: Why is it that some people have all the wealth they would ever need and are miserable, yet others live on a meager salary and are some of the happiest people in the world? Or why do many of those who have achieved celebrity and success through their talents end up being some of the unhappiest people in existence, resorting to drugs and alcohol to find comfort and sometimes even suicide? If wealth, fame, success, possessions and power do not bring happiness, then what does? I'll tell you. The answer to the *million-dollar question: contentment. It may sound like an oversimplified answer, but it is true. Think about it. Humankind strives for all the things I mentioned earlier in hopes that they will achieve—think about it—contentment. They know what they are striving for, but they go about finding it in all the wrong ways. As you said, what they are missing is God. Without God, all efforts to achieve true contentment are futile."*

�֍

If you remember back to one of their previous conversations, Garrett and Clarence were discussing the relationship between the human nature and the Holy Spirit, both existing within each Christian. They are constantly at war with each other, striving toward opposing goals. Our human nature is driven solely toward fulfilling the desires of the flesh, seeking self-gratification and immediate pleasure above all else. This contradicts the goals of our spirit nature, which are to maintain a personal relationship with God and follow His commands above all else. This entails prioritizing His two greatest stated commandments, as seen in *Matthew 22:37–40.*

When we seek to feed our human nature, we soon discover that its appetite is insatiable. It never has enough. To make sense of this concept, let's first look at what the human nature desires. The common denominator to all its cravings is fulfillment of our fleshly desires through worldly means. Let's go through the ones that I mentioned. Our human nature seeks after wealth from the worldly perspective, which refers to money and possessions. Financial wealth in itself is not evil. The love of money corrupts. No one was ever better equipped to validate this point than King Solomon, as confirmed in *1 Kings 3:3–13.*

As the verses explain, Solomon, in addition to being made the wisest that ever lived, was also the richest person to ever live. Therefore, if anyone would have a clear perspective on how material wealth affects a person's life, it would be him. Yet despite all his wealth, his view regarding it would shock most believers. He found that despite all his riches, he could not find happiness through them. They allowed him to buy things, but they did nothing to fulfill the hunger of his spirit nature. A question has been used for years to address this very issue: How much money is enough? A simple question on the surface, it is a very complex one when thought about because the answer with regard to the human nature is there is never enough. In fact, in *Ecclesiastes 5:10,* he explains why we cannot find contentment in material wealth alone.

Just as a drug addict must use greater amounts of a drug over time to achieve the same effect or an alcoholic must consume greater amounts of alcohol over time to achieve the same effect, the same principle applies to those who have a love for money. The craving for it is insatiable. They are never content with any amount. In effect, they are chasing the proverbial carrot on a string, and Satan is the one dangling it out in front of them. As a Christian focuses on the carrot rather than God, Satan merely aims the carrot off the narrow road, and before the person realizes it, he or she is lost somewhere in the vast wilderness far from God's plan for him or her.

This is where the difference between a Christian who is financially wealthy and a person who simply has a love of money can be seen: their priorities. Christians may have abundant finances, but as long as they keep their primary focus on God, they will not stray from His will. In fact, they will desire to be obedient to God with regard to their tithes and offerings, which will result in opportunities for others to be blessed by them, through such things as charities, hospitals, ministries, mission fields, soup kitchens and many other great organizations. In this manner, Christians will find contentment, not because of their money but in spite of it because they put God first. One of the greatest demonstrations of this perspective is found in the verses of *Luke 21:1–4*, not from a wealthy person but from a poor person.

I would guess that if the widow mentioned in *Luke 21* could be transported to the present time and see the impact that her gift of two small coins has had on the millions of Christians who have read of her deed, she would be left speechless as to how what she would probably perceive as a meager offering could make such an impact for God. But this is the beauty of how God works. He does not see things as the world sees them. He is able to see into people's hearts and evaluate their motives. What the world saw as two small coins, God saw as a huge sacrifice from a humble servant. She didn't just throw in a couple of coins; she gave everything she had! It may seem insignificant to the average person, but it would be the equivalent of a billionaire giving every penny he or she owned away at one time as an offering. As incredible of an act as that would seem it would be no different from what the woman actually did. In fact, the widow's gift would still be greater because Jesus states that the widow gave out of poverty rather than out of wealth. To perform such an act, she truly had to have a godly perspective, which means that she had true contentment in her life. Those who love money unfortunately do not find true contentment. They soon discover that when their primary goal is to achieve wealth above all else, their moral compass becomes an obsolete tool. Wealth will be sought after through any means, whether by using others, cheating, stealing, lying or compromising one's character. And although this may allow one to increase their financial state, it will not bring them contentment, as we see in *1 Timothy 6:9–10* and *Proverbs 11:18.*

God designed us as spiritual beings that happen to exist in a physical body. Our human nature craves the carnal things of this world, but we soon realize that this is tantamount to a person living solely on a diet of candy. Our bodies may crave sweets, but we know all too well the effect of eating too many sweets. Eventually, our bodies become sluggish from too much sugar and not enough nutrition, resulting in nausea, fatigue and muscle weakness. Whether we like it or not, it is only when we feed our spirit a nutritious diet of God's word, prayer, faithfulness and love that we find true peace and contentment. Once again, Solomon's perspective on this issue rings true, as seen in *Ecclesiastes 6:1–6.* This is where Solomon hits the nail on the head. He keeps his focus on his heavenly home rather than his earthly home. He realizes that worldly possessions mean nothing once we leave this world, as articulated in *Ecclesiastes 5:15* and *1 Timothy 6:6–8.*

When we focus on things eternal and strive to further our relationship with Jesus daily, the things this world has to offer soon begin to lose their luster. They no longer appeal to us, because they are empty calories or spiritual junk food, if you will. This is how we attain the attitude that brings us true contentment. Our happiness is no longer dictated by how many possessions we have or how much money we have accrued; our joy comes from knowing that we have been saved through Jesus's sacrifice and looking forward to sharing eternity with Him in heaven. Paul touches on this in *Philippians 4:11–12,* and *Hebrews 13:5* expands on it as well. Solomon elaborates further in *Ecclesiastes 5:16–20.*

This answers the question posed earlier by Clarence as to why those with money and possessions often times are unhappy while others who live paycheck to paycheck are often so much more content and fulfilled in their lives. The latter group focuses on feeding their spirit rather than their flesh, resulting in true contentment despite their external circumstances. This does not mean that if they are poor, they do not strive to better themselves or to make themselves more successful. Rather, it means that their contentment is not contingent on the outcome of their attempts. They have achieved the perspective that God wishes all to obtain:

* Even if they have very little compared to worldly standards, they are thankful for what they do have and do not focus on what they don't have.
* They praise God for providing for their needs rather than despairing over not having the things they want.
* They understand that everything they do have belongs to God in the first place, which allows them to be more generous to those around them.
* They carry a glass-half-full view of the world rather than a glass-half-empty one.
* They understand that when they go to the grave, all their possessions, money and positions of power will be absolutely worthless with regard to their eternal standing.
* They love those around them more than worldly things.
* Their love for God does not change when faced with trials and hardships.

As I grew up in church as a young child, I would often hear the phrase "the peace that passes all understanding" used a lot. It wasn't until I became an adult that I gathered the true understanding of its meaning. Godly contentment brings about a peace to one's soul that the unsaved will never comprehend. This peace says, "No matter what tomorrow brings, whether fair weather or storm, whether living or dying, whether prosperity or poverty, whether sickness or health, whether joy or sorrow, whether gain or loss, I will rejoice for I know that I have Jesus in my heart and an eternal reward waiting for me in heaven." This peace allows the Christian to live in a world of sin, surrounded by every form of evil imaginable and yet hold true to their calling without despair. And at the end of the day, this peace tells the world, "You may beat me, you may curse me, you may mock me, you may imprison me, you may take everything I own or even take my life, but you cannot take the love of God out of my heart nor harm my immortal soul." Once we have achieved this peace, we will have true contentment in our lives and be able to truly live life to the fullest.

As I looked across the great gulf that lay between Clarence and I, a moment of clarity and understanding swept over me, and I finally started to understand all that was taking place before me. The road that Clarence was trapped on is the road that was meant for him and no one else. As he sat with his back to the high, sheer cliff, I realized that the cliff is representative of people's mortality and their inability to escape death. The bottomless chasm before him is symbolic of the futility of people trying to intervene in God's plans when it comes to His timing and will. The rockslide to his right demonstrates God's ultimate authority regarding our lives and the number of days He has planned for us. Finally, the cave to his left signifies the transition that takes place as we cross from this world to the next. Although its dark entrance may initially be intimidating to enter, we, as Christians, know that this is a temporary darkness because we walk by faith. Although we cannot see beyond the opening of the cave, we know that God is there waiting for us just out of sight and that we have nothing to fear.

"Well, my friend, I believe my time has come. I'm glad I was able to speak with you one last time before I left this world. I pray that God will continue to bless you as you continue on your journey."

"Good-bye, Clarence. I don't know how I can ever repay you for all that you have done for me. Thank you once again for being such a good friend to me," I told him with tears in my eyes.

"We'll continue our walk again when God calls you home someday. Stay strong in the Lord!" he said with his final words.

He looked over his right shoulder and turned his head to the left toward the opening as if watching something go by. Then he slowly got to his feet, struggling to stand straight. As he stared at the doorway before him, he turned his head one last time toward me, produced a smile and gently waved to me. I waved back to him, unable to speak any longer as tears streamed down my face. He looked back to the cave and suddenly seemed to stand a little taller. He took his final steps along the last couple of feet of his narrow path on this earth and then stepped into the darkness before him. No longer able to see him, I stared numbly at the entrance, trying to take in the fullness of the moment. Suddenly, I was amazed to see what appeared to be a faint glow of light emanating from the opening. Then suddenly, dust billowed forth from the mouth of the cave as rocks fell to block its way.

I sat on the path and began to weep, overcome by emotion from what I had just seen. After several minutes, I wiped the tears away and stood to continue my journey. As I rose, I took one last look at the cave. Dust continued to settle from the commotion. Just as I was about to turn away, I noticed something coming out of the smoke toward my path. I looked up and smiled, realizing that it was a white dove. He flew farther down my path and out of sight. I took my staff and began walking once again, contemplating that one day, I, too, will find myself in the same situation as Clarence. But just as a twinge of concern began to rise, a peace came over me, and I knew deep down that when that day arrives, I will walk confidently ahead in faith, just as my good friend Clarence did. And who knows, maybe it will be Clarence that I see first when I enter that doorway. I gripped my walking staff a little firmer and pressed on ahead, seeing the world around me a little differently and thanking God for another day's journey.

We see from Garrett's interpretation of the scene before him a true perspective of man's mortality. The sheer wall behind Clarence as mentioned signifies our inescapable mortality, the fact that we are all destined to die, as we read in **Hebrews 9:27–28.** The chasm reminds us that God is ultimately in charge of our days. We cannot interfere with His plans and His ways. Despite the innovations that have come about, the technology that has been created and the wisdom that man has accrued, humankind still has not been able to come up with a solution for one universal occurrence: death. In all its pride and arrogance regarding its worldly wisdom, humankind still has to hang its head in defeat when it tries to battle God over the body's limited time clock. This is confirmed in **Ecclesiastes 3:20.** The rockslide represents God's awesome authority with regard to our days on earth. We can fight Him over this and become angry with Him, but it is a futile deed.

A great example of this comes from God Himself when He is speaking to Job in **Job 38:17–18.** The cave is analogous to death itself. Just as no living person on earth knows what to expect when he or she crosses that bridge, so too is Clarence faced with a visual representation of this act. He looks to a small, dark entrance of a cave, not knowing what lies just inside it. Yet he enters into it confidently despite this fact, which is due to his faith in God.

We, too, have to do the same as we face our own mortality. Throughout my life, I have always been extremely curious as to how I will meet my end. Of the billions of people that have come and gone on this earth, each person has had his or her own unique set of circumstances surrounding death. The following are some questions I ask myself:

* Will I die young or as an old man?
* Will I die alone, surrounded by friends and family or among strangers?
* Will I die in my sleep?
* Will I die early in the morning, midday, evening or late at night?
* Will I die in a hospital bed?
* Will my cause of death come from a disease?
* Will my family have to make the call?
* Will my body be left disfigured?

* Will I have my mind when I die?
* Will I have to die without my wife?
* Will I have full use of my body when it happens?
* Will I have grandchildren when I pass?
* Will I have seen my son married before I go?
* Will I go before my parents?
* Will I go before my wife?
* Will I be at work when it happens?
* Will I be taken during the rapture?
* Will I be worried or at peace?
* Will I be hot, cold or comfortable?
* Will I see a light and a tunnel as Garrett described?
* Will I feel content, or will I have regrets?
* Will my death be painful, or will I drift into it painlessly?
* Will my death be due to a tragic accident?
* Will my death come at the hands of another person?
* Will my death come from an attempt of saving another person's life?
* Will my death be during a holiday season?
* Will my death take place along with others?
* Will my death come as a result of not denying my faith?
* Will my death be a catalyst for someone to accept Christ?
* Will it occur suddenly and unexpectedly, or will I have time to prepare?
* What age will I have my last birthday?
* What age will my son be when I go?
* What is the last song I will hear?
* What day of the week will my death occur on?
* What month of the year will my death occur in?
* What season will it take place in?
* What will the weather be like?
* What will the last sermon I hear be on?
* What will my last sunrise look like?
* What will my last sunset look like?

* What will my new body look like?
* What will I be wearing when it happens?
* What will be the last meal I eat?
* What will be the last words I ever speak?
* What will be the last words I ever speak to my wife and son?
* What will be the last thoughts going through my mind?
* What will be the first thing I see in heaven?
* What will be the first sound I hear in heaven?
* What will be the last Bible verse I read?
* What will be my last prayer to God?
* What will be the last movie I watch with my wife?
* Who will be the first relative I see in heaven?
* Who will be the first person I see in heaven?
* Where will I be when it takes place?
* Where will be my last vacation?
* When will my last Christmas be?
* When will my last New Year's Eve be?
* How many people will be affected by the news?
* How many people will weep for me?
* How many people will I have led to the Lord?

We cannot see what lies just beyond this life, but we have faith in God's word that we can cross into that dark unknown world and enter into the light of our heavenly reward. This challenging concept is beautifully articulated in *2 Corinthians 5:1–10* and *1 Corinthians 15:54–55.* Paul demonstrates an awesome perspective on this issue, found in *Philippians 1:21–24.* As Paul's death draws near, he continues to hold to the same godly perspective concerning his own mortality, as seen in *2 Timothy 4:6–8.*

Day 199

Lately, I've been thinking a lot about Clarence and all the things he taught me since I crossed the river. I was reminded of him just this morning as I reached back into my pack to get a snack. Suddenly, I remembered that he gave me this pack in the first place. The memory brought a tear to my eye, leaving me feeling a little emotional. I decided to take a break and sat down at the edge of the path, leaning against an old oak tree. I removed my pack from my back and started to open it, when suddenly I realized what a relief it was to have the heavy load taken off. As I began to dig into the pack looking for some food, I soon realized what made the pack so heavy to carry. About two-thirds of the pack was filled with small, smooth stones. At that moment, I suddenly became aware of what had been taking place under my very nose. I was the one who had put those stones in the pack, one by one over the months.

When I began walking the narrow road, I soon became aware that from time to time, the path would draw near to the river, bringing me close to those living in the Southern Lands. On seeing them on the opposite river bank, I would try to strike up a conversation with them, as a friendly gesture. Unfortunately, the majority of the time, things would not go so smoothly. It would not be uncommon for them to reach down to the ground and grab stones to throw at me in anger. I was caught by surprise the first time it happened, but then I recalled when I myself used to live among those across the river and the negative view I myself had regarding those traveling the narrow road. Realizing why they threw the stones didn't make it any more tolerable, but at least I understood why they were doing it.

In the beginning, when I was new to this side and immature in my walk, I would bend down and retrieve the stones they threw and throw them back at them, trying to even the score with those against me. It didn't take long to realize that the more I threw, the more they threw. We were merely fueling each other's fire. Another consequence that came about from my actions was that to get a better shot at my attackers, I would often step away from the path and draw as close to the river as I could go in order to better reach my targets. This always resulted in me wearing egg on my face. Once I stood on a grassy knell and fired rocks back at them. As I stretched my arm back to make another attempt, my feet flew out from under me, a result of damp grass producing a slippery slope. I landed on my backside, leaving me with a sore tailbone and grass-stained clothes. Another time, in the process of launching my projectile, I stepped forward, only to discover that my foot planted itself in a groundhog hole. This resulted in several days of limping down the trail because of my sprained ankle.

But my worst experience had to be the time that I reached down for a stone that landed directly in front of me, grabbed the stone, started to rise and then suddenly became blinded by some force that came from the tall grass in front of me. It only took me a second or two to realize that I had inadvertently agitated a skunk, which caused him to nail me square in the face with his pungent spray. Needless to say, I carried the consequence of that mistake for quite a while.

Surprisingly, at times I would even encounter stones being thrown at me from the hills to the left of the road as well as the land between the road and the river. After suffering defeat after defeat in my rock battles, I finally gave up trying to beat those throwing stones at their own game and left the rock throwing to them. But even though I no longer threw stones back at them, I would out of anger pick up the stones they threw and put them in my pack, physical evidence to use against them. Sometimes I would pull some out of my pack and show others the proof of what I had endured. But mainly it was a way for me to take possession of the objects intended to hurt me and to provide a constant reminder for myself of how I had been wronged.

The rocks themselves possessed a very unique characteristic. They all had strange symbols carved into them that I did not recognize. Many a night, I would sit by the campfire and pull them out to examine the strange markings, having no clue as to what the symbols meant. It was only by chance that while reading the Guide Book *one day, I came across the very symbols that I had so many times seen on the stones. I was elated to finally have my riddle solved and began comparing the markings on the stones with those in the book. To my surprise, each symbol translated into a different word. Here is a list of the words that I discovered:* hate, jealousy, bitterness, self-righteousness, arrogance, slander, discord, rage, gossip, envy, selfishness *and* pride. *Looking back, I now realize that in some twisted way, I hung on to those stones and regarded them as trophies to fuel my self-pity.*

As the months went by, I accumulated quite a little collection. I never usually thought much about the combined weight of the stones, but in hindsight I now realize that during the uphill portions of my journey, my pace was significantly slowed as a direct result of my pack. Subconsciously, I knew my pack was heavy, but I had become accustomed over time to it being that way and soon learned to accept it as a normal feature of my gear. But now, as I sat here for the first time and gazed at my pack full of rocks, I was left wondering why I would unnecessarily burden myself with such a heavy load. The rocks truly served no purpose other than my hanging on to them for my own selfish reasons.

As I sat and stared at the ridiculous sight before me, I realized what I had to do. Strangely, part of me seemed to want to hold on to them, as if I were giving up some sort of perverted power over those who threw them at me. But after several minutes of introspection, thinking about the toll the load took on me daily, I finally grabbed the pack, carried it to the edge of the path, turned it upside down and emptied every last stone into the weeds. For several seconds, I stood holding on to the empty pack, realizing that without the weight of all the worthless souvenirs, the pack felt light as a feather. I placed the few remaining essential items into my pack and placed it on my back.

I'm not sure if it was simply my own imagination, but I felt like I stood a little taller than I had for a long time. A huge burden had been lifted from me, and now that I was aware of its source, I did not want to go back to carrying such a load. I realize the folly in what I was doing. In my efforts to hold what in effect were physical representations of wrongs done to me by others, the sole purpose was for the gaining of sympathy from others and justification in my mind to hold grudges against my persecutors. The result of this thought process did nothing to exact revenge on my enemies, but instead only slowed down my journey on the narrow road and provided a heavy burden for me to carry unnecessarily. In fact, my decision to pick up the stones and hold on to them had a greater negative effect on me than the actual act of the stone throwing itself. I had done my enemies' job for them. I realized that I might not be able to stop others from throwing rocks at me, but I could choose to leave them on the ground, where they could do me no harm. I no longer had any use for them, and they would never slow me down again.

The rocks that Garrett carried in his pack represent the hurts he received from others in various forms. The fact that he held on to them represents an unforgiving spirit on his part. Unfortunately, this is a common occurrence, even with many born-again Christians. They feel that by hanging on to these stones, they hold some kind of power over their adversaries, when, in fact, they are suffering under the terrible weight of an unforgiving heart. Considering the rocks that came from across the river, they would, of course, represent hurts that nonbelievers inflict on us in a nonphysical way. Garrett's act of throwing the stones back across the river represents his trying to repay evil with evil or exacting revenge on his persecutors. To address this first point, we can look to *1 Peter 3:8–9.* In reference to revenge, *Romans 12:14–21, Proverbs 20:22* and *Proverbs 24:29* provide a powerful perspective regarding how a Christian's attitude should be in the matter. And as for those who threw stones at him from the left side of the road, which would represent born-again believers not behaving like Christ, the Bible gives us directions for correcting a fellow brother or sister in Christ, found in *Matthew 18:15–17.*

Rather than throwing stones back at those wronging us, by practicing the previous verses, we may be able to convince the rock throwers to drop their rocks and repent from their wrongdoings. This is how we practically apply God's love to our Christian family. Throwing rocks back at them may appease our human nature and bring us temporary fulfillment, but in the end, we will only be hurting ourselves spiritually and fueling our fellow Christians' sinful actions.

This point is further elaborated in *James 5:19–20*. The tragedies that occurred to Garrett as he tried to throw stones back at his attackers signify the dangers that can befall us as we step away from God's will and respond by thinking only with our carnal nature. *Galatians 6:1–2* mirrors this warning. As Christians, if we truly understand the definition of God's love, we will not feel the need to cast stones back at those who hurt us. We will instead feel compelled to pray for them, just as Jesus did for those who mocked Him as He hung on the cross, as seen in *Luke 23:34.*

No one in the universe is better qualified to speak on the subject of having stones thrown at them than Jesus. And there is no better role model for how to deal with stone throwers than Jesus. He spent His life with a bull's-eye on His back, drawing fire from every angle, yet He never threw a single stone back. Examples of the bombardment He endured during His short existence in this world can be found in *Matthew 12:22–24, Mark 6:1–3, Luke 5:21, Luke 15:1–2, John 8:13, John 8:52–53, John 9:16, John 9:24, John 10:31–33, John 19:15–16, Mark 15:17–20, Mark 15:31–32, Matthew 27:43–44, Mark 15:36* and *Luke 23:39.*

After considering the previous examples, we have no reason to complain about anything this world throws at us. Jesus, who endured the most punishment, did nothing to deserve even one of the rocks thrown at Him. Yet He endured them for us. Leaving the beauty of heaven to clothe Himself in humanity, living a life of poverty and sacrifice, being mocked, taking on beatings, being denied and abandoned by friends, being spat on, carrying a cross, enduring the nails piercing His body, hanging on a cross, having His side pierced and, most punishing of all, taking on the full weight of our sins and bearing the wrath of His Father in heaven as the sin offering for all humankind, resulting in the Father turning His back on Him and separating from Him for the first time since before time began—there are not enough stones on earth that could be thrown at us in a lifetime to equal what He endured.

For this reason, we love Him, serve Him, praise Him, endure hardship for Him and devote our lives to Him—not out of fear of punishment, not because a book tells us to and not because we want to impress others, but because we see the full measure of His love for us demonstrated through His sacrifice, a sacrifice, we must remind ourselves, that He didn't deserve and that He didn't have to make. But He did make it, and that is why He deserves our all. And as followers of Jesus, we are told to expect persecution from the world, just as He did, in *John 15:18–21.*

Not only are we called by God to accept the stones without bitterness, we are also expected to delight in the trial, as seen in *Matthew 5:11–12, 1 Corinthians 4:12–13* and *2 Timothy 3:12.* We only have to look to God's word to find His perspective on forgiveness. A great place to start would be *Matthew 18:21–22,* which describes a conversation between Peter and Jesus on the subject. It is obvious that Jesus's intent was not to say that after seventy-seven offenses, we are to no longer forgive. It was a figurative statement to represent that we are to forgive as many times as needed. In *Luke 17:3–4,* Jesus is again recorded making a similar statement to His disciples. Here we have two instances recorded where Jesus, in His own words, made it crystal clear as to His view on forgiveness. If we combine these two examples with *Matthew 6:14–15,* we gain a more complete perspective as to God's thoughts on the subject.

In reviewing the three examples together, we find that not only are we commanded to forgive each other as many times as needed, but also that if we disobey this command, God will not forgive us. These examples, when applied to the story, would represent forgiving the rock throwers when they ask for forgiveness and not carrying the rocks and using them as reminders to be lorded over the heads of the throwers. What Garrett did not initially realize was that for every stone thrown at him, he himself had thrown many, many more at God through his disobedient acts during his life. If he had chosen to continue to carry the stones instead of dumping them, God would have had an even bigger backpack to show him as he stood before Him in the future. We all are guilty of being rock throwers at different points in our lives, yet when a rock comes our way from another, we stand flabbergasted by the very idea that someone would dare do such a thing to us.

The rocks we use to throw at each other represent manifestations from our sinful nature that we unleash on those we attack. These manifestations stem from specific qualities that are produced from our sinful nature. These were described in the story as the special markings found on the stones. We find some of these mentioned in *Galatians 5:19–21* and *Romans 13:12–14*, along with the severe consequence that accompanies those who follow a life of such choices. Each of the qualities listed has its own unique characteristic, but all share a commonality in that each provides an arsenal of weapons that we can choose to use on those around us for unrighteous purposes. The first one to examine is rage. Rage is basically uncontrolled anger. Much to the surprise of many, anger in itself is not a sin. We see examples of righteous anger in response to such injustices as child abuse, rape, murder, assault, theft and other such crimes perpetrated on the innocent. As holy people, we should despise sin just as God does. One verse that confirms this point is *Psalm 97:10*.

Jesus does not mince words in this matter when speaking to His disciples in *Luke 17:1–2*. Righteous anger can be seen confirmed in a very short but effective verse, *Psalm 4:4*. It does not say, "Do not sin by being angry"; it says, "In your anger do not sin." Therefore, we know that anger is a normal and healthy emotion. We can even find examples of God being angry, such as *2 Kings 22:13*. Even Jesus can be found in *John 2:13–16* becoming angry and taking action against the offenders. When our human nature taps into the anger and uses it as rocket fuel, we see the transformation of anger to rage occur. Once it has been converted, we become blinded by it and unable to make rational decisions from our spiritual nature, making it about as easy to control as a shooting rocket. This puts us in a position similar to that of an intoxicated person: making bad decisions, doing things we wouldn't normally do and providing a foothold for Satan to take advantage of the situation, as clearly seen in *Proverbs 29:22, Proverbs 14:16–17, Proverbs 15:18, Proverbs 14:29, Ecclesiastes 7:9* and *James 1:19–20*.

Next are jealousy and envy. The two are very similar, both meaning a covetousness attitude toward another. With envy, its meaning always signifies a negative attitude. But just as with anger, there are some instances in which jealousy is not a sinful act. This fact is proved in that there are many verses that attribute this term with God. Because God cannot sin, and we find verses that show that He at times can be a jealous God, the argument that jealousy is not always sinful is solidified. We can find our first example within the Ten Commandments themselves, illustrated in *Exodus 20:4–5* and *Deuteronomy 4:24.* We also find a reference from Paul confirming this point in *2 Corinthians 11:2.*

As Christians, we should be jealous for the things of God. For example, for a husband having a certain level of jealousy for his wife or for a wife to have a certain level of jealousy for her husband is healthy in the same context as the previously mentioned verses. Having made a vow before God to be faithful to one another, it would be natural for each to want to keep his or her spouse from the advances of another, thus maintaining the bond. When we become covetous for things outside of God's will and plan for us, we cross over into parallels with envy, producing sin. If we look back to the earlier mention in *Galatians 5* regarding the acts of the sinful nature, we find both jealousy and envy listed. Paul makes an accusation of jealousy to believers in *1 Corinthians 3:3.* We are called specifically to not envy the things of this world or those who are unsaved, confirmed in *Proverbs 3:31–32, Psalm 37:1, Proverbs 24:1–2* and *Proverbs 23:17.* We find in *Psalm 73:1–22* a very candid passage describing the author's admission of envying the prosperity of the wicked and then his return to a godly perspective.

Next are bitterness and hatred, another similar pair of terms. Bitterness and hatred can both be described as an intense ill will or disdain toward something or someone. Just as we saw with anger and jealousy, there are times when hatred is justified and not sinful, as made clear in *Psalm 5:4–6, Psalm 45:6–7, Psalm 97:10, Proverbs 8:13* and *Romans 12:9.* We see a common theme throughout the previous verses. As Christians, we are called to hate evil and wickedness. Yet a difference between evil in general and sinners who commit evil exists. Per scripture, we are called to hate the evil done by others but to love the person. Many times, it is described as "loving the sinner but hating the sin." We see the Bible's confirmation on this perspective in *Matthew 5:43–48.*

It is a basic human reaction to become upset when someone harms or offends us or our loved ones. If we follow the will of our sinful nature, that emotion can easily simmer and over time boil into bitterness and hatred toward the offender. Satan attempts to have us fixate solely on our hurt and rationalize our sinful reaction through the lenses of self-pity and self-justification, which act as spiritual blinders placed alongside our eyes, blocking out any input from the Spirit. *1 John 2:9–11* reiterates this point.

This is the complete opposite reaction that the Spirit wishes for us to have. Despite our initial anger toward a situation, the Spirit reminds us that as children of God, we are called to love our neighbor, even if he or she is our enemy. He reminds us to forgive our neighbor for his or her wrongdoing, or God will not forgive us of ours. Ultimately, how the Spirit achieves His goal is by having us take a step back and look at the situation not from the narrow view of self but from a broader perspective that allows us to examine our mind-set in light of God's will. From this standpoint, we are able to see the big picture and remind ourselves that our primary goal in this life is to live for God and grow daily in our salvation. It is not to take on the role as an avenger. God has that job covered; He does not need our help. Again, if we refer to *Romans 12:14–21,* we are reminded of this point.

The next dynamic duo of devilish deeds is slander and gossip. Unlike anger and jealousy, there is no context in which either of these two deeds can be considered righteous. They share similarities in that they both involve a negative verbal attack on another person. *Slander* is defined as a false, ill-motivated statement about somebody, meant to harm them. Gossip, on the other hand, can potentially contain true information, but its broadcast is done with a malicious intent as well. Both forms of speech are used to tear down another in order to try and elevate the deliverer. Let's start by taking a look in *Proverbs 10:18–19, Proverbs 11:9, 11–13, Proverbs 12:6, 18, Proverbs 13:3, Proverbs 16:27–28, Proverbs 18:6–7, 21, Proverbs 20:19* and *Proverbs 26:21–28.*

After examining the previous verses, it is more than apparent how much God despises gossip and slander. They are the spiritual equivalent to a set of whips, used to slash the spirit of another and to inflict open wounds. Considering that we are all God's creations, it is no wonder that His stand is so strong against such behaviors. What parent would stand and watch another inflict physical harm to his or her child and not become angry? In the same way, God is able to see our spirits and their wounds just as we would see a physical wound on another. If we use the analogy of a spiritual whip, then the tongue would be that whip. The Bible puts great emphasis on this body part and the power it wields, as seen in *James 3:3–10*.

We find in the previous verses several items to which the tongue is compared: a bit in a horse's mouth, a ship's rudder, a spark of fire and a restless evil, full of deadly poison. All the objects listed share one common denominator: they are all catalysts. A catalyst is an item that is used to initiate or trigger a greater effect or a series of effects. An example of this would be a pebble thrown into a pond. Even though the pebble is very tiny and in itself does not contain much power, when thrown into a still pond, it creates a ripple effect that emanates from its point of entry into the water and travels outward in every direction, ultimately affecting a large amount of the water's surface. The same can be said for the items used to describe the tongue. The bit used in a horse's mouth is similar to the pebble in that it is actually a small and seemingly meaningless object. But when it is placed in a horse's mouth, the rider can control the horse's speed and direction through its use. A ship's rudder is a very tiny object in comparison to the large ship it is attached to. But when used, it determines the course for the entire ship. A spark is actually the best analogy of the three for the tongue in my opinion. If we consider what a single little spark springing from a campfire can do to a forest, we begin to better understand the potential spoken of in the verses.

Fire again makes for a great comparison. Fire itself is neither good nor bad; it is just a tool. When lost in the woods and night begins to fall, there is no greater friend to the lost soul than a roaring fire from which to keep warm, cook food, provide light and ward off danger. But when used maliciously, fire can burn the body, destroy property, produce dangerous smoke and even cause death. The tongue can be seen in a very similar way. From our mouths, we can produce praise, blessings, instruction, prayers, comfort, motivation, kindness, guidance and teaching. But from the same mouth, we can also choose to produce slander and gossip. We can use the tongue to steer others in a wrong direction as with the bit and rudder. We can use the tongue to inflict injury on others as with a spark. We can even use it, as the verses stated, as a deadly poison. Just as a small hypodermic needle can contain enough poison to kill another through injection, so too can the tongue be used to inject spiritual poison into those around us if we choose. Ultimately, the decision is ours. We make the choice regarding how it will be used.

This brings us back to an earlier discussion, the battle between the sinful nature and the spirit nature. For this analogy, I would like to compare our bodies to airplanes. Each plane carries a large amount of cargo, consisting of such things as food, water, medicine and other helpful resources that can be parachuted to those in need. But also attached to each plane are several missiles, along with numerous bombs and a machine-gun turret. Each plane carries three passengers: the person whom the plane represents and two pilots. One pilot represents the spirit nature within each of us, the other the sinful nature within each of us. In the plane's cockpit, we find that there is only room for one pilot to fly the plane. We make the choice as to which pilot flies the plane at any given time.

When we choose to put the spirit nature at the controls, we find that our plane serves to help those around us by delivering assistance to those in need, such as food to the hungry, water to the thirsty and medicine to the sick. But when we put the sinful nature at the controls, we find our plane being used to spread harm and destruction to those around us, through missiles that pierce the heart and soul, bombs that explode and emotionally cripple and machine-gun fire that assaults indiscriminately. In considering this analogy, we realize that the plane that is able to bring so much blessing to people is the same plane that can inflict havoc and death to those it encounters.

We each are given an airplane to control. What ultimately determines the plane's function is the pilot flying the plane, which we choose. And the device that the pilot uses to fly the plane is the tongue. It is the control mechanism that provides either blessing or destruction to those around us. In the same way, we are judged by those things that come from our mouths, either blessings or curses. This is why we as Christians must discipline ourselves to keep the Holy Spirit in command of our bodies. Once we relinquish power to the sinful nature, it has an entire arsenal at its disposal with which to inflict pain and destruction to others. Slander is just one of the weapons used, as demonstrated in *Matthew 15:11, 18–20*.

The next sinful act to address is discord. This term is basically defined as disharmony producing strife. It describes a person who, rather than seeking to live in peace with those around him or her, strives to produce conflict and arguing. Another term synonymous with *discord* is *dissention*. We find the Bible speaking very clearly in regards to a person of this nature, as noted in *Proverbs 6:12–14, Proverbs 10:12, Proverbs 15:18, Proverbs 16:28, Proverbs 28:25* and *Proverbs 29:22*. I find it very interesting that the Bible so clearly specifies the type of people who are associated with dissention, the list including a scoundrel, a villain, a hateful person, a hot-tempered person, a perverse person, a greedy person and an angry person. To find oneself listed among such a group is not a very flattering position to brag about.

But those mentioned all share the common denominator of a contentious spirit. Dissention differs from all the other acts mentioned in that it is not unique in itself as the others are. Hatred is different from jealousy, and jealousy is different from bitterness. But dissention is a by-product of the other acts. When hatred flares up, dissention is produced. When jealousy raises its angry head, dissention is produced. When a person is filled with bitterness, dissention is produced. It is the obvious result of those led by the selfish nature resisting those led by the Holy Spirit. Therefore, that God takes such a negative stance on those who strive to produce conflict and prevent others from living out God's commandment of love is no surprise. The following verses are powerful in that God gives specific traits that He "hates" and that He finds "detestable." Of the seven listed, dissention makes the list, reemphasizing the danger of possessing such a quality as described in *Proverbs 6:16–19*.

I spoke earlier about how a single spark can bring about so much destruction. To further that analogy, dissention would be the tool used to produce the spark. When we consider what takes place spiritually through the actions of a contentious, quarrelsome person, it is not unlike a person walking about a forest, striking matches and throwing them aimlessly about. Sometimes nothing occurs because the ground is damp from morning dew or saturated from a rainfall. This would represent a Christian's heart quenched by the Holy Spirit. This person takes on the role of a spiritual firefighter, standing ready with a fire hose that is connected to the living water Jesus spoke about. But sometimes the match finds a dry and flammable forest floor, produced by long periods without rainfall. Under these conditions, a single match is more than enough to ignite the forest floor, spreading flames out of control and destroying everything around it.

The same occurs when confronted by a quarrelsome person without the Holy Spirit in control. The sinful nature does not have access to water hoses and living water. It attempts to put the fire out by stomping on it, which is very dangerous, not to mention very ineffective. It doesn't take long to realize how fast a spiritual fire can spread and destroy our lives without the assistance of the Holy Spirit. Possessions, relationships, careers, positions and loved ones can all become collateral damage when placed within the line of fire of a spiritual inferno, brought about by dissention. *Proverbs 26:21* beautifully corroborates this perspective.

This brings us to our final group of sinful acts, self-righteousness, arrogance and pride. I name these three together because they share so many similarities. Self-righteousness is defined as having an overinflated opinion of one's own righteousness compared to others. Arrogance is defined as a sense of superiority over others. Pride is defined as, once again, an overinflated opinion of one's self compared to others. In a nutshell, all three can be tied together through a common bond, that being one of conceit and selfishness. There is no shortage of verses or examples in the Bible regarding this topic, as demonstrated in *Psalm 119:36, Proverbs 18:1* and *James 3:13–16.* What a coincidence that once again we see dissention being connected to acts of evil. If we go back to the list of personality types the Bible connects to dissention, that being a scoundrel, a villain, a hateful person, a hot-tempered person, a perverse person, a greedy person and an angry person, the book of James gives us two more to add to the list, an envious person and a selfish person. Once again, when a person becomes green with envy, dissention is produced. When people feed their selfish nature, resulting in self-righteousness, arrogance and pride, dissention is produced. This is because sin in any form will always be in conflict with God's perfect will. Anytime an act of the sinful nature exists, it will compete with our spirit nature to be fed, resulting in conflict or dissention.

To reiterate, we go back to the sinful nature–spirit nature seesaw. The sinful nature within us is the poster child for selfishness. This trait is the cornerstone of its foundation. Every motive and deed stemming from the sinful nature originates from selfishness, or the fulfillment of self. Therefore, it is accurate to conclude that if selfishness ranks so high with the sinful nature, its standing with the spirit nature would be the polar opposite. It also stands to conclude that if selfishness runs so counter to the spirit nature, it would also be highly despised by Jesus. This conclusion can be drawn not only from understanding biblical principles, but also by observing how Jesus lived His life according to the four Gospels. We first look to *Philippians 2:3–8* to establish the point of putting others before ourselves as Jesus did during His time on earth, which counters the principle of selfishness.

If anyone in the universe would have the right to be arrogant, it would be Jesus because He *is* God. He could have come to earth and taken the role of self-righteousness if He would have chosen, since He in fact is the Creator of the universe. He could have accumulated wealth unimaginable, mansions, servants, monuments constructed in His honor, anything He wanted. He could have lauded over us the fact that He is God revealed as man, been dressed in the finest clothes, ate the finest foods, drank the finest wines and enjoyed a life of complete comfort here on earth. In fact, I would imagine that a high percentage of people, if given the same opportunity, would have chosen such a path.

But here lies one of the greatest enigmas facing humankind since the beginning of time. Jesus, equal partner in the Holy Trinity (*Mark 1:9–11*) who had no beginning and has no end (*Revelation 1:8*) who is spotless, having never committed a single sin (*2 Corinthians 5:21*), took it upon Himself to leave the majesty of heaven and its splendor (*Hebrews 2:6–7*), leave the company of His loving Father for the first time ever (*John 1:1–2*), clothe Himself in humanity with all the pains and discomforts connected with it (*Isaiah 53:2*), not only come to earth but start as a newborn born in a barn (*Luke 2:6–7*), choose for His parents not a wealthy couple but a poor, simple couple living in a poor, simple town (*John 1:45–46; Matthew 13:55*) and devote His life on earth not to being served but to serving others (*Matthew 20:28*). Accepting persecution from others despite His power (*Isaiah 53:3*), taking on humankind's punishment for their sins even though He was the only one who didn't deserve it (*Isaiah 53:4–5*), enduring a slow, horrible death even though He could have quickened it (*Matthew 26:39*) and forgiving those who were mocking Him and crucifying Him even as He hung on the cross, as told in *Luke 23:34.* This is what the opposite of selfishness looks like.

This brings us back to our final three sinful acts that, as we have clearly established, were not present in Jesus. In fact, of all the acts I have covered, the one that I believe Jesus finds most reprehensible to Him would have to be pride, shown clearly in *Proverbs 8:13, Proverbs 11:2, Proverbs 16:18* and *Proverbs 18:12.* The reason I believe that Jesus would put pride at the top of His most-hated list is this: this trait brought Satan to the point where he believed he could overthrow God the Father and usurp His position of authority. Pride blinded him, causing him to make war against God and the angels in heaven, resulting in his expulsion, along with a third of the angels who foolishly followed him, as revealed in *Luke 10:18* and *Isaiah 14:12–15.* As a result of Satan's pride, for God to remain holy and punish sin, He was forced to create hell, a place of eternal fire and damnation, as the punishment for rebellion against Him, as shown in *2 Peter 2:4.* And it is pride among those who do not accept Jesus's sacrifice on the cross that forces God to assign them a place in hell, which initially was intended for Satan and the fallen angels and ultimately the lake of fire after the great day of God's judgment, described in *Matthew 25:41,* where the believers are separated from the unbelievers.

Pride and its effects have done more to separate God's creations from Him than anything else. When we choose to allow pride to dominate our being, whether we realize it or not, we are declaring Satan as our god and letting him lay forth the paths we will follow. Think of it this way: When God looks into our hearts and sees pride existing there, He is reminded of the one who through pride dared to challenge His authority, thus creating war in heaven. He also is reminded of the great price Jesus had to pay for us because of pride. How then can we be surprised when God, as a Father, observing day after day the millions of prideful hearts that ignore, mock, downplay and even deny His Son's amazing sacrifice, places such a heavy penalty on unbelievers?

Pride was the sound produced from every stone thrown at His Son, every curse directed toward Him, every lash of the whip across His back, every fist striking Him, every step He took as He carried the cross, each cast of the die on the ground by the soldiers playing for His belongings, every pound of the hammer against the nails that tore through Him, every drop of blood that fell from Him and landed on the ground, the spear that pierced His side and the stone scraping as it rolled to seal His tomb.

The culmination of pride's echoes resounded all too clear for the Father, and He remembers them all too well. Just like any earthly father, He did not wish to see harm come to His one and only Son, but He was willing for it to happen so that we might be with Him as well. But also just like any earthly father, He is protective of His Son and will deal harshly against those who trample His Son's sacrifice under their feet. He was more than generous toward us in that He allowed His Son to pay such a price for us, one that He didn't deserve. After this, if we continue to ignore the priceless gift offered to us, His generosity then ends and is replaced by a just and righteous wrath against any who would reject His Son, as soberly spelled out in *Hebrews 10:31.*

Day 255

As I sit this evening staring into a roaring campfire along the side of the road, I am processing something that caught my attention just a couple of hours ago. Today was a drab and rainy mess. All day long, I trudged down the path in the midst of a steady drizzle, not a torrential downpour but just enough to soak me to the bone. By the time night started fading and the sun went down, I soon became cold and wet rather than just wet; thus, I decided to build a fire to warm myself and dry my wet clothes. I began to gather firewood and kindling as usual and piled it into position for a campfire. After several attempts, it soon became apparent that I was not making much progress. It didn't take long until I realized that my efforts were in vain because I was trying to start a fire with wet wood. The day's rainfall had saturated everything around me, making the job of starting a fire a mission impossible.

I was steadily growing colder as the moments went along, starting to despair about my situation, when I noticed along the edge of the woods a large piece of tin laying on the ground, obviously blown from the roof of somebody's barn or shed. It was about four feet by eight feet and was rusted around the edges, most likely from its long rest in its current location. I walked over to it and slowly lifted it, hoping to avoid some woodland creature springing out from under it and lunging at me. To my relief, no such thing occurred, but what I did find exceeded my hopes: dry wood. The tin had been lying on top of some fallen down tree branches and limbs of all sizes, shielding them from the effects of the rain. I hurriedly gathered up the wood and used it to make a new pile for the campfire. With the dry kindling that I found under the tin, I was able to start the fire, and soon, with the help of the dry larger limbs, I had a roaring campfire blazing in the night, despite the steady drizzle. I placed some of the damp wood around the fire's edge and found that after a short time even the wet wood became ready to burn as well, having been dried out by the heat from the fire.

This brings me back to what I was reflecting on earlier. As I was thinking about how lucky I was to find some dry wood, I remembered something that I had learned back in my high-school science class. We had discussed the principle of converting potential energy into kinetic energy. Potential energy is also known as stored energy; kinetic energy is basically energy in motion. Regarding the campfire before me, an obvious change takes place with the wood because it has the ability to transform into a roaring fire. It's not like trees have fires burning within them that come out once we open them. So how does the transformation take place? The wood itself possesses potential or stored energy within its very makeup. Using the right catalyst, the potential energy is able to transition into kinetic energy, which occurs as the wood converts to fuel for a fire, resulting in the production of heat and light. The energy is always present within the wood. It just needs a catalyst for starting the transformation process, which in this case would be a spark or a match.

I then began thinking about how we actually possess a quality similar to the wood. We all possess a potential or stored energy within ourselves, which is symbolic of our gifts and talents. It remains dormant, like the piece of firewood, until a catalyst begins the transition to kinetic energy. In our case, the Holy Spirit would be that catalyst, transforming our potential energy into a kinetic energy, which has as its by-product the blessings of light and warmth. But just as with the wood in the forest, when we allow ourselves to become saturated in the things of this world, the Holy Spirit is unable to perform the role of a catalyst within us, due to the wetness. We must remain as the wood under the tin, shielded from the corrupting influences of the world and ready to be used when needed.

With regard to helping those around us, we are of no benefit to them as long as we choose to remain as firewood. But when we allow the Holy Spirit to become a catalyst in our lives, we become to those around us as a campfire is to one who is cold and wet. We become a light to those in this dark world and warmth to those who are left out in the cold. And just like the damp wood that was placed around the campfire, when those who are unsaved spend time with us, they too will find themselves beginning to dry out from exposure to the world. They become kindling with potential energy that is ready and willing to be converted to kinetic energy and set ablaze by the Holy Spirit. (See **2 Timothy 1:6–7** and **1 Thessalonians 5:19.**)

Day 289

Today's weather was exceptionally beautiful: clear blue skies, ideal temperature, no humidity, a slight breeze in the air—a perfect autumn day to be alive and outdoors. At one point, I decided to stop and take a break in order to take in the sheer beauty around me. I walked to the far right side of the path, which brought me to the edge of a steep drop-off overlooking the mighty river below. As I sat along the rim, my eyes followed the river along its course, eventually winding into the rolling hills beyond. For a while, I became lost in the moment, my senses just absorbing all that was taking place around me.

Then a thought came to me, and I started looking at my surroundings a little differently. I began to focus on the scenery with different eyes. Gazing on the distant hills blanketed with a dense forest, I started examining the plethora of colors within it. The reds, oranges, yellows, all blending to form a beautiful quilt that enveloped the countryside as far as the eye could see until it eventually merged with the crystal-clear blue sky above, which was totally empty except for a couple of small puffy clouds meandering slowly by. At the bottom of the cliff lay a rolling green field, beautifully contrasted by the bright-yellow sunflowers growing sporadically within it and the sparkling blue river along its border. Looking up, I noticed several birds flying by, a gorgeous red cardinal and a stunning blue jay, which came to rest in a tree limb beside the path. For the first time in my life, I *finally started to take notice of something that had been right in front of my nose. I began considering the simple gift of color.*

It may sound silly at first, but I realized that I had never fully appreciated God's gift of color to us. We are surrounded daily by a world of vibrant and diverse colors. At first, it may seem like no big deal, but God could have just as easily designed us to see only blacks, whites and grays. It was His prerogative. But the fact that He created a world with an abundance of colors and gave us the ability to perceive these colors shows that He not only wanted us to merely exist on this earth, He wanted us to know us how much He loves us by giving us a place of beauty to live in.

It is not unlike what earthly parents do for their newborn child. They could choose to simply place their baby in a plain, functional room with no colors or design as a nursery, but more often than not, they spend great time, expense and effort to create a room that is not only livable but appealing to the eye as well. They paint the walls a beautiful color, place pictures and decorations around the room and fill it with cute toys. These are not mandatory requirements for parents. They do these things because brings they experience joy when seeing their child happy. They do these actions out of love for the child.

*In the same way, God loves us so much that He took the time to hang a sky above us that sometimes appears crystal blue, that sometimes appears red and pink during sunrise and sunset, and that occasionally turns green during a storm. He complements the base color of the sky with various accessory colors, such as a bright beautiful rainbow containing a number of stunning colors within its arches; puffy white clouds; shining celestial bodies such as the sun, moon and stars; and, in some places, the breathtaking northern lights, which twist and dance across the sky. Instead of nursery-room carpet, He provides luscious green fields, accentuated by a myriad of flowers with colors more diverse than the rainbows, for us to walk on. And just like the stuffed animals parents buy, God surrounds us with beautiful animals of every color just for our pleasure. And once again, we must remind ourselves that He didn't have to make things this way, but He did. (See **Genesis 9:13.**)*

Next, we have to take into consideration the sense of smell. Again, He didn't have to give us this ability, but thankfully He did. Because with it, we have the pleasure to savor the scents that bring us so much joy, such as the sweet fragrance of flowers, the salty mist of an ocean breeze, the warm spice of cinnamon rolls baking, the smell of pine and various other foliage experienced during a walk through a forest and millions of others, too many to name. Along with scent, taste is closely tied, yet another blessing from our loving Father. He could have simply made food tasteless, something we eat simply for the sake of survival. But He gave us taste buds for the sole purpose of delighting in the food we eat and taking pleasure in the various delicacies afforded us. Once again, rather than simply give us what is needed to maintain existence, we find He accentuates the gift to bring us more joy. (See **Psalm 34:8.**)

Sound is the next sense to look at. It appears obvious that He would create this sense, in general, because of the need to communicate to one another in an efficient manner. What I want to focus on more specifically is not just the gift of sound in general but the gift of music. I've always felt that music transcends humanity on some level. We read in the Bible about the angels singing praises to God before His throne, not to mention the many verses calling us to praise God through song and instrument. As speech allows us to communicate to one another mentally, I feel like music allows us to communicate to one another and to God on a spiritual level. Just as we see parents winding up a music box for a baby's delight, God gives us the gift of sound, as well as the gift of music, to bring us delight and to provide an outlet for us to express our emotions to Him and others. It is as if music is the language of heaven, and God shares it with us as yet another undeserved blessing. (See **Ephesians 5:19–20.**)

Yet another sense that we can take for granted is that of touch. We don't often consider it as something to be thankful for, but as with the others, touch, too, is a source of pleasure that God didn't have to give us. We obviously have the ability to perceive sensation within our skin as a safety measure against the dangers of extreme cold, hot or painful stimuli. It is a basic survival tool without a doubt. But once again, we see God taking a basic need and expanding it to allow for pleasure. The feel of soft material, a gentle breeze, the touch of a spouse's hand and a warm tub of water all create within us a sense of delight and comfort, which was the intention of God. He provides the means for us to experience comfort, not unlike parents wrapping their baby in soft, cozy blankets.

*As we consider all the mentioned blessings, we are forced to conclude one thing that is certain. God loves us without a shadow of a doubt. Not only does He love us; He loves us before we accept Him as Savior. This is apparent in the fact that we are given the blessings listed even as sinners. He loves us unconditionally. But unfortunately for those who reject His offer of salvation, His love will not prevent Him from passing judgment on unbelievers after this life because He is a just God and cannot be reconciled with sin. The comforts we experience on this earth are but a shadow of what we will be granted in heaven. The joys we find in this life should be an incentive to experience even greater joys in the next. But if we take His blessings for granted in this life and refuse to accept His offer, then we will experience an eternity of sensations that will leave us in anguish, such as the smell of brimstone, the feeling of heat and the sight of darkness, rather than the blessings that are found in heaven. (See **Revelation 20:10, 14–15.**)*

Day 360

This morning I finally reached the top of the large hill that I have been tackling for three days now. As I stand at the edge peering out over the valley below me, I take time to scan the surrounding landscape. The view is breathtaking, as my high elevation gives me a 360-degree view at the lay of the land. From here, I am able to see a number of high peaks jutting up above the forests to the north. To the east and west, I observe miles and miles of thick forests blanketing the land. To the south across the river, are sprawling flatlands stretching into the horizon as far as the eye can see. My perspective from this point is strengthened because I am afforded such an extensive view of the world around me.

I look back to the west, where I have just traveled from, and gain a bird's-eye view of the course I've taken over the past several weeks. As I journeyed that course, my ability to see what lay ahead at any given time was very limited, due to the dense forest I was walking through and my lower elevation. But as I look at that same course from where I am now standing, I can see the hills, the bends and the valleys all with one glance. It would have been great to have this knowledge of the terrain during the past several weeks, as I would have been more confident in knowing what lay just around every bend.

I next turn and look to the south, at the land across the river. So many times during my walk on this path, as I face uphill walk after uphill walk, I find myself glancing at the level terrain across the river and for a moment become envious of *the easy life afforded to those on its shores. As I go forward sweating and toiling, they walk about unfettered and carefree. In these times, I start to despair and question my choice to follow the path. But as I stand looking across the river from this elevated point of view, I find my spirit renewed by the perspective given to me. I am able to see the bigger picture across the river, and I am reminded why I continue to follow the course I currently take. Those who live across the river may experience an easy walk in their day-to-day lives, but they will never be fortunate enough to see the world around them as I do at this point. They will never have a full and complete perspective of how desolate and barren their world is since they live their lives focused only on their immediate surroundings and instant gratification. If they could stand where I am standing and see the never-ending wasteland in which they reside and compare it to the beauty found on this side of the river, there would be mobs of people standing at the river's edge in search of bridges in order to cross over to this side. Yet unfortunately, they go on living day after day, blinded from seeing their impending doom because of their insatiable hunger for the good life.*

Finally, I turn and look to the east, the direction of my journey, and again I see the miles and miles of forest stretching out before me. Within the blanket of trees, I can make out many valleys, hills and fields. One would think that this would allow me to plan my route for the immediate future, knowing what to expect along each section of the way. The only problem with this suggestion is that even though I have a bird's-eye view of the land, I am not able to see the path specifically. I could literally take thousands of possible courses through this dense foliage. It's one thing to see an overview of a forest. It's a totally different thing to be in the heart of the forest and under its canopy, following a course with very limited foresight due to the thick vegetation in all directions.

As I ponder this thought, I experience an epiphany. The hidden path to the east, which lies out of sight, represents "walking by faith, not by sight," a concept that Clarence had discussed with me that he said came from the Guide Book. *Looking back to the west, I am able to see my prior course and the surrounding terrain. I can examine the choices I made in regards to roads taken from an all-encompassing view. I am only afforded this perspective because of my temporary elevated position and hindsight knowledge of the route I took, adding value to the expression "hindsight is twenty-twenty."*

But regarding my future course to the east, I understand that even though God occasionally places me in positions such as this, which allow me to see my world from a broader perspective, I still am not able to see the exact course that He would have me follow. Even though I can see rolling hills, deep valleys and high peaks for miles ahead, the vast green forest hides from my view the path that God would have me take. I am given only a limited view of the path at any given point of my journey. This, I believe, is part of God's plan to keep me turning to Him daily and relying not on my own wisdom. I am given knowledge as to the general direction I am to travel, I am even occasionally given a vantage point from which to see my future course in the bigger picture, yet only when I am communicating with my heavenly Father during my day-to-day travels am I given specific directions regarding each step I am to take.

Whether I choose to hear the directions or even obey them is a different matter altogether. As I trust in God to guide me on my Christian walk, He presents my course to me in His timing and fashion. I realize that He has each twist and turn of my life plotted out. Every uphill climb, every valley I must walk through, every rocky path, He knows about them all before I even draw near to them. He also knows the points where I will falter and wander off course through my own weaknesses or disobedience. Yet for every wrong turn I make, the Holy Spirit calls from the path, beckoning me to return and repent from my sinfulness. Once I find my way back on course, He continues leading me on toward my destination.

The explanation of the landscape is as follows:

* The north with its towering, impassable peaks signifies God's ultimate will and His power in keeping us from certain courses in life.
* The south with its broad, flat plains represents the world and the choice we have to take the easy way rather than the narrow road God expects from us.
* The west represents our past and the roads already traveled. As Garrett explains, he is able to look back and see the course he has taken, for

better or for worse. While walking that course, he was only able to see very short distances before him at a time, which represents how God has us walk daily by faith. But looking back on our lives, we are given the hindsight perspective, seeing past events as a whole. From this position, it is easy to look over the roads already covered and point to alternate paths we should have taken. But we must remember that during those times, we were only given a limited view of the course ahead of us. We can use these times to learn from our mistakes, but we can't dwell on them and incapacitate ourselves for upcoming paths ahead of us.

* The east represents the course we take, as Christians, toward Christ and His calling. Again as Garrett explains, he is given an overview of the terrain ahead of him, but he is unaware as to the exact course God will have him take through the forest. Some areas contain valleys, some contain hills, some contain dense woods and others may offer level fields. As to which of these he will travel through, only God knows.

* The thick covering of the trees represents our future being hidden from us. As Garrett noted, he could look out to the east and set a course in his mind from the perspective given him at that time, but the minute he treks into the woods, he is at the mercy of the terrain and the obstacles that lay ahead of him. This is why God expects us to walk by faith and not by sight.

* The elevated vantage point represents a temporary perspective that God has given Garrett during his journey. This could be symbolic of a Christian having a time of success and prosperity in life, a time void of hardship or testing. As he looks out over the landscape before him, should Garrett use this blessing from God to try to plot his own course by judging the lay of the land himself, this would be prideful. He would not be following the Holy Spirit. A good example of this is found in *Luke 12:16–21.*

There may be times in our lives that God will bless us with prosperity and success. But we are expected to accept it with a heart of humility, knowing that it may be temporary and fleeting. In the verses, we see a person who used his financial security as an excuse to no longer rely on God's will but his own. God quickly reminded him how foolish his relying on material wealth was, as He informed him he would be granted not a single day more on this earth in which to enjoy that wealth. This correlates to being able to see over a far distance, but not being able to see under the tree cover just a short distance ahead. God doesn't mind us setting our sights ahead for the future and making plans, but our ultimate statement to Him should be, "If it is Your will…"

* The elevated vantage point in itself is not a wrong thing; in fact, it comes naturally to Christians who follow the Spirit's call. The Christian is given a view of the world that is not afforded to the non-Christian. This is because the Christian is able to discern spiritual matters and the unsaved person is not. We find this confirmed in *1 Corinthians 2:10–14.*

As I stand upon the same hilltop deep in thought, another epiphany strikes me in regards to perspective. Having just written about perspective in the sense of comparing my past journey to my future journey, as well as comparing my current location to that of the world across the river, I suddenly begin to look at my surroundings and see them from yet another separate point of view all together. The forests that surround me blanket the earth in several shades of green stretching into the horizon. What I begin to think about is the fact that my current viewpoint merely exists due to the simple fact that I stand making my observation during the middle of summer.

Because of the season, my view of the world around me is one of endless green forests, intense heat and high humidity. Yet if I were to have arrived at this same point in the fall, my description would be totally different. I would be describing a sea of red, orange and yellow foliage spreading throughout the land, with occasional patches of green from the pine forests and a cool, crisp breeze enveloping me. If I had stood at this same spot and described it during the middle of winter, yet another entirely different description would exist. I would be speaking of a wonderland of white stretching out in all directions with very little color to speak of, other than once again the occasional pine forest and a cold winter chill cutting to the bone. And finally, a fourth perspective would exist had I stood here during the peak of spring. A world of flowering trees and buds would be observed, the forests breaking free from the long winter's hold and the warmth of the sun's rays. All four descriptions of my surroundings would be accurate yet totally unique from each other. At first this may appear to be a contradiction, but as mentioned earlier, each description owes its differences to the time of year it was described in.

This brings me to my epiphany. As Christians, we must be aware of the fact that just because we have traveled the same path as another, we may have two completely different perspectives on the same experience. Not understanding this concept can significantly impede our growth and effectiveness as Christians. Putting the analogy into the context of our everyday lives, the seasons would be representative of the highs and lows of our lives.

*   *Spring would represent times of growth, renewal and rebirth, such as marriages, job promotions, births, graduations, career changes, purchases of new homes or any other optimistic event that brings us to a place of hope in our lives.*
*   *Next, we have summer, which represents the periods of our lives in which we experience contentment, security and peace of mind, which would include periods of financial stability, job security, good health for ourselves and our immediate circle of friends and family or any other experience that brings us a positive outlook on our lives.*
*   *Then we have autumn, which represents those times in our lives of reflection, pondering and soul-searching—such as retirement, anniversaries and maturing of children—that lead to an empty nest, birthdays or any other experience that involves closing a chapter in our lives.*
*   *And, finally, we come to winter, which represents times of hardship, despair and loneliness, such as illness, death, bankruptcy, divorce, abuse, poverty or any other situation that tries the soul.*

As humans, we experience all four of these seasons throughout our lives. For every summer in our lives, there comes a winter, for every spring, there comes a fall. That is the beauty of life; it is constantly changing, just as the seasons do. We can almost schedule our clocks around it. For this reason, we must mentally prepare ourselves as Christians to not become comfortable and complacent within our lives. If you are experiencing a stretch of warm summertime in your life right now, enjoy it while it lasts. But don't become too dependent on it, for Old Man Winter is right around the corner, and he is bringing the wind and the snow to shake your world up for a season. And if you are walking through life at this moment taking in the intoxicating smell and beautiful sight of flowers around you, thank God for blessing you, but be ready to see those same flowers and leaves wither and fade with the coming of fall.

If we do not mentally prepare ourselves for change, we will continually find ourselves grieving and struggling to accept the fact that change is an essential component in our lives. Jobs come and go, children are born and grow up, birthdays come every year whether or not we like them, sickness and disease occur around us without rhyme or reason, death takes the young and old alike without being required to give explanations and our bodies reveal their "wear-and-tear nature," slowly betraying us as we age. As time goes on, we cannot be naïve and think that as Christians we will be exempt from the consequences of human nature, only to lash out at God when our lives fail to remain pain free. It makes about as much sense as standing on our rooftops and screaming at the sky for snowing on us.

༖

We must learn to be content in every season of our lives. I often laugh when I observe certain people who seem to find a way to be discontent no matter what season they are in. In the winter, they complain that it's too cold, that the snow is a pain to drive in and shovel and that it gets dark too early. In the spring, they complain that there is too much rain, that the ground is too muddy and that the flowering trees cause their allergies to flare up. In the summer, they complain about the heat, about mowing the grass and about the bugs. And even in the fall, they complain about the leaves in their yard, about the fact that summer flew by and about the fact that winter's coming again. Without realizing it, they put themselves in a perpetual, never-ending spiral of pessimism and discontentment. These are the people we inevitably end up sitting next to on the bus, plane or subway. They never seem to have a good thing to say about anything. I've developed the theory that because they have complained for so long, they have mentally crippled themselves in a way and therefore are forced to use complaints as a crutch to function. What God asks us to do as Christians is to be content, regardless of the season, as described in *Philippians 4:11–13.*

We as Christians must be the examples to the unsaved around us. If we cannot be content with God's love living within us, how can we possibly expect for those around us in the world to be? And why would they be inspired to become a Christian if, after watching our lives, they see nothing but complaining and misery? This is not to say that as Christians we can never have a bad day, never complain about something or never get the blues. There is an appropriate time for mourning. There is an appropriate time for grieving. As we can see, this is clarified in *Ecclesiastes 3:1–8.* But there is a significant difference between having a bad day and being the Eeyore of the group. We must resist the temptation to be negative and try to find the positive in any situation possible, if not for us then for those around us who we may be able to reach for Christ. And it is a choice. We cannot always control the things that happen to us, but we have the choice as to how we respond to those things. Are we going to be like those following Moses in the desert, bellyaching for forty years, or are we going to be like Job and praise God through the storm, even if it means we have everything taken from us? How we as Christians handle adversity often speaks more to our faith than how we handle the good times in our lives.

Day 365

One year ago today, I crossed over the bridge and began my journey on this side of the river. How the time has flown by. It seems like it was just yesterday. It is a bittersweet day, joyful in the fact that I've been granted a year's journey and tearful in the fact that it makes me remember Clarence, the reason I'm here. As I hold my water cup in my hand, I raise it up in the air and make a toast to him. "God bless you, Clarence! When last we walked together, it was on this narrow road. When next we walk together, it will be on the streets of gold."

Day 399

What a mess I found myself in today! Earlier this morning, as I was strolling down the path, I heard the sound of laughter off to my right, faint at first but growing louder the farther I walked. I came to a point where I could see a group of people in the distance gathered along the edge of the cliff near the river. They were scattered about, sitting on the ground around a campfire, appearing to be having a wonderful time. It was obvious that there was a lot of drinking going on, as I could see them holding the cans, not to mention the ones strewn about them.

As the jovialness continued, I watched as two of the guys approached each other, each with a woman on his shoulders. They appeared to be having some kind of contest in which the women attempted to knock each other off the guy carrying her. I found myself entertained by the whole situation and watched for a time. At times it became difficult to see the action, as there was a wooded valley running between the path and where they were. As they moved about, occasionally the top of a tree would obscure my view of them, temporarily frustrating me.

I found myself taking several steps closer to see the action better. Then after a time, I realized that I was several feet off the path. For a second I thought about turning around and moving back onto the path, but then something inside me made me stop. Although I knew I had no business being off the path, I suppressed the small voice telling me to turn back and chose to get a closer look at the party.

I began walking down the slope through the woods, planning to reach the other side of the valley in order to have a better view of the activities. As I began reaching the center of the valley, I noticed that the ground was becoming increasingly muddy the farther I went. I wasn't very happy about the fact that my shoes were becoming filthy, but I pressed on, trying to not think about it. Suddenly, as I took a step, I felt my foot plummet down as if into thin air, bringing my waist level with the ground. I had stepped into quicksand.

The rapid change of vertical view left me frozen in shock. For several seconds, I couldn't move. Then I began to look around me and process the reality of what had just happened. After the initial shock, I decided to attempt to get myself out of the mess I was in. Slowly, I started to turn back toward the path, hoping to find some footing. But I soon found that the more I moved the farther I began to sink. A fear ran up my spine, making me begin to wonder if I was going to get out of this alive.

I began yelling as loud as I could, hoping the people I had been watching could hear me. But unfortunately I soon came to two depressing realizations: the first that no one appeared to hear me over the festivities and the second that the more I yelled, the deeper I sank. I sat frozen in fear, unsure what to do. As much as I wanted to keep trying to get out on my own, all attempts became futile. I began screaming at myself inside my head for being so stupid as to leave the safety of the path; this was entirely my fault.

After several minutes passed, which seemed like days, I found myself passing from a state of panic to a state of acceptance for the error of my ways. I began weeping openly, feeling completely helpless with the situation I found myself in. Then in the midst of my tears, I heard a sound that brought me back to reality: the white dove sat in a nearby tree as I looked toward the path. Instantly, I found myself focusing on the dove, watching as it stared intently at me. The feeling that came over me from seeing the bird was a mixed emotion; as much as I was glad to see it, I also felt a wave of shame crash over me. I had gone where I should not have gone, and now I had to face the consequences.

As I stared at the dove, I began to cry out to God to forgive me and to help me in my time of need. After a minute or two, I watched as the dove rose from the limb and flew toward me. As crazy as it sounds, for a brief moment I had expectations of it swooping over me and pulling me out of my mess. I soon realized how silly that thought was. Yet I watched as it flew closer to me then up above me. Following it with my eyes, I saw it come to rest on a limb high above my head. Then I noticed it. Hanging down from the same limb over my head was a long vine that I had not noticed before.

My heart began to dance with excitement at the discovery of this new revelation. Ever so slowly, I began to reach up for the vine, as it was only about a foot or so above me. Grabbing the end of the vine, I mustered all my available strength and began to pull. Inch by inch, I began to ease out of the muck, but it was a daunting task. Soon my waist was out and then my knees and then finally my feet were out. There I was, exhausted and hanging on to the vine for dear life. I knew what I had to do to complete the rescue. Slowly, I began swaying my body back and forth, attempting to swing the vine back over to the safety of the hard ground. Little by little, I picked up speed and distance until finally I saw that I had an opportunity. Praying that the vine would not break, I took one last swing over the quagmire toward the path and made a leap for it. I hit solid ground!

For nearly ten minutes, I could only lie on the ground, physically and emotionally spent from the grueling ordeal. Then finally, I found the strength to stand. The weight of my clothes was ridiculous from the mud, making my gait pattern appear to look more like a lunar walk. Slowly, I walked back up the hill I had just previously climbed down, toward the path. As I finally reached the path, I sat for several minutes and gathered my strength once again. Looking down at myself, I became disgusted with the decision I had made to leave the path. It is very frustrating when one has no one to blame for his unfortunate circumstance but himself.

Walking over to a nearby stream, I removed my clothing and began to wash it in the water. After some time, I had removed the mud, but the clothes remained soaking wet. Unfortunately, I had to put the same cold wet clothes back on and continue my journey in them. This did not make me overly excited, to be honest. For the rest of the day, with each step I took, I was reminded of my foolishness by the chaffing of my wet pants on my legs and the excess weight of my clothes.

As I now sit here this evening by the campfire, my damp clothes drying above it, I thank God for showing me mercy in my time of need despite my disobedience to Him. Looking back, I realize that the more I tried to save myself through my own actions, the further I sank. It was only when I surrendered my will and looked up to God and asked Him to help that I found my salvation from my crisis. All I can say is, "Thank you, God, for saving me once again."

⌗

Here we find the perfect analogy in which to describe the consequences of disobedience to God. When we stray from the straight and narrow path and disregard the conviction of the Holy Spirit, the result tends to mirror the story above. Initially, our stepping off the path stems from some form of distraction or temptation from the world, thus the story's mention of Garrett wandering to the right of the road, which is representative of the world. Examples of things that can make us lose our focus and cause us to wander off course are temporary pleasures of the world, such as drunkenness, debauchery, earthly possessions, financial gain, positions of power, sexual gratification and illicit drug use. As we begin to focus on these things rather than the path we are called to follow, we find ourselves walking farther and farther into the muddy reaches of the world.

Initially, as we take the first couple of steps, the sight and feel of the mud on our shoes causes us to reel back in disgust. For some, this is enough to turn them around and send them back to the path. But for many, the allure of the temptation on the other side of the quagmire forces them to block the reality of the messy transformation they are experiencing. With each step, the mud climbs farther and farther up their body, and with each step, they become more and more desensitized about what is taking place to them. Focused only on reaching the forbidden fruit, they press on, not heeding the danger sign of the ever-increasing depth of the mud they are heading into. Finally, they reach the point where their ground gives way. The sudden sensation snaps them out of their carnal fixation and brings them rushing back to reality, but by this point it is too late. They are slowly sinking into a swampy nightmare.

Their initial reaction is to panic as they try desperately to regain control of their situation. But as was described in the story, the more they attempt to solve their situation through human wisdom, the more Satan pulls them into a downward spiral by the weight of their own sinful actions. The sad reality of this is that many times people continue this process to the point of their own demise. Yet there are times during which, as in the story, people find the courage to stop fighting on their own and reach out for God in their moments of need. It is only then when they reach up to God for help that they find the safety line God has made available to them, as detailed in *Psalm 40:1–2*. Symbolically, just as in the story, even though the vine of escape is made available to them by God, they have to put forth the effort and make the difficult climb out of the quicksand. This is representative of putting faith into action. As *James 2:14, 17* shows, faith without deeds is worthless.

Once people have freed themselves from their near-death situations and regained solid footing, it is then that they often gain an improved perspective on their situations, realizing the foolishness of their decisions. From this point, even though they return to the path, they do so carrying the consequences of their actions. In the story, the consequences were walking with cold, wet, muddy clothes. In real life, the consequences are usually much worse. Although the forgiveness that Jesus offers is all encompassing, He doesn't guarantee to take away the pain and suffering that result from our actions. We are often left to walk through life for a time in our cold, wet, muddy clothes. As uncomfortable as this may be, often times it works out to be a blessing in disguise, as it can serve to be a constant reminder to us each time we consider straying off the path.

Day 415

About midday, as I was walking down the trail, I began hearing ahead of me the sound of running water. It wasn't as loud as the great river off to my right, but I could make out the distinct sound all the same. The farther I walked, the more obvious the noise became. As I reached the edge of the woods, I found myself standing on high ground, the clearing before me sloping downhill and eventually coming to a drop-off. From there, a span of about twenty or thirty feet lay until the land began again. From where I stood, I was not able to see what lay at the bottom of this gulf. I walked down the hill and came to the edge of the land. Peering over the edge of the drop-off, I was able to observe a very deep and narrow canyon that ran between this side and the other. Even though the distance between was not extremely wide, it was enough to make it impossible for me to reach the other side without assistance. I looked to my left and then to my right in search of a way across without luck.

As I stood pondering my next move, I heard a rustling coming from the trees behind me. I looked back in time to see the white dove fly out from the forest and toward the right, disappearing around a bend in the canyon. I decided to walk to the right and see where it was heading. I had no sooner rounded the bend when I noticed a pleasant surprise: a bridge. The old but sturdy-looking bridge would make the crossing rather effortless. I slowly walked across the bridge, looking down at the fast moving stream that raced below me to join the great river. Finally, I reached the other side and breathed a sigh of relief, knowing that if it were not for the fortune of finding the bridge, I would still be somewhere on the other side wandering aimlessly in search of a way across, most likely taking myself way off course in order to find it.

Then I began to realize something for the first time. The act of following God on a daily basis by faith is a spiritual representation of crossing a bridge. As I come on dead ends during my journey, as in situations where I find God calling me to go a certain direction, but with my human wisdom, it seems an impossible task; He provides the means for me to continue despite daunting obstacles. Just as I was facing an impossible situation from my human standpoint, the fact that I could not jump from one side of the span to the other, with the help of the bridge, it became possible with very little effort on my part. Similarly, through faith in God, when I face a spiritual dead end and cannot see any way humanly possible to continue on the path that God is leading me, He provides a spiritual bridge for me to use to reach my destination that I would not have been able to reach using my own power and knowledge. Instead of wandering about aimlessly and trying to find an alternate way across on my own, with faith, I simply wait on God and then follow the white dove as He guides me to a bridge, allowing me to continue on my journey without straying from the path that He would have me travel.

The challenge comes in applying patience. Even though a bridge is guaranteed, it is not always guaranteed to present itself in our time; rather, it will appear in God's time. This is why many may lose patience with God and try to find it on their own. We have to remember that not only does He have a plan for where regarding our journey; He also has a plan for when. Also, once we have been shown the bridge, we may look across to the other side and see that it leads to a location that forces us to question God and His direction for our lives. This is the danger of trying to predict God's next move, thereby becoming disappointed when it doesn't play out like we anticipated. And finally, there are bridges that the world tries to construct, but they are weak and unsafe, not to mention the fact that they lead away from God's true course for our lives. It's only when we put our trust in God that we will be shown the true way and true timing to cross any valley.

As Garrett mentions, we not only have to look for God's will but His timing as well. A perfect example of this concept can be seen played out in *Genesis 15:1–5.* As we see, Abram was given a course to follow and a destination from God. This destination was to be the father of many, beginning with a biological son. God Himself stated this to Abram as His will. Abram started this journey on the right foot, as we read in *Genesis 15:6.* Even though Abram started on the right course, we find in the very next chapter that, rather than wait for God's timing to accomplish His promise, Abram decides to produce a son with his wife's maidservant, Hagar, described in *Genesis 16:1–4.*

At this point, if we compare Abram's situation to Garrett's scenario, we have God setting Abram on a path toward becoming a father. Abram comes to the ravine, as did Garrett, and sees no bridge to take him to the other side. He knows that God's will is for him to go to the other side, but in his human wisdom, he cannot understand why there is no bridge waiting for him. Here is where he makes his error. Rather than sit at the edge and wait for the Spirit's direction, he wanders off to the south in search of his own way across. He finds a bridge but not one made by God's hands. This one is made by human wisdom, and it is called Hagar. The bridge does the job of taking him across the ravine, but no sooner does he cross than the bridge collapses from his weight. He has no way to return to the other side, where God has planned to reveal His true bridge to him. As he attempts to travel north on his new side of the span to the location God had ordained for him, he unfortunately realizes that even though he has crossed a ravine, a new one that he was not aware of exists. In his haste, he became more concerned with getting where he wanted to go than going when God wanted him to, thus resulting in his stranded situation, as we read in *Genesis 17:15–19.*

Abraham sat at his dead end for over a decade until the Lord finally decided to fulfill his promise. He had received a son through his own workings but not the son that God had promised him. Finally, a bridge appeared and allowed him to travel to where God had intended for him all along. Had he waited patiently as God had asked him to do, maybe God would have given him Isaac even sooner. In the end, he ultimately received his promised son, but at the cost of contending with an illegitimate son as well, which was not in God's original plan for him. This goes to show that when we lose patience with God's plan and travel off course, He can still bring us to where He wants us, but that does not mean that we escape any consequences that we might have brought on ourselves through our impatience.

In *Genesis 22:1–2, 9–12, 15–17,* we find Abraham in another situation that draws a parallel to Garrett's story, only this time he makes the right choice. In this scenario, Abraham was once again brought to a ravine. To gain access to the other side, God told Abraham to symbolically "throw Isaac into the ravine" to test his faith. Abraham was obedient and brought his son all the way to the edge, ready to go through with the act. But at the last second, God stayed Abraham's hand and blessed him for his impressive faith. God provided the bridge across the ravine, allowing Abraham to walk into history as the father of many nations. God does not always say that the choices are going to be easy, but then again, that is why it is called faith, as we find exemplified in *Galatians 2:20, 2 Corinthians 5:7, Romans 5:1–2, Romans 3:21–22, Romans 1:17, Mark 11:22, Matthew 17:20* and *Habakkuk 2:4.*

I can vouch from my own experiences that Garrett's bridge analogy is true. One great example would be the details of my dating life leading up to meeting my wife. Early on as a young man, I had always dreamed about finding my soul mate, falling in love, getting married and living happily ever after. The quest was an honorable one because marriage was a God-ordained institution. Where my difficulties came about was when I, like Abraham, decided to find my own bridge rather than wait for God's bridge. Every time I would come to a ravine, rather than sit back and wait for God's timing, I would travel in every direction in an attempt to get to the other side, wherein lay the future spouse I longed for. In the process, I wandered constantly from God's chosen path, resulting in my tramping through numerous briar patches, swampy areas, slippery slopes and rocky terrain. Of course, these obstacles listed are meant to describe relationships that ended in disappointment. It seemed that the harder I tried to find the right person, the more scratches I would attain, the muddier my boots would become and the more grass stained my clothes would become. I would find myself wandering back to God after each failed endeavor with my head hanging low, disappointed and ashamed for trying to accomplish the task on my own.

Not until January 2000 did I finally have enough. After looking back and reflecting on failure after failure, I had finally decided to give in to God and wait for His timing. It was difficult to do, but I knew that I would never grow spiritually unless I learned to become obedient in this area of my life. Ironically, the timing of this choice also coincided with my beginning a new career and a new job. Deep down, I felt at peace with God. Then on May 4, 2000, when I wasn't looking for it or expecting it, God decided it was time to build a bridge for me. That was the date that I met my now wife of twelve years. I had turned my dating life over to Him, and He was faithful to bring me my soul mate, in His time. Recently, my wife and I were discussing this topic and the timing of everything. We ultimately concluded that if we had met at an earlier time in our lives, there was a strong chance that we would not have made the same connection with each other because of the different circumstances going on in our lives.

It's sobering to think that throughout all those years, during all my frustrations with God, all my failed relationships and my questioning of His plan for my life, He was sitting back waiting patiently, knowing that on a certain day in a certain year, His plan for my life would be revealed to me in regards to my marriage partner. When I think of all the time I wasted, all the opportunities I missed for serving Christ and all the needless worrying I wrapped myself in during my lost decade, it saddens me. Obviously, hindsight is twenty-twenty, but I wish during those years I could have been Abraham offering up his son to God in faith rather than being Abraham running off with Hagar. As with Abraham, I have been graciously blessed by God with a loving and beautiful wife despite my shortcomings and impatience. But also as with Abraham, I carry the weight of lost years and a compromised witness before others. If you are sitting at the edge of a ravine and becoming frustrated because God has not produced a bridge for you, just remember that He has not forgotten you, just as He did not forget Abraham or me. And you can be sure of one thing. If He asks you to wait, it's for a good reason. And if you are patient and have faith in God, whatever He has in store for you will be well worth the wait. Don't compromise and settle for a Hagar; wait on the Lord and receive His perfect will for your life! You won't be disappointed.

Day 453

I have to admit that today did not start out especially well for me. In fact, it was like a Monday on steroids. It began last night with a terrible storm that gave me broken sleep because of the howling winds, the thunder and the rain pounding on the roof of the cabin I stayed in. By morning the storm had passed, but as I went to get my boots, I suddenly realized that I had left them outside overnight because they were very muddy and I was trying to avoid tracking mud into the cabin. I reached down to pick them up and found that they were completely soaked! My heart sank at the thought of having to wear wet boots on a cold, damp morning. I reluctantly put them on and instantly felt my socks becoming soaked with water. My joints were responding to the weather, making me feel about twenty years older than I am. Every step felt like I was walking through desert sands, between the weight of my boots and the effort required from my body to move my legs. But eventually, I was able to get moving and set a steady pace.

There were puddles scattered about everywhere like a landmine field. As much as I tried to avoid them, I seemed to be drawn to them like a magnet, resulting in muddy water splashing up and soaking the bottom of my pants. As the sun started to rise, the comforting warmth of its rays was soon forgotten, as the heat started to evaporate all the moisture, resulting in an uncomfortable level of humidity. I started sweating more and more profusely the more the morning went on. My shirt competed with my boots to see which could become the wettest. Every

couple of steps, I found myself wiping the sweat from my face and swatting at an-
noying gnats that left the mud puddles in order to swarm in front of my eyes. It
was a most miserable day, with my mind seemingly fixated on negativity. Nothing
was going right.

I trudged on in a most foul mood, mad at the world and a little disappointed
at God. It didn't make sense to me. Here I was following the narrow road, trying
to live in a way that was pleasing to God, and He goes and lets me have a day
like this. I would expect Him to allow those across the river to experience such difficulties, but people like me? In my mind, I began compiling my list of grievances
for God, even though I didn't foresee any specific meeting with Him in the near
future. He must have been temporarily distracted by someone or something else for
Him to allow me to suffer in such a way. I continued to walk in an almost trancelike state for quite a while, fixated only on my sad state of affairs and constructing
an ever-increasing pity party for myself. As I brooded over my miserable circumstances, I could feel my frustration rise within me.

Slowly my mood turned from frustration to bitterness, and I found myself
stomping down the path a little more sternly. I had fixed my gaze downward
at the path several feet before me when I suddenly noticed a clump of colorful
mushrooms growing along the right edge of the path. I decided these objects were
going to be the recipients of my anger, a way to physically take out my frustrations
and release some steam. I walked over to them, bent my knee back, aimed for the
mushrooms and gave the hardest kick I could muster. My foot made direct contact
with its desired target, sending particles of mushrooms spraying in all directions.
What I should have taken into consideration though was the fact that the path
was still wet and muddy, which as a result caused my other foot to slip out from
underneath me, sending me rolling down the wet hillside along the path's edge.

After passing through tall weeds, twigs and several thorn branches, I finally
came to a stop by smacking into a large oak tree. The force of the impact with the
tree briefly knocked the wind out of me, leaving me gasping for breath. When I
was finally breathing normally again, I slowly sat up, wincing from the pain to
my right side each time my ribs expanded and contracted from my breathing. In
addition to being wet, muddy, hot and miserable, now I could add bruised and
scratched up. At that moment, I would have loved to have had someone to yell

at or to blame, but unfortunately, I had no one to point the finger at except for myself. This made the situation even worse, adding insult to injury.

As I slowly crawled back up the embankment to the path, my anger only intensified. I reached the path and stood for several minutes, simply contemplating everything that had just happened. It was like some sort of bad nightmare that had just taken place. Instead of trying to kick anything else, I allowed my rage to turn inward and fester. I thought, "What else could go wrong? If anyone ever tries to say that God does not have a sense of humor, I will argue with him or her until doomsday." In a pure example of His comedic timing, as this question ran through my head, an acorn from the overhanging oak tree plummeted, landed directly on top of my head, ricocheted off it, and fell to the ground before me. This was the final straw.

Since that morning, I had endured wet clothes, profuse sweating, mud, grass stains, scratches, bruised ribs, having the wind knocked out of me and, last, a knock in the head from falling foliage, the cherry on top of my "banana-split day." Walking to the side of the road, I found a large rock and plopped down on it. I had moved past frustration and anger, and I had now reached the stage of emotional numbness. Resting back against the rock, I closed my eyes and tried to gather my thoughts. For several minutes, I replayed the day's events back through my head. The more I thought about everything, the less I wanted to continue on the path.

When I opened up my eyes, I noticed that I was seated in a position where I could see across the river to the Southern Lands. For a moment, I envied those on that side of the river. I started to think how much easier life would be sometimes without hills to climb and obstacles to overcome. Is this what I have to look forward to for the rest of my journey? Are trials, hardships, pain and suffering my new normal? My spiritual outlook started becoming very bleak, and I felt like I was beginning to regret this destination choice. Sadly, I even found myself looking down over the hill to see if any bridges were in sight that would take me back over to the other side. A small part of me felt uncomfortable thinking this way, but my emotions seemed to be overriding any voice from that part of me. I sat fixated on the river, looking down the steep hillside, deep in thought.

Suddenly, at the bottom of the hill I saw movement through the trees. I wasn't able to make it out at first because it was fairly far away, but eventually I saw through a clearing that it was a man. He stopped for a second and appeared to be resting. He looked around at his surroundings, taking in everything. Then suddenly he seemed to notice me sitting at the top of the hill. Waving excitedly at me, he yelled out, "Hello there, my friend!" My reflexes kicked in, and I cringed without realizing it. The last thing I wanted right at this moment was someone bugging me. I would have got up and hurried off if I hadn't still been in such a funk. I just did not have enough energy. Looking back down the hill, I watched him start moving again along a path that, as I followed it to its end, led right to my path. A very steep and windy course, it would be challenging to the best hiker. My focus returned to the hiker, as I observed him trudging along the course.

It became apparent that the man was not a fast hiker by any means, which was fine with me, given my lack of interest in any company at this point. He walked with a staff, slow but steady, and every couple of minutes, he would look up the hill toward me and wave excitedly. Some of the bends seemed to challenge him as he walked, but he carried on nonetheless. After he had traveled about halfway up the hill, I finally began to realize something. He was not walking with a normal gait. He held the staff in his right hand, and he used it partially as a crutch when he went to move his left leg through. His left arm and hand, which was drawn up against his chest in a closed fist, as well seemed to be affected.

Then something quite amazing and unexpected started to occur to me. A warm sensation began to course through my body, seeming to break the cold, icy demeanor that I had wrapped myself in. As much as I wanted to hang on to my foul mood, my emotions would not let me. I was being overwhelmed by emotions I had never experienced before: compassion and empathy. I could feel the very muscles of my face transition from my previous scowl to an utter state of relaxation. Step by step, he carried on up the hill. I watched his face and was amazed that despite the obvious physical handicap he bore and the difficult terrain he faced, he never once lost his smile. His right foot would take a step; then he would thrust his weight to the staff and drag his left leg through with a determination that I had never known before. He walked as a man with a mission, strong and proud.

Suddenly, I noticed that he started to go out of focus. Then I realized that it was because of the tears welling up in my eyes. Within my chest, my heart began to feel like a wax candle melting by a campfire. The closer to me he drew, the greater *my physical reaction. My previous emotions of anger, bitterness and self-pity were rapidly being replaced with emotions such as shame, humility and sympathy for the stranger's affliction. As he drew even closer, I could start to see the features in his face more clearly. He was probably about my age but in some ways seemed to be much older. I assumed this was most likely due to the fact that he had endured a much tougher life than I had, which had physically aged him more. Sadly, what also became apparent was the fact that one side of his face had been severely burned at some point in the past. As he continued to walk, I found myself mentally putting myself in his shoes. I tried to imagine myself facing the same handicaps that he lived with on a daily basis, and I suddenly shuddered at the thought. Then my thoughts were interrupted by the sensation of warm tears running down my cheeks. I began weeping for this man I had never met, heartbroken over his obvious struggle.*

My mind began thinking back to my thought processes just prior to this stranger coming into view. As I reviewed them in the light of this man's difficulties, shame and self-loathing began to overtake me. Compared to this man, I had nothing worth complaining about. Wet clothes, a little sweat and a couple of scratches—all these were temporary inconveniences compared to this man's permanent scars and limitations. Could I have been any more selfish and ungrateful? I lowered my head and simply began to weep. I wept like I had never wept before. All the built up emotions from earlier seemed to undergo a process of condensation, transforming into tears which flowed uncontrollably. My body convulsed as waves of brokenness swept through me. My mind forgot about everything else, as I just simply wept.

Suddenly, I was snapped back to reality when I felt a hand on my back. I jolted out of my zone and looked up to see the stranger standing above me, looking down sympathetically at me. He was smiling at me, though with a crooked grin due to his burn injury on the left side of his face. "Are you OK?" he asked me, with a note of sincere concern.

"Yes," I choked out, wiping my eyes and embarrassed at being seen in such a state. "I'm fine," I replied, halfheartedly. "Just having one of those days, I guess."

"Is there anything I can help you with?" he asked as he leaned on his walking staff.

As he talked, I looked at his tattered clothes and his worn shoes. It was obvious that he had endured a rough life, his face bearing horrible scars, his body impaired physically. Yet here he stood in front of me without complaining about his circumstances, not bitter and despondent about his lot in life, but offering to help me in some way. I was being humbled like I had never been before. How could this man maintain such a positive attitude despite the many hurdles that lay before him? And, more important, how could I have such a miserable attitude about my own life when my troubles seemed so trivial compared to his? How do I tell him that my day is so devastating because I took a little roll down a hillside when he walks around daily with use of one arm and limited use of one leg? How do I tell him that my life is so terrible because I obtained some grass stains and muddy clothes when his own clothing is in such a sad state of affairs? How do I tell him that I had actually contemplated just minutes ago looking for a way across to the Southern Lands because of a couple of scratches and bruises when he lives daily with a horrible physical reminder of some tragedy etched on his face? For several seconds, I couldn't find any words to answer him back. I found myself looking down at his feet out of embarrassment. Suddenly, to my surprise, he patted my back. I looked up at him and saw a grin and an expression of sympathy. My heart melted even further.

"Thank you for your offer," I shakily said. "I thought I was having a bad day, but I'm starting to realize that it wasn't as bad as I thought. I greatly appreciate your generous offer though, more than you know."

He smiled down at me, understanding, I believe, what I was talking about. I thought about how easy it would have been for him to have adopted my attitude with everything he had gone through, yet here he was using those same tragedies as a means to minister to me. Suddenly, I began wondering if the circumstances of his life were not allowed to take place by God specifically for this reason. Had he not endured such a traumatic accident, would his attitude have been more like mine? Did this hurdle that God allowed to be placed in his life actually provide a means for him to be strengthened spiritually beyond what the average person experiences? Many would have most likely become bitter, resentful people given the same circumstance. But God must have looked deep into his character and saw another Job. He saw someone who could take adversity in his life and use it to show the glory of God through a life of humility.

"I'm glad to hear that," he said. "Well, I must be going then. Got to take advantage of such a beautiful day you know! Take care and God bless, my friend."

And with that, he turned and started walking again, slowly swinging his body with each step down the path. I watched as he traveled a short distance and then turn to a path that branched off to the left of the road. That path wound up the hill rather than followed a level course like the main one I was following. Looking ahead, I could see the white dove resting on a branch along the level path, farther beyond where the stranger had exited the path. Once again, I was ashamed to compare my present course of easy walking to the uphill climb the crippled stranger was tasked with. I watched him until he was no longer in view, sitting for several more minutes after that and processing everything I had just experienced. No longer did I notice the things that had troubled me up to that point.

Then I realized that the gloomy outlook I spent all day with stemmed from me narrowing my perspective very selfishly to my immediate surroundings. I was focusing on a tree without seeing the forest. It took a complete stranger to open my eyes and for me compare my situation to the world around me. When I viewed myself and my problems through a self-centered lens, I became bitter and resentful. But when I viewed myself and my problems through the lens of God's love, my trials and complaints began to appear very insignificant and petty compared to what others are forced to deal with on a daily basis. It is a very humbling experience when we realize that the world does not revolve around us, when we discover that we are not the center of the universe and that no matter how bad things seem, there is always someone worse off than we are. We cannot always control the circumstances that surround us, but we can control how we choose to cope with those circumstances.

As Garrett found out, the adage "I had no shoes and complained, until I met a man who had no feet" holds much truth. I can attest to that fact personally; nothing humbles me quicker than seeing a person faced with a handicap, a birth defect or a mental impairment who, rather than allow the difficult circumstance to make him or her a victim, chooses to overcome the hurdle and live life to the fullest. During these times, I am reminded about how fortunate I am to have been graced with so many blessings that are easy to take for granted, such as sight, hearing, speech, full cognition, use of both hands, use of two legs, intact motor skills, no significant disease, no disfiguring physical appearance, no birth defects, no painful conditions, normal eating capacity and numerous others.

Having spent more than two decades in the health-care field, I have seen more heartbreaking circumstances than I would like to say. Yet somehow I never seem to stop being amazed and inspired by those I have the privilege to interact with. During one such period in my life, I was working in a pediatric unit in a large naval hospital during my hospital corpsman training. While there, I encountered a small boy, most likely five or six, who had been significantly burned. On first glance, one's heart skips a beat to see such a tragic and heartbreaking sight. As I began to work with him, I was blown away by how he went about his day playing just like any other little boy would, oblivious to the fact that he carried such horrific scars. Even though I only spent a very short time with the boy, the memory of him haunted me for years after. At one point, I finally sat down and tried to put my feelings into words, composing the following poem:

One cold, dark morn to my dismay, I wake to hear the newsman say,
"Rejoice, for 'tis Thanksgiving Day, our blessings to be thankful for."
But as I run back through my mind, the many days I've left behind,
The only thing I seem to find is hungering for so much more.
My small five-digit salary leaves not much room for luxury,
Lest I should hit the lottery, oh how my life shall be a bore.
I own a house; it's much too small. My hair is thin; I'm not too tall.

No talent or looks have I at all; my shoes worn thin, my coat I tore.

My dreams to traverse far-off lands soon turn to naught but sinking sands

That fall upon hard-callused hands; what have I to be thankful for?

I ponder this while driving to have dinner with a friend or two,

And looking back, if I but knew what miracle God had in store—

For suddenly, before I know what's happening, a tire blows;

Swerving into a ditch I go, my world a blur, then nothing more.

Realizing I am not dead, slowly I wake and lift my head,

Only to find I'm in a bed, my arm in sling, my head so sore.

With shaking fist held in the air, teeth clenched in rage—how does God dare

To let this be? Does He not care? To Him I'll turn to nevermore.

Then suddenly I hear a sound; beside my bed I turn around.

Taken aback by what I found gazing upon me near the floor.

For sitting in a metal chair, two soft green eyes and long blond hair,

So sad a sight I could but stare, this precious child no more than four.

Speechless I found myself to be, gazing at such a tragedy,

My heart o'ercome with sympathy, a shell of a child, nothing more.

Such pain I see behind those eyes; on shriveled legs her body lies,

Amazingly, I realize, despite it all, a smile she wore.

My anger breaks the silent air. "Oh, little girl, how can you bear

To wear a grin from in that chair? Surely there's naught worth living for."

Despite my words she does not flee, but slowly moves her chair toward me.

Taking my hand, says, "Come and see all I have to be thankful for."

So down the hall I follow her; a thousand thoughts within me
stir.
Then suddenly my mind's a blur at what I see through open door.
Inside this room I stop and stare at broken children everywhere,
Roaming about with not one care of handicaps their bodies bore.
Pointing, she says, "Look over there, that small boy sitting in a
chair."
So pale was he, and not one hair upon his tiny head he wore.
Oh what a tragic sight to see, the scars of chemotherapy,
Found on this child no more than three, never to see the age of
four.
Then walking by hands in the air, a small boy passing blankly
stares,
Two blinded eyes left unaware of what each step would have in
store.
A little girl looks up my way; then kneeling down, I gently say,
"And how are you, my child, today?" A smile, a stare, and noth-
ing more.
Then suddenly I realize upon deaf ears my words do lie.
It therefore comes as no surprise the sadly puzzled face she bore.
Across the room I look and see a sight that takes the breath from me—
A face so badly burned that he the scars to bear forevermore.
Yet as he plays, he shows no cares, ignores the other children's
stares.
He smiles as if left unaware the tragic scars his body wore.
Turning, I can no longer take this pity causing my heartbreak;
From this bad dream I wish to wake, returning to it nevermore.
Then from the chair comes suddenly, the small voice of reality,
Spoken so empathetically of that which she is thankful for.
"How blessed am I with eyes that see, share life with friends and
family,
To suffer not from some disease—for these I'm truly thankful
for."

"But as for sitting in this chair, oh please, kind sir, do not despair,
For one day when I go up there, I'll walk with Jesus ever more."
God works mysteriously, they say, as from the mouths of babes that day,
God spoke to me in such a way that changed my life forevermore.
The wealth of man is measured not by earthly things that can be bought
Or that which human hands have wrought—oh no, my friend, it's something more.
This sinful world has naught to offer from which immortal souls can prosper.
I'll gladly live this life a pauper to one day stand at heaven's door.
If only we could realize God's precious grace is where wealth lies,
We'd see our lives through different eyes and have so much to thank God for.
How sad I find it all to be—it took a blinded child for me
God's blessings in my life to see, so long I'd chosen to ignore.
And even though it seems absurd, God used a child who'd never heard,
A single sound, no, not one word, to hear His knock at my heart's door.
And in the last expected place, I found God's beauty and His grace,
Seen in a small child's burn-scarred face, despite the twisted mask he wore.
Oh Lord, on this Thanksgiving Day, as I bow down my head to pray,
A thankful heart I send Your way for granting me another year more.
I own a house—it might be small but is better than none at all,
And one day when God makes His call, I'll have a home forevermore.

We as parents attempt to teach our children to appreciate what they have and to not take things for granted. We try to avoid raising a spoiled and self-centered child who grows up to be a spoiled and self-centered adult. Yet how many times in our own lives do we find ourselves being petty and ungrateful, taking the gifts of God for granted? Sometimes I believe those facing obstacles in their lives actually are given a spiritual advantage by God because overcoming the hurdle grants them an opportunity to become stronger in a way not available to the rest of us. We have to remember that God does not see our lives as we do, self-centered and nearsighted. He is the master quilt maker, and each life represents a small piece of material within that quilt. The billions of pieces of material are sewn together in various combinations, each united alongside other pieces. As pieces of material, we are granted a very limited view of our immediate surroundings, thus bringing us to often question the reasons why we are positioned where we are in the quilt and why with certain pieces of material. Some pieces of material are very beautiful and colorful in themselves, while other pieces of material appear at first to be plain and ordinary. This can often make a plain piece of material question its importance and significance within the quilt.

Yet, as stated, God is the master quilt maker, and as such, He is granted an advantage over each individual piece of material. He is granted the perspective of seeing the beauty of the quilt's pattern from a better advantage point. Oftentimes, those pieces that originally seemed plain end up making the most significance in the outcome of the quilt's pattern. As quilt maker, He has a pattern from which He works, and He does not make mistakes. He doesn't make too many or too few pieces of material. He makes just enough to complete the job that's needed.

With this in mind, when we are faced with those around us that society likes to deem unfit, unworthy or unwanted, we must remember that each human soul holds a place in God's ultimate design. Who are we to question where He places, how He positions, how He designs and how He uses each piece of material? Who are we to complain when we do not know and cannot see the pattern of the quilt? There will come a day when the last piece of material is sewn into the quilt by God and we will all be granted an opportunity to see the completed design. Then and only then will His glorious and perfect work of art be revealed for all to see.

So when we are faced with physical, mental or emotional scars, just remember that God is merely making adjustments to His quilting material to perfect us for His grand design. (See *Isaiah 53:2–5, 7, 10–11* and *Romans 8:18.*)

Day 499

While traveling the road today, I had a valuable lesson revealed to me through an accidental analogy. It began as I was merely walking, just enjoying the day. The stretch of road I was walking on winded along a large rocky hillside. To my right, the hillside sloped down very steeply, almost cliff-like, to a valley with another path running through it. I could see several other travelers walking along the path, although they were too far away for me to make out much detail about them. Coming to a stop, I decided to take a little rest break and enjoy the view from where I stood. Staring out over the expanse, I shuffled and felt my foot bump against something. Looking down, I noticed a rock on the ground about the size of a plum. Out of reflex, I began moving it about with my foot in a playful manner. After several minutes of doing this, I bent my knee and gave the rock a forceful kick, sending it cascading over the side of the hill. I watched as it fell, rapidly traveling about fifty feet before it struck against the hillside.

Suddenly, from the location where the rock hit, I spied another rock a little larger begin to roll down the hill. I did not think much of it at first, but as I watched it roll, it soon struck another rock that was a little larger, setting it into motion along with about a dozen other smaller stones. I watched in horror as the chain reaction continued to unfold before me, each set of rocks breaking loose another set of larger rocks below them, eventually transforming into a full-fledged avalanche. All of a sudden, I remembered the people walking along the path in the *valley. Crying out at the top of my lungs, I tried to warn those down below, but the roar of the falling debris drowned out my cries. I was left standing helpless, unable to do anything but watch and pray. My hands flew to the top of my head, watching the event unfold. Finally the rocks reached the bottom and erupted in a belch of dust and a roar that echoed throughout the valley for what seemed like forever.*

    I stared down in disbelief, my stomach in a huge knot, my knees feeling like they would buckle. For several minutes, I waited for the dust to clear, petrified that I had killed someone under the weight of the rockslide. Finally, the dust began to clear, and I could begin to see people standing in the path on either side of the rocks. I cried down to them in utter panic, asking if everyone was OK. After several minutes, I received a confirmation that everyone was fine, much to my relief. They had fortunately heard the sound of the rocks coming and had cleared the path before they reached them. I fell to the ground in utter disbelief, my legs no longer being able to hold me because of the shock coursing through me. Even though no one was harmed, I couldn't shake the picture of someone lying beneath a pile of rubble, dead because of a stupid careless act performed by me.

    As my head spun, a moment of clarity somehow broke through, and I became aware of a life lesson presenting itself during this calamity. Beginning as a random act of kicking a small stone over a hillside, the situation quickly transformed into a devastating landslide that nearly cost many innocent people their lives. The small stone I kicked did not have the power by itself to harm the people below me, but it held enough weight and force to move a couple of stones that were larger than itself, positioned vulnerably on the hillside. Likewise, those stones by themselves were not large enough to produce bodily harm to the travelers, but just like the initial stone, they held enough weight and force to move a second set of stones a little larger than them positioned loosely on the hill. The stone I kicked set in place a chain reaction that ultimately resulted in the landslide.

    Then I began to realize the analogy that had just played out before me. I had to wonder how many times a careless word uttered by me or a careless action performed by me took the same spiritual course as the rock I just kicked, acting as a catalyst and setting in motion a chain of events that brought about a destructive end to innocent people. A quote that Clarence once gave to me came to mind: "No one single drop of water considers itself responsible for the flood." As I had just witnessed, I guess it could be similarly said that no one stone considers itself responsible for the landslide.

Day 504

As I journal today's events, I do so with the notation that today will stand out as one of the most poignant days since I started on this path. I've traveled up hills, across plains and through valleys, all to reach the place where I am today. I have come to expect storms, animals, hard climbs, humidity, cold weather, weary legs, obstacles in the road and even other travelers along this journey, but I had not prepared myself to encounter one thing, and that one thing is named Gabriella.

Early this morning, I began walking as I usually do without anything out of the ordinary taking place. The weather was uneventful. The trail was easygoing. It was just a typical day. Or so I thought. I was looking up at the clouds as I strolled along, my mind wandering aimlessly as I rounded a bend. Suddenly, my foot came into contact with something, nearly tripping me and causing me to reflexively fight for balance. Broken out of my daydreaming, I looked down to see what the cause of my stumble was—a backpack that belonged to a woman sitting on the edge of the path. My initial emotion from this embarrassing act was mild frustration. Why would someone be so careless as to leave a pack in the road for someone to trip over, namely, me?

Looking at the woman, I bit my tongue, but my facial expression spoke volumes about my state of mind. But the expression lasted for only seconds because I quickly realized that she was crying and holding her knee in pain. I walked over to her and knelt. "Are you all right?"

Choking on tears and appearing embarrassed for the condition she found her-
self in, she replied, "Not exactly. I twisted my knee on a root sticking out of the
ground. I don't think I can walk on it." Looking down at her knee, I noticed that
it had already begun to swell significantly.

"Is there someone I can get for you? Are you walking with anyone?" I asked.

"No," she answered. "I'm walking alone."

My mind began processing furiously. I tried to think of what I could do
to help her. "Let me get something for the swelling," I blurted out. Before she
could say anything, I jumped up and jogged to the small stream at the edge of
the path. I reached into my pack, grabbed a small cloth, then knelt and placed
it into the water, which was ice cold. After wringing it out, I ran back to the
woman. "This will be a little cold." As I draped it over her knee, she jumped
from the shock of it.

"That's freezing!" she yelled out. "Are you trying to kill me?"

I became instantly indignant. "Excuse me? I'm simply trying to help you, you
big baby. You're very welcome by the way." I couldn't believe she would snap at me
after I took time out to help her. "Women," I thought.

"I'm sorry," she said sheepishly; "I didn't mean to snap. I'm just so mad at
myself for being this careless."

My dander quickly subsided. "That's fine," I said. "I guess I'll live." It was
then that I noticed for the first time how attractive she was. I felt myself staring at
her, feeling like a nervous schoolchild. "Does it seem to be helping?" I asked her, a
little more nervousness in my tone this time.

"Yes, actually it is," she said. "And thank you. By the way, my name is
Gabriella, Gabriella the big baby."

I caught myself blushing a little at having my words brought back up. "Nice
to meet you; my name is Garrett. And I apologize for calling you a big baby. That
was rude of me." She cracked a grin, obviously because she got me to blush. "Did
you have somewhere you needed to be today?" I asked.

"Luckily no, but this is not the way I had planned to spend my day."

"Do you think you can handle putting weight on that leg?" From the looks of
her knee and her expression, I was guessing not.

"I'm not sure, but I guess I have to try sometime."

Slowly, she began bringing herself up, and I reached down to help her. I brought her arm around my neck and tried to support her as much as I could. As soon as she started putting weight on the leg, she winced from the pain and shifted the weight back to the other leg.

"I guess the answer is no unfortunately." She sat back down on the ground. "Looks like I'll be making myself comfortable here for a while."

I could sense the discouragement in her voice.

"I appreciate all you have done for me, but I don't expect you to stick around all day on my behalf. Thank you for your help."

I stood there for a second, processing the situation. It was true, in fact, that I had no obligation to stay with her. She was a total stranger, and I would have every right to just turn and continue with my journey. But a strange thing occurred within me that I had never experienced before. I had crossed paths with many other female travelers in my days on the path, but for some reason, today was different. There was some kind of chemistry, a spark taking place that I could not explain. To put it into words, the best analogy I can come up with is from Bambi, *when the words* twitter pated *were used by the owl to describe to the woodland creatures the process of falling for someone. "Now what kind of gentleman would I be to leave a helpless woman by the side of the road? I think I can rearrange my schedule to accommodate a damsel in distress." I tried to make my motives sound as altruistic as possible, but in all actuality, I stayed more for my benefit than for hers, I hate to admit. If that is selfish, then I'll take the label.*

"No, that is too much to ask. I couldn't impose on you like that."

"It's too late. I already cleared my schedule, so you are stuck with me." I plopped down beside her and made myself comfortable. Her expression showed that she understood her protests would be in vain. We sat and talked for well over an hour, learning a lot about each other and exchanging witty banter back and forth. At one point I discovered that she had a scarf within her backpack, which I then took and used as a wrap for her knee. Once again, I helped her to her feet and found that she was able to tolerate weight bearing much better with the wrap, but still not completely.

Chivalry prevailed, and I offered myself as a human crutch in order for her to resume her walk. We continued at a slow pace, not covering too much ground on the trail but covering much ground on a personal level. As the day came to an end, I reflected on the change that had taken place within me over the last twelve hours and realized that, for better or worse, I would never be the same person again.

I laugh to myself as I write this section of the book because of its parallels to how I met my wife. I've worked in physical therapy for more than fourteen years, starting my career out in a little outpatient clinic. My job duties consisted of not only treating patients but also scheduling them for their appointments. Early in the spring of 2000, I took a call from a young lady named Kim wishing to schedule an evaluation for therapy due to a knee injury from a fall while ice skating. The date of May 4 was chosen. When the day arrived, she entered the clinic and received an evaluation as normal. I was taken aback by how attractive she was, but I did not think too much about it; our relationship was a professional one. She remained on therapy for about a month and then was discharged. During her time at the clinic, we came to be good friends through the numerous conversations we had. Sometime after her therapy was over, we decided to go out for a bite to eat as friends. Even at that point, I did not think too much about it, as I just assumed that our relationship would continue to stay as friends. Fortunately for me, God had other plans.

I was twenty-six at the time we met, and I had been in a number of relationships, some short-lived, some longer. I had even been engaged at one point during a two-year relationship but had broken it off because I felt God was moving me in a different direction. So when I began dating Kim, I was amazed that things progressed as quickly as they did. After only several months, I was clearer and more confident of God's direction for us than I had been even with lengthier relationships. It probably flew in the face of common sense, but in September of that year I proposed to her, with the interpretation of God's will obviously a mutual thing, as she said yes. On January 27, 2001, we were married at the church we attended at that time on a cold and snowy day. And as Garrett stated, for the better, I have never been the same person again since that day. Thus began our joint adventure, kicking off Garrett and Gabriella's as well.

Day 772

As I pick up my pen today, I do so for the last time as a single man. In just a short while, I will be joined with my bride to be, Gabriella. Looking back over the past nine months, I never would have imagined in a million years that the waylaid stranger I stumbled upon would turn out to be my future wife. We hit it off in a surprising way right from the get-go, quickly becoming friends and then growing even closer as we traveled the road together. At first I was afraid that it was too good to be true, being the eternal pessimist that I am when it comes to relationships. But then I began to realize as the days passed that I could no longer imagine traveling the road without her.

Then came the day that had me on pins and needles, the day I proposed to her. We began the day no different than usual, or so she thought, strolling down the trail. We came to a large oak tree along the right side of the path. Hanging down from a fork in the tree about seven feet up was a long piece of pink yarn with a piece of paper tied to it at the end. I looked at her quizzically, shrugged and motioned for her to investigate it. She walked over to the tree, grabbed the folded piece of paper, opened it and read aloud.

"When I'm with you, I feel all squirrely inside!" She looked up and laughed at me, asking, "What in the world?"

I looked back at her as if I was also confused. "Beats me; that's an odd thing to write."

She peered up and saw that the yarn ran into an open fork of the tree. Slowly, she pulled on it and began drawing it out from the tree. Suddenly, a large cluster of acorns rained down from the notch and fell atop her head, sending her jumping back, laughing in surprise at the woodland waterfall. As the falling stopped, she walked back over to the string that came from within the notch and found another piece of paper tied to it. She opened it and read it aloud.

"I'm nuts for you!"

She turned, her mouth open, and laughed hysterically. I played along with the act, laughing as well as pretending to be in the dark as she was. Finally, she grabbed the string once more and, stepping away from the tree, gave it one final tug, wincing as she did, expecting to be pelted by another barrage of acorns. But this time, only one thing flew out of the tree, and it was tied to the end of the string. It sailed through the air and bounced off her head, causing her to turn and look dumbfounded at me with a silly grin. I laughed even harder, partially for the knock on the head, partially because I knew what was about to happen. At the end of the yarn was a final note folded.

She opened it, began reading once again and only managed to get the first word out, "Gabriella..." In a flash, her head spun around with her eyes wide; she stared at me before looking back to the paper and continued reading. "I love you, no 'jOAK.' Will you marry me?" She read the last few words with crackling voice; then with teary eyes, she turned and looked down at me, on bended knee and holding up a ring.

"Well?" I said sarcastically. "Are you going to make me wait all day down here?"

"Yes!" she screamed, tackling me to the ground in a ferocious bear hug. "No 'jOAK.' I will marry you!"

And that sealed it. And now here I stand, moments away from making it official. I guess the only thing I can say is I'm glad Gabriella fell for me, literally.

❦

In hindsight, that probably would have been a clever way to propose, but I'm sad to say that was not my method used. One of the many things that my wife and I discovered we had in common early on in our relationship was a mutual love for coffee. So on the day I proposed, I drove to pick my then girlfriend up from work. Having made a pit stop prior to this, I walked across the street to a Starbucks and set up a plan. I informed the workers there what I had in mind, and they became excited to play a role in the act, which resulted in them giving me a free mocha.

By the time I walked over to get Kim, I was not only nervous about pulling off the proposal; I was wired to the hilt from chugging my large drink. As we crossed the street to go to my car, I told her I wanted to stop in the Starbucks for a coffee. As I approached the door, my heart initially sank because the sign on the door said CLOSED. Then I saw one of the girls run over and unlock the door from inside, much to my relief. As we walked in, I pulled out a kazoo from my pocket, in unison with the workers from the store and their kazoos. We began humming out the tune "Let Me Call You Sweetheart" to her, as she stood looking on very confused. Then one of the girls reached over and started a CD player I had brought in, playing a preselected song. I assumed the position, pulled out the ring and asked her if she would marry me, with her answering the same as Gabriella, thankfully. Once again, we received free coffee from the giddy girls before they sent us on our way. Thus we began our engagement, caffeinated and carefree.

Day 773

Yesterday I wrote as a single man; today I write as a married man for the first time. The ceremony was beautiful but not as beautiful as Gabriella. A pastor I've become acquainted with over the past year or two graciously provided us with a simple, private ceremony. After we exchanged rings, the pastor gave us an interesting gift, one that is customary on this side of the river but not from where I came from. A lengthy bundle of rope, it was the kind one would find a rock climber using to climb or rappel a cliff. I have to admit that initially I was confused about the gift because it did not seem to be a normal wedding present. He went on to explain why this gift is routinely given to couples when taking on marriage vows.

The rope was used to join the two people physically as they travel the road together. As rough terrain is a common feature on this side of the river, the rope was to be used as a safety measure, should one of the two lose their footing during their travels. He made an interesting point, stating that the closer the two are, when one loses his or her footing, the easier it is to correct the other as there is less tension on the one bearing the load. The rope could be lengthened or shortened as the two traveled, depending on how far apart the two traveled from each other. As a rule of thumb, he recommended couples to travel close to each other whenever possible, in order to maximize the rope's strength. For example, if a partner loses his or her footing while five feet from the other, little tension is placed on the rope or the stable-footed spouse. But if the rope is given twenty or thirty feet of slack, and one of the two should lose their footing and slide down a hillside, by the time the rope becomes taught, the sure-footed spouse will have his or her work cut out for him or her as the momentum of the falling one at that distance will place a significant amount of strain on the rope, magnifying the force of the partner's weight as compared to a closer distance.

As a rule of thumb, we were told to walk side by side, using the width of the path as the measure for judging the proper distance to be from each other. If the path became too narrow for us to walk side by side, I was to take the lead and keep the length of the rope as minimal as possible between us. He also referenced to the fact that there would be days when one of us would be weaker than the other, whether from illness or simply fatigue. During such days, the other would be able to give assistance by walking slightly ahead and providing some pull to the other, thus helping him or her keep up the pace until becoming stronger.

Along with this wisdom, he also offered us a warning. As much as humanly possible, we were to try to avoid becoming an unbalanced relationship. By this he meant we were to avoid having one person purposely lag behind, expecting the other to constantly pull more than their share during the walk. The result of this behavior, he stated, would be a growing resentment by the overworked partner, placing a significant strain on the entire relationship. Balance was the key, give-and-take, mutual respect and a servant's heart for each other.

In addition to this, he emphasized the importance of maintaining the integrity of the rope itself. If we were to neglect it, letting it become dried out and frayed, and a situation should arise where it was put under significant strain, such as a fall by one us, it would most likely snap under the weight of the load. But if we devoted attention to it, keeping it oiled and intact on a daily basis, it would maintain its strength throughout the years, able to support our weight should one of us stumble.

It seemed odd to me at first, but after hearing him describe the theory behind it, I could see the wisdom in it. Across the river from where I came, marriage vows were taken on a more casual basis, easily broken and discarded. There was not the support of a rope should one partner stumble or fall. With this tool at our disposal, I now felt that we could say we tied the knot.

Day 851

Well, the honeymoon is officially over. After today, we discovered the reason for the line "for better or worse*" in the wedding vows, as we both demonstrated our worse side to each other. The morning started out as a typical one, but by midday, it had taken a 180-degree turn. What started the argument, I couldn't even tell you. Maybe we both woke up on the wrong side of the bed this morning. Whatever it was, harsh words were spoken to each other that can't be taken back, feelings were hurt, and several trees bore the brunt of my foot as I kicked them in frustration. By late morning, we had our rope slackened to the point where I was several feet off the path to the left and she was several feet off the path to the right. We were bound and determined not to walk next to each other at any cost. This resulted in me walking through high weeds and thorny bushes and her walking through a swampy, muddy mess. We continued for hours like this, both of us too stubborn to admit that we were wrong and apologize.*

Finally, as evening was approaching, Gabriella came across a small slope on her side, which forced her to walk on uneven ground, her left foot stepping at a higher elevation than her right. With the ground being so muddy on her side, it didn't take long for her to lose her footing, sending her sliding down the hill. Even though we had lengthened the amount of rope between us, we were still connected, which meant that as the rope went taut, I caught the unexpected pull from her weight, which dragging me through the briar patch and into the middle of the road. Frustrated, I began yelling, asking her what in the world had just happened. As she came to a stop, she got back to her feet, climbed her way back to the road where I was and yelled back at me in return. After a minute, we simultaneously stopped midyell and looked at each other. There I stood with burrs attached to my clothes and hair, scratches all over my arms and legs and weeds sticking out of my pockets. There she stood covered in mud from backside to shoes, grass-stained jeans and dandelion-stained face. As much as we tried to fight it, we could not contain ourselves and busted out laughing at each other. And just like that, we survived our first lovers' quarrel.

Assessing each other, we realized how foolish we were to leave the path in our anger, only inflicting pain and discomfort to ourselves in the process. Looking at the rope, we were amazed at how frayed it had become while being drug through bushes, weeds and mud. We took some time to clean it up and repair the damage to it, learning a valuable lesson through the experience.

༉

Communication is a key component to a healthy marriage. Most of us take much longer to realize this than we should. When placed in a situation of frustration, too often our human nature takes on a "Hulk-like" transformation, growing in disproportionate size and overpowering our spiritual wisdom with carnal instincts. Just like the Hulk, while in that phase, we leave a trail of destruction behind us, blinded by anger and resentment, as so clearly described in **Psalm 37:8, Proverbs 30:33** and **Ecclesiastes 7:9.** Instead of large green fists of fury, we use words that cut and injure, their sole purpose to inflict hurt to the one who has made us hurt, whether intentional or not, spoken about in **Proverbs 12:18.** And just like the Hulk, once the rage passes, the only thing left is a small and battle-weary man who is faced with the turmoil he has caused. As Christians, we are held to a higher calling.

Day 919

Yesterday, during our daily walk, Gabriella and I came upon an interesting scene. We began our traveling early that morning, the weather clear and warm. As we were talking to each other, I caught something out of the corner of my eye. Off to the right, I had seen a quick flash of white moving among the trees. Walking to the edge of the path, I looked about, trying to find what I had seen. Strangely, I noticed amid the high grass and shrubs the faint outline of a path winding up a grassy knoll and continuing out of sight. As I scanned the horizon to where the path ran, I caught the flash of white again traveling the course of the hidden path and then out of view. In my mind, I was pretty confident about what I saw, but I was trying to make sense of it, as the path seemed so unclear.

I took Gabriella's hand and led her into the tall grass while she gave me quizzical looks. We walked a short distance, eventually coming to the top of a knoll and found the faint outline of a path continuing through a field and into a clump of trees. We continued into the trees and noticed that the path began to become more pronounced. As we approached a bend, I looked ahead and found confirmation as to what I thought I had seen. Sitting on a limb above the path was the white dove.

Coming to the point where it sat, I looked ahead to the right of the path and saw a couple looking down a deep hole. The woman was crying, and the man was attempting to console her. As we approached them, we asked if there was anything we could do to help. The man tearfully stated that at the bottom of the hole was their son, who had fallen in several days ago. They had initially tried to rescue him by lowering their rope in, but as they began pulling him up, the rope snapped, trapping him at the bottom with a rope too short for him to reach. They had spent the past couple of days dropping food and water to him, attempting to keep him alive and waiting for someone to come along that could help them. Amazingly, we were the first travelers to come upon them since the fall took place.

I took off my backpack, reached in and pulled out the spare rope that I carried. Fortunately, it was a rope of significant length, able to reach the bottom of the hole. Because of the age of the child and his weakened condition, we realized that he would not be able to hold the rope while we pulled him up. We decided to tie the rope to the boy's mother and lower her in and have her hold the child while we pulled them both up. We tied the rope around her, lowered her down the hole and waited for the tug, which was her cue for us to pull them up. The man, Gabriella and I began pulling the two of them slowly out of the hole, finding that it took the strength of all three of us to bring them out. Finally, after much effort, we saw the two heads pop up out of the ground, the mother clinging tightly to a dirt-covered boy, who appeared weakened and frail.

Immediately, we laid the boy on the ground and began to tend to him. He was conscious but clinging to life. We spent the rest of the day rehydrating the boy and getting food into his system. He had been rescued from the hole, but he still was not out of danger. We spent all that night and the next morning watching over him and praying for him, asking God to provide a healing.

When the boy woke in the morning, we were astonished to see the transformation that had taken place in him within less than a day. After just a couple of hours, he was on his feet, wanting to move about. Some of the effects of the ordeal were still noticeable, such as his wobbly legs and his balance deficits, but with each hour that passed, he seemed to grow stronger and stronger. We talked with the couple throughout the day, getting to know them and discussing the incredible timing of our arrival on the scene. It was apparent to us that it was not a coincidence, but rather the hand of God that had our paths cross. By evening, it appeared that the boy was going to make a full recovery. We exchanged hugs and agreed to keep in touch with each other, as we had developed a close friendship in a short amount of time.

Walking away, I began thinking about how different today's events might have been if I had not followed my gut and pursued the white dove. It would have been just as easy to continue on the course I had been following, but I realized that God had other plans for Gabriella and me that day. Whether it was because I just happened to be in the right place at the right time or that God had guided my course specifically to be in that place to see the dove at the exact time, I wasn't sure. But ultimately I realized more than ever that being attentive to the dove and letting it guide me not only affects my course but the course of many others. The thought of that weighs heavy on me, but I realize it's true. Then I began to wonder how many other times in the past I had let similar opportunities like today slip by due to a lack of focus or a lack of discipline. What happened in the past cannot be changed, but I made a decision to do what I could from this point on. I'm devoting my life to being a full-time bird watcher.

ॐ

The story behind the story in this case revolves around a miraculous incident that occurred a year after I was married. Prior to my marriage, when I was in the navy, I had registered to be a bone marrow donor. About a year or so later, I received a letter in the mail stating that I was a match for a person needing bone marrow. I was excited that I would be able to help in such a way and waited to receive more information. However, a short while later, I received a second letter informing me that a second donor had been found who was a closer match than I was for the person. Hearing this left me a little sad that I would not be able to help, but I was happy for the person receiving the donation.

Years went by, and I met my wife. While we were dating, I was able to introduce her to some friends of my family. They were a couple whose daughter was about seven years old and whose son was about five years old. During the period that we dated, we discovered some devastating news. The boy had been diagnosed with leukemia. It was beyond heartbreaking. Illness and disease is bad enough in this world, but when it affects someone so young, the grief is elevated to a completely different level. Much prayer took place regarding the boy's condition, as the community rallied behind the family. Surprisingly, throughout the ordeal, the boy remained upbeat and optimistic, even as he lay in the hospital. He became a witness to the hospital staff, often speaking about heaven and spiritual matters. Despite being on the list, sadly I was not found to be a match for the boy. Shortly after my wife and I married, the boy lost his fight to the illness and went to be with the Lord. It was such a surreal experience because the boy was so young. The grief was great, requiring much spiritual healing for the immediate family as well as the friends throughout the community.

Then, about a year after being married, I received a second letter stating that I had once again been identified as a match for a person. I reluctantly became optimistic, wondering if this would be a repeat of the previous experience. Yet as time went by, I began to realize that this time was for real. I traveled to Pittsburgh to begin the process, filling out paperwork and undergoing a physical. The name, age, location or any facts about the person receiving the marrow was kept confidential, leaving me curious as to whom my marrow would go to. Just prior to the scheduled day, I returned to Pittsburgh three separate days to receive injections that would increase my body's production of stem cells, which would be harvested and delivered to the person waiting.

Finally, on September 19, 2002, I drove once again to Pittsburgh to have the bone marrow withdrawn. From what I had heard prior to this event, I assumed the marrow would be withdrawn through a series of needles placed into the pelvis. But I was surprised to find that a new and improved technique was being used, resulting in a significant decrease in pain. The new method consisted of a setup similar to a blood transfusion. An IV was inserted into my arm and a tube drew blood out of me and into a machine. This machine then separated the excess stem cells from my blood and returned the blood to my body through a second IV site. The procedure was completely painless, which did not produce any complaints on my part.

After several hours, the task was completed and the stem cells were flown to the waiting donor. I was given the information that the marrow was going to a six-year-old boy in Michigan, but no further information. My part was done. I was kind of sad having no information in regards to how the procedure went, as this kind of information was not privy to disclosure. The rules stated that after one year, if both parties were in agreement, names, addresses and phone numbers could be exchanged. The following year, near Easter, I received a peculiar letter from the marrow donation center. Inside it was a page from a coloring book that had been colored. It was from the boy who had received my stem cells; he was alive! It had been about six months since the procedure, and this was the first information I had received regarding his status. I was elated! I began to think about how peculiar the circumstances had played out. I had not been able to help our friends' son, who lived just miles away from me, but I ended up being a match for another boy the exact same age as our friends' son whom I had never met and who lived two states away. It made me begin to consider how God's will is worked out and how He doesn't follow the earthly strategies we design in our logic. It was His will for our friend's son to join Him in heaven, but it was also His will that another boy be healed. It made me think of Job's statement in *Job 1:21,* where he said, ***"The Lord gave and the Lord has taken away; may the name of the Lord be praised."***

We may not always understand God's reasoning and purpose for certain events in our lives, but ultimately we have to trust Him and accept His will. I had given permission to the marrow center to release my information to the family should they be interested in contacting me. I was hopeful but knew there was a chance that they would not want to. That is why, later that year, when I received a letter from the family, I was delighted to know they were interested in contacting me. Soon, we were having our first phone call, followed by our first visit. The family of five drove out to meet us for a weekend, staying at a nearby hotel. We learned that Vincent, the boy who received the marrow, had been diagnosed on May 10, 1998, with acute lymphocytic leukemia (ALL) at the age of twenty-one months. He was lethargic with yellowish skin. His hair became brittle and was not growing. He had stopped eating and drinking, was taking longer naps and was sleeping more often. Despite this, his eighteen-month checkup with his doctor noted him near a two-and-a-half-year-old mentality with vocabulary and communication skills. He went into remission on June 10, 1998.

For the next three years, Vincent was on daily chemotherapy and weekly spinal taps. Eleven months after his last chemotherapy drug and spinal tap, he relapsed. At one point, they were informed that he had a 50 percent chance to live. He was once again diagnosed with ALL, but this time it was more aggressive and found in his spinal fluid. They placed him on an aggressive chemotherapy regimen, requiring frequent treatments throughout that summer. He ended up spending his sixth birthday in the hospital receiving a double-port catheter and a single broviac tube surgically placed. In early September, before his stem cell transplant, he had multiple radiation treatments at the University of Michigan, making him even weaker. Then, on September 19, 2002, he was able to receive my stem cells.

A strange thing was discovered after he received his transplant: the antigens in my blood matched the antigens in his blood ten out of ten! The doctors decided to research this further and found that even the subantigens were ten out of ten! This was a first in the history of the University of Michigan. God had made us a perfect match! Vincent was the first patient to not get mouth sores as a result of the transplant. He was discharged within two weeks, the earliest in the University of Michigan's history. He had the quickest return of a white blood cell count to normal in the University of Michigan's history. His amazing recovery was even discussed at the International Oncology meeting in Germany later that year. Since that meeting, Vincent and I have met several times, and we keep in touch regularly through phone and e-mail. Our families have grown together as one family, united through the procedure that took place that day. It never ceases to amaze me how mysteriously God works.

With regard to Garrett, the rope in the story is symbolic of the antigen match that Vincent and I had. The parents of the boy in the pit were unable to bring him out simply because their rope was not long enough. When Garrett arrived on the scene, he was fortunate to have a rope long enough to reach the bottom. It was simply chance that afforded him this opportunity to assist in saving the boy. The same could be said for me. If Vincent's parents or family would have had a matching antigen, they would have easily undergone the same procedure that I had. Yet for some reason, God chose to not have them match. Instead, He had me, a total stranger to the family, be the one with a match for Vincent's antigens. Just like in the story, I was the one who just happened to have the right size rope to accomplish the task needed. But through that connection, our family has been blessed with the opportunity to get to know Vincent and his family, which has resulted in an ongoing bond. In hindsight, it might have been easier for God to have made his parents the match for him, but then my family and I would not have been afforded the blessing of sharing in such a tremendous miracle.

Day 1,225

This morning, I caught a whiff of something burning. The last thing a traveler in the woods wants to smell is smoke. As I looked around, I could not find the source of it, but I was concerned all the same. When I checked with Gabriella, she confirmed that she smelled it too. We hadn't traveled much farther when above the trees we could see smoke rising in the distance. The path we were on seemed to be heading in the general direction of it, so we picked up our pace, wondering what type of scene we would come upon. Soon we rounded a corner and found the source of the billowing smoke. Sadly, it was coming from what used to be a house.

As we approached, we could see several people standing around the charred remains. The fire, now extinguished, left nothing but ashes in its wake. The owners of the house stood staring at the tragic sight, somber and covered in soot. Despite losing their home, they seemed to be more thankful that they were alive and well, without injury.

As we came to the remnants of their home, it was clear that nothing was left. Even the beams had been reduced to nothing but small clumps of charcoal. I picked up a stick and began poking through the remains, hoping to find something of value that the family could salvage despite so much loss. For quite a while, I found nothing but ash and soot. Then suddenly my stick hit against something solid with a different feel to it. Brushing away the debris on top of it, I discovered something about a foot long resting on the ground. I reached down, picked up the curious object and began brushing it off. After a minute or two, I realized what I had in my hand but couldn't understand how it had survived such intense heat. Looking down, I was staring at a fully intact copy of the Guide Book. *The leather cover that surrounded it had been charred and damaged, but the entire book was intact and unharmed. It just didn't make any sense to me. Everything around it had been reduced to ash, but this book, made of paper, had somehow survived.*

I carried it over to one of the homeowners and handed it to them. As they opened it and began turning the pages, giant tears rolled down through the soot on their face. They looked up at me and thanked me for finding it. Despite losing so much, I was glad that they could walk away with something of sentimental value. In hindsight, it seemed logical to me that if anything would have been salvaged from a fire, it would be a Guide Book. *As Gabriella and I walked away, I took one last look at the smoldering heap, just in time to see a white dove fly out from within the blackened pile, its contrasting color to the charred debris making it stand out all the more. Turning around, I grabbed Gabriella's hand and continued walking.*

༄

This analogy is directly influenced by a real-life event of my parents. During my high-school years, my parents decided to take a trip to Hershey, Pennsylvania. My brothers and I stayed with my aunt and uncle while they were away. Early one morning, I was awakened by my aunt. She began to explain to me that my parents had been in a car accident. Luckily, they had walked away from the accident without any major injuries, but they were in a lot of pain. In addition to this, their car had been totaled in the accident.

My grandparents left that day to drive to where they were, which was about a four- to five-hour drive. The next day, they returned with my parents, who were suffering from severe whiplash. As my parents recalled the events to us, they explained that they had been sitting at a red light. As a tractor trailer was slowly approaching them from behind, a driver of a car behind the tractor trailer decided to blindly pass the large vehicle at a high rate of speed and whip in front of it. Tragically, the driver of the car did not realize that a red light and my parents' vehicle were in front of the tractor trailer, which resulted in the car slamming into my parents' car from behind at full speed, sending them flying through the intersection.

As my parents' car finally came to a stop, my father quickly released his seatbelt and sprang from the car. Looking back, he realized that my mother was still in the car. As he investigated, he found that her seatbelt would not release, leaving her trapped in the wrecked vehicle. A sense of urgency came over my father, and he reached for what had always been a companion of his as long as I could remember: his pocketknife. Taking the knife, he quickly cut the seatbelt, freeing my mother from it. Then, to their horror, they realized that my mother's car door would not open. Thinking quickly, my father reached through the driver's side door, grabbed my mother and pulled her out of the car. Like a scene from an action movie, my father began running away from the car with my mother in his arms. Suddenly, as he was running, he heard the sound of the car exploding behind him as the gas tank had caught fire. The heat of the explosion was so intense that it burned the hair off the back of my father's legs as he ran with my mother. He had saved her just in time.

As they returned to the burned car the next day, they found it had been reduced to merely a frame. Pictures of the car showed the charred remnants. Everything had been destroyed; nothing remained but burned and warped metal. They discovered the miracle that had occurred. Sitting on the floor of the backseat, on burned metal, was a charred but intact Bible cover. As they removed the object from the remains of the car, they opened the cover to discover a scientific improbability, a fully intact Bible. Hundreds of thin, flammable pages that contained the inspired words of God had somehow remained untouched, despite the tremendous heat that lapped around it, a heat that melted the material from all the seats, that melted all the carpeting on the floors and that was hot enough to bend the metal of the car, yet did not burn a paper book clothed in a simple cover.

My parents have made a full recovery from the accident. For years now my parents have shown that Bible to numerous friends, giving the testimony of its miraculous and unexplainable existence. We may never know the full reasoning of why they had to endure such a horrific accident and near-death encounter. But I like to think that God used that situation to show that even when under fire, His word will always prevail. (See *Matthew 24:35.*)

Day 1,366

I awoke this morning from a most interesting dream. It was a very vivid and moving dream, the details of it still etched in my mind as if the events had really happened.

Shortly after falling asleep last night, I began dreaming that I was walking along the path with Gabriella. In the dream, the path ran closely alongside the great river that separates this side from the Southern Lands. As we walked, I looked to my right at the river and was astounded to see that it was full of people from the Southern Lands! They weren't drowning or in trouble; in fact, they were drifting down the river aimlessly in various types of flotation devices and appeared to be having the time of their lives. Some were floating on round tubes, some on rafts, some were kicked back on small row boats, but all were simply just floating down the river toward the east, the same direction that we were heading.

I also noticed that none of the people were actively propelling themselves in any way. They all were content to be carried at the mercy of the river's direction. As we walked, they happened to look up and notice us on the narrow path, at which time they began laughing at us and taunting us for having to hike rather than floating downstream like they were. This did not make me very happy to say the least because the road we were on had headed uphill, adding insult to injury.

I must admit that for a second, my human nature got the best of me, and briefly I envied those in the water who seemed to not have a care in the world while Gabriella and I had to physically drain ourselves by hiking up the path before us. Attempting to ignore them, we pressed on and tried to act as though they weren't there, but doing that was difficult because they seemed to be fixated on torturing us. Their numbers were staggering, and they seemed to fill the entire surface of the river, hooting and hollering back and forth to each other as if they were having the time of their lives.

After we had covered some ground, I began to notice a peculiar thing; the water in the river seemed to be flowing a little stronger and quicker. The people in the river seemed to be oblivious to this, but from our perspective, it was noticeable. Then I came to a realization that I had not thought about before. As tiring and frustrating as the path could be, we who walk it ultimately have the ability to determine our course; but as for the people in the river, even though their traveling is carefree, they are ultimately at the mercy of the river regarding their course and the direction they travel. Ultimately, they sacrifice freedom for leisure.

As I looked down at the river from our higher ground, it became more and more obvious that the farther we traveled to the east, the quicker the waters of the river became. Some of the people in the river began to notice this and, out of fear, began paddling to the banks of this shore and ditching their rafts for the dry ground. Standing along the shore were some from this side of the river positioned to reach out their hands and assist those coming to dry land, but the majority seemed to not care about this fact; instead, they just continued their celebrating, mocking those standing at the banks of the river. In my dream, the opposite shore of the river had high, sheer cliffs, making this shore the only opportunity for anyone to escape the river.

For a short time, river riders would occasionally be seen making a break for our shore, but sadly as we watched, some who seemed to have a desire to reach our shore were on the opposite side of the river and caught in a powerful current, leaving them unable to break its grip. Occasionally, large jagged rocks would stick out in the river, right in the path of those floating downstream. As much as they would try, they seemed unable to avoid the obvious collision course, ultimately ending up smashing into the rocks, their flotation devices destroyed, resulting in their being pulled under the waves, never to be seen again.

After traveling a little farther, I began to notice that the land on this side of the river began to resemble that of the opposite side, with the shoreline transitioning *into steep hills rather than level ground. As people would float to our shore, rather than having level ground to pull up to, they would encounter the walls. The people from this side of the river did not let this matter deter them from helping the river people. All along the wall stood travelers from the path; they held out their copies of the* Guide Book, *resulting in the books transforming into long ropes and rope ladders that the travelers would then hang over the side for the use of those in the river. It wasn't as easy, but it still continued to be an effective means for those in the river to escape, as they would grab the devices and climb up to the top, leaving the treacherous waters behind. But the further we traveled, the higher the walls became.*

There finally came a point where the river transitioned into a torrent of raging rapids. Some in the river continued to celebrate, oblivious to the danger; yet others became aware that they were in serious trouble. As the people clung on to their devices for dear life, fewer and fewer of the people seemed to make it to our safety ropes along the wall. As I looked ahead down the river, my mouth fell open at the horror I saw approaching. About a mile down the river, I could see the foaming splashes of a huge waterfall! This explained the quickening of the river; they were trapped in the powerful pull of a mighty waterfall. After several attempts, I soon realized that my distance from the river prevented any of them from hearing my cries of warning to them. I could do nothing. I was powerless to prevent the horrible disaster I saw coming for them.

It didn't take long for the people to finally come around a bend and see the waterfall lying ahead of them. But by this point, it was far too late for them to alter their course, as the force of the water was simply too powerful. I could hear the screams coming from them as they approached the waterfall and were quickly pulled over its banks to their deaths. But even with a steady flow of people crying out in panic, the majority of those in the river remained oblivious to this end because the bend in the river prevented any from seeing the waterfall that lay ahead of them. Only when they rounded the bend did they catch a full glimpse of what they were heading for.

Gabriella covered her eyes and buried her face into my chest at the horror of the sight and sounds coming from the people plummeting to their doom. We pressed on down the path, each step bringing us closer to the waterfall that lay below us. Finally, we reached the point in the path where the waterfall lay parallel to us. The sound was deafening, as the roaring of the water drowned out all other noises, even those who were pulled down into its hazy depths.

There came a point where we watched the remaining people tumble over the falls, and then there were no more. Looking back, we could see the river was clear of any other passengers floating in its grip. With my arm around her, we followed a bend in the path to the left, taking us away from the mighty falls. The farther we went, the quieter the sound of the falls became until at one point, we could no longer hear any noise coming from behind us.

The path we took was a narrow ledge that hugged a vertical mountain, with a sheer wall to our left and a straight drop-off to our right. How far the drop-off ran to the right was unclear because fog prevented us from seeing the bottom. But the fog itself laid hundreds of feet below the path, so either way, a fall from the path would mean instant death. The path snaked along the side of the mountain, with numerous bends that made it impossible to see what lay too far ahead.

As we finally rounded one particular bend, we nearly fainted at the sight that lay before us. Spread out in all its glory from horizon to horizon was heaven! Angels flew to and fro, and throngs of people dressed in white stood on what appeared to be the very clouds themselves. We were overcome with a combination of fear and awe; we were totally caught off guard. Resting in the center of it all was the most beautiful throne I had ever seen. It would have been the envy of any earthly king who had ever reigned.

Walking slowly closer to the scene, we could hear the most beautiful music all around us. It seemed that the very air was filled with it. As we finally reached the edge of the cloud on which everyone was standing, I looked to the throne and noticed a ball of light directly above the seat. Suddenly, it began moving in our direction, growing in size as it traveled. Simultaneously, we both became weak in the knees and fell to them as this strange orb approached us. Eventually, it reached us and stopped several feet from us. When it stopped, the light began to take shape, transforming into a silhouette of a person. Despite our fear and awe, we also sensed an overwhelming sensation of love coming from this figure.

Suddenly, it appeared as if it were reaching out to us, and in its hands were what appeared to be two garment boxes. Fascinatingly, the only human feature that could be detected in the glowing silhouette was its hands, with each appearing to have a hole in the palm. Taken aback at first, we eventually reached out and took the boxes, opened them up and found that each contained a sparkling white robe within it! As crazy as it sounds, the only way to describe them is that they were whiter than white, almost glowing. We instinctively took off our filthy traveling clothes and put on the robes, which felt softer than anything I had ever worn before. Looking at Gabriella, I could see tears of joy running down her face along with a beaming smile. As we looked around us, everyone present on the cloud was dressed in an identical white robe.

Then a most peculiar thing occurred. The figure before us moved its right hand and pointed off in the distance. As I looked to where it was pointing, I could see a most mind-boggling sight. Stacked as far as the eye could see were millions and millions of boxes, just like the ones Gabriella and I had received. It was an amazing sight. I couldn't even fathom the existence of such a horde of any item. At first I was puzzled at what I was looking at, but then I noticed something that made things begin to make sense to me. When the figure before us pointed, I noticed its head begin to hang down, as if in sadness. It was then that it all clicked. The boxes I was looking at each contained a robe just like the one I had received. I thought back to the waterfall and made the connection; each of the boxes had been intended for a specific person. Then I understood why the figure seemed to be sad; the owner of each box had chosen the river rather than the path, thus missing out on their opportunity to spend eternity in heaven as well as receiving their robe.

Looking at the total number of boxes stacked put things in a whole new perspective. I began to comprehend just how many people had missed their opportunity to be where we were, and the realization was staggering. I turned to Gabriella and hugged her; she hugged me in return. I closed my eyes as I held her, trying to hold back tears of my own.

Suddenly, the music that filled the air around us came to an abrupt stop, and the light that was detectable through closed eyes seemed to fade. In place of the music was what sounded like…snarling? Hesitantly, as I reopened my eyes, I received the shock of my life. We were no longer in heaven. The angels, the music, the throne, the clouds and the figure before us were all gone; I was still clutching Gabriella, but we were in our regular bed. The snarling sound I heard was, in *fact, Gabriella snoring. Looking down, I could see that the white robes had ceased to exist; in their place were our bedclothes.*

With my looking about, Gabriella abruptly woke up and began looking at me with a half-asleep, confused look on her face. "What?" she said, rather frustrated.

Confused myself and a little heartbroken, I replied, "Nothing. Go back to sleep."

As I lay my head back down, she plopped hers down as well and said in an agitated tone, "You go back to sleep! And stop snoring!"

I knew far too well at that point that it had only been a dream, because there could definitely not be any snoring in heaven.

ᘐ

The analogy of the path and the river should be obvious. The path represents the journey that we Christians take. The river represents the world. The contrast between the two demonstrates the spiritual difference between Christians and non-Christians. Those in the world symbolically are similar to those in the river. Because they do not walk in the Spirit, they choose to take the wide path of the world and its easy ways. This easy way is signified by the fact that they simply rest on the waters and let the currents direct their course.

As mentioned in the story, even though they are free from having to walk, they are held captive by the course of the river and its currents. This represents those who follow the ways of the world. Without the direction of the Holy Spirit, they are pulled along by their fleshly desires, their addictions, their temporary wants, their quest for instant gratification and their carnal hungers, much in the same way as a person floating on a raft in a river. (See **Proverbs 16:25.**) The people in the river scoff at those on the path, just as those in the world scoff at true Christians who take the moral high ground on issues, choosing the right way rather than the easy way. Often this is done because those on the river know that they should be on the path but lack the discipline to do so. (See **Proverbs 14:8.**)

The description of the river flowing faster represents the increasing pull of sin as a person spends longer and longer periods in the world. As mentioned in the story, some begin to realize what is happening and make a dash for the shore. These people represent those who are unsaved and respond to the calling of the Holy Spirit. They leave the world and exchange their floating days for walking the narrow road. But as also mentioned, some attempt to make it to shore but are unable to beat the current and crash into rocks, sealing their doom. This represents those who hear the truth and have an initial desire to pursue it but ultimately fail to do so through lack of discipline, hardness of heart, addiction or any other earthly stronghold that holds them hostage to their sin. (See *Philippians 3:18–19.*)

The people along the shore represent Christians providing opportunities to reach those in the river, or in the world. As in the story, some respond to the invitation, yet most do not. The description of the shoreline transforming into a high wall represents the reality of our modern culture as we draw closer and closer to the end times. As mentioned in the Bible, the closer we come to the end, the harder it will be for those living in those years. The people using their *Guide Book*s, transforming them into ropes and rope ladders, represent Christians using scripture to save the lost. Symbolically, our bringing the lost to salvation is similar to someone offering a rope to those drowning in the river. We pull them out of the world and offer them solid ground on which to walk. (See *Mark 16:15–16.*)

The waterfall clearly represents death, not death to all but to those in the world who have never accepted Jesus's offer of salvation. It is the perfect analogy of an unsaved person facing death. They are being steadily drawn to an untimely demise, each day coming closer and closer to their doom. As easy as floating on the river is, people on the river must constantly live with the uncertainty of what lies ahead for them. They give up their free will in exchange for a comfortable ride down the river, but the end is the same for all of them, a plummeting death. In contrast, we see the person walking the path. They endure a physical hardship not known to the people on the river, but with each step, they come closer to their eternal reward. So what we find in place is an interesting contrast: on one hand, a life of ease and pleasure resulting in eternal destruction and, on the other, a life of toil and hardship resulting in eternal reward. (See *Matthew 10:28.*)

The bend in the river just prior to the waterfall signifies the blindness of the unsaved to their impending doom. As the waters pick up speed, this signifies the approaching of the waterfall. But with their fixation on themselves and their immediate satisfaction, the river people do not concern themselves with what lies around the bend just out of sight. Only when the unsaved travel around the bend and find themselves face-to-face with their own mortality do they finally begin to think in terms of an eternal perspective. But usually by this time, it is too late. The strong currents of the waterfall have these people trapped in their clutches. Occasionally, a few are fortunate and catch a last-minute rope cast from the hillsides, but this is a rarity. This would be representative of the deathbed scenario, a last-minute cry out to God and receiving salvation as the thief on the cross did. But living life with this exit plan in mind is a risky scenario, just as counting on grasping a dangling rope while headed for a waterfall would be. (See *2 Corinthians 4:3–4.*)

As Gabriella and Garrett discovered, waiting at the end of the narrow road for every born-again believer is heaven, eternity with our Creator and Lord. The road may seem to be long and hard at times and may test us to our core, and the sight of the river may be tempting to us in our times of weakness, but for those who endure this difficult journey, just around the bend past the waterfall sits the reward that we have long awaited. (See *1 Corinthians 2:9.*)

Day 1,492

Earlier this evening, as Gabriella and I sat by the campfire carrying on a conversation, I noticed that the flames were slowly dying down. Moving over to the fire, I tried to figure out why this was happening. Looking at it, I realized that some of the larger logs had shifted place and fallen directly over the coals. Without the space that had existed earlier between the logs, it seemed that the flames were being choked out. I grabbed a long, sturdy stick and began moving the logs around, creating an opening between them and the coals. Within seconds, as a slight breeze worked its way over it, a giant flame burst forth, reigniting the wood and sending fire blazing high above it.

Out of curiosity, I opened the Guide Book to see if campfires fell under its expertise. Surprisingly, I found that they were addressed in there. It mentioned that three key components are needed to produce fire: oxygen, heat and fuel. In the absence of even one of the three, fire cannot be produced. I began looking at our campfire and thinking about how this information applied to it. There was plenty of wood in the fire, thus meeting the fuel demand. There was heat because the coals were more than hot enough below the wood. But then there was the oxygen component, and that was lacking. When the wood collapsed and smothered the coals, it prevented any oxygen from moving within it, thus choking out the flames. The minute I lifted the logs from the coals and a breeze blew over it, a flame erupted forth.

As I sat watching the fire dance, an analogy sprang to mind. I began to think about how we as Christians are similar to a fire. Just like a fire, we also need the same three components to produce a spiritual flame within us.

Representative of the oxygen would be the Holy Spirit. Just as the fire before me was smothered out when its oxygen was cut off, so too is our spiritual flame extinguished when we block out the influence of the Holy Spirit. We may have fuel and a heat source, but without the flowing of the Holy Spirit, the fire goes cold.

Representative of the fuel would be the word of God. The individual scriptures would be similar to kindling, the chapters like large sticks and the books of the Guide Book *like logs. With these, we are given a fuel source from which to supply our fire. But without them, the oxygen and the heat source become useless, as they have nothing to feed them.*

Finally, representative of the heat source would be our passion or zeal for the Lord. As the Holy Spirit convicts us and empowers us, we begin to have a burning passion to do the will of God and share His word to those around us. Without the heat of our zeal, the oxygen and fuel remain cold, producing no flame in our spiritual lives.

As I prepared the campfire earlier, I began by stacking some kindling in the center and then taking some larger sticks and leaning them in a conical pattern around the kindling, making sure to leave some space in between the sticks and the kindling. I then lit a match and applied it to the kindling, starting a chain reaction that began by the fire consuming the small tinder. This in return, as it gained momentum, began to ignite the larger sticks surrounding it. As a breeze would blow through the structure, the flames would gain momentum and begin burning hotter and faster. Larger logs were then applied to the burning pile, with those too becoming ignited eventually as the smaller pieces were consumed; the result, a campfire.

Looking back at the analogy, the setting up of the kindling would represent the reading of God's word. As a new Christian, we begin with a basic knowledge of the scripture. The match would represent the igniting of our zeal. As the flame of the match meets the dry kindling, we have fire. Slowly, we begin to add larger and larger sticks to the existing flames. This represents our gaining spiritual knowledge through maturity over time. The more we read of God's word, the more the Holy

Spirit moves through our lives. The more the Holy Spirit moves through our lives, the higher our passion for Christ grows. The more our passion for Christ grows, the more we want to read His word. The cycle just continues until one of the three components is removed.

The benefits of a campfire are numerous. First, it provides a source of light. This becomes imperative when in the woods at night. Similarly, we Christians live in a world of darkness brought about by sin. As we build up our spiritual campfire, the light produced not only helps us; it sheds light to others in the darkness as well. In addition to light, the fire produces heat. When night falls in the woods, the surrounding temperature falls as well. This correlates to the spiritual coldness found in the world, as it is generally devoid of God's love. When we maintain our spiritual campfire, the warmth of it often draws the lost to it just as the light does. The fire also becomes useful for cooking food and boiling water when in the woods. Oftentimes, water found in the wild contains harmful bacteria that, if consumed, can produce dire consequences. But when the water is boiled over a fire, the water becomes healthy to drink, as the contaminants are killed. Similarly, when raw meat is exposed to the flames, the food becomes cooked and safe to eat. The same could be said of our lives as Christians. We live in the world, but we are called to not follow the world. As we take the things of our daily lives and place them over the spiritual fire within us, the power of God transforms those things and purifies them, making them spiritually safe for us. By this, I am referring to the power of the Holy Spirit to provide spiritual discernment within us for the things of the world.

Just as with a campfire, we as Christians must maintain the integrity of our spiritual fire within us. The following are some ways in which our spiritual fire can become compromised:

*   *Lack of oxygen, representative of hindering the Holy Spirit (See **1 Thessalonians 5:19.**)*
*   *Lack of fuel, representative of neglecting the word of God (See **Colossians 3:16.**)*
*   *Lack of heat, representative of losing our zeal and passion for serving God (See **Romans 12:11.**)*

* *Wet fuel, representative of allowing the things of the world to flood our interpretation of scripture* (See **1 John 2:15.**)
* *High humidity, representative of imbalanced priorities dampening the movement of the Holy Spirit in our lives* (See **Matthew 6:21.**)
* *Wind, representative of gossip, godless chatter, slandering and senseless debates that blow out our attempts to ignite our zeal, or our "spiritual match"* (See **2 Timothy 2:23.**)
* *Improper fuel, representative of studying false doctrine rather than the word of God, the equivalent of burning plastic or tires rather than wood, resulting in exposure to toxic smoke* (See **2 Peter 2:1–2.**)

Day 1,591

Gabriella and I were taught a valuable lesson today in regards to being obedient to the voice of God. This morning found us walking the path as usual, the weather exceptionally good. As we came around a bend in the road, we looked and saw a spectacular sight lying before us. Spreading out for roughly a mile was a flower-filled field within a small valley with the most diverse assortment of color I had ever seen in one place. A gentle breeze made the tall grass dance about, sending waves of green rolling over the land. It was truly one of the most beautiful sights I had ever seen. It was one of those scenes you see portrayed in movies, where the man and the woman run toward each other; dance and skip with huge, silly grins on their faces; finally meet in the center and embrace; hold each other's hands and spin; and then walk away hand in hand. The path leading to the field ran down a gentle slope before us and then followed a straight level course directly through the grassy land. To our left, a rough partially grown up path ran up the hill that created a half circle around the field, rejoining the straight path on the other side of the field.

As we stood looking at the scene, I suddenly heard to my left the distinct call of a whippoorwill from a nearby tree. Looking over, I watched it chirping for a time and then turned to begin walking down to the field. Grabbing Gabrielle's hand, I took a step and then found myself being pulled back unexpectedly. Turning around and looking quizzically at her, I saw her staring at the whippoorwill, which bounced off the limb and flew away, following the course of the steeper path. The expression on her face was one of concern. "What are you looking at?" I asked her.

Stoically, her brow still furrowed, she said, "The white dove."

Looking about, I asked, "Where? I don't see it."

She looked at me with a puzzled expression on her face, like I had three heads. "It just flew away. You were looking right at it. How could you not see it?"

Confused, I said, "I saw a brown whippoorwill fly away, but I didn't see a dove."

Her expression remained the same. "Are you blind? The bird wasn't brown; it was snow white. Didn't you hear it cooing?"

"No," I answered, "in fact it was making the classic whippoorwill cry, you know, 'Whip-poor-will, whip-poor-will!' I don't think a dove makes that kind of call."

Her facial expression slowly transitioned from one of concern to one of frustration. "Are you sure the bird didn't say, 'Cra-zy-still, cra-zy-still!' Because that is what I think you are right now."

Biting my tongue, I didn't respond, mostly because I didn't have a comeback quite as pithy as hers. Then she turned to the left and began up the alternate path. "Where are you going?" I asked.

Begrudgingly stopping, she turned to me. "I told you. I saw the white dove fly up this way, so that is where I intend to go."

"But that way is uphill, and it bypasses the entire field. Why would we go that way? We have a perfectly easy path right before us."

"You can go where you want, but I'm going this way. The dove appeared to me for a reason, and I'm not ignoring it. So are you coming with me or are you going to make me go up here alone?"

By now I was fuming. I had not seen the dove she was speaking of, and I had been looking forward to walking through the beautiful field. But I knew that if I didn't follow her desired course, I would never hear the end of it, and the rest of the day would be a long walk with her. Turning sharply to the left, I stormed up the hill, exaggerating my strides to make my feelings known to her. I stayed ahead of her, marching uphill under protest as I stared down at the beautiful valley to my right.

Eventually we reached the halfway point of the roundabout way, which brought us to an elevated hill overlooking the field. We decided to stop and take a rest because the inclined path made for quite a challenge. Pouting, I sat and watched as a gentle breeze blew through the tall grass and flowers below, wishing we were amid them at this moment. I looked across the field and found the path that we would have been on had we chosen the way I wanted to go. Gabriella sat behind me, not saying anything because she knew I was still frustrated with her. Finally I broke the silence and pointed to the path below. "We could be down there right now, but no, we had to take the high road. What would have been so wrong with taking a nice easy walk through such a beautiful field?"

Perturbed, she said, "I told you. I saw the white dove follow this course, and I feel He was leading us in this direction for a reason."

"I didn't see a dove! The only bird there was a whippoorwill. I think you were seeing things, and now we are doing all this work for no reason." I stared at her, armed and ready to continue the argument between us.

She turned her head in frustration away from me and stared down at the field. I watched her closely, waiting for a rebuttal so that I could return fire upon her. Then, strangely, her countenance began to change from one of bitterness to one of shock. Curious, I turned away from her and looked down to the field where she was staring. A huge knot began to form in my throat, as I looked down in horror to see two bear cubs strolling down the path through the field, followed by a huge mother bear. They were coming from the opposite direction as us and, had we taken the path through the field, would have collided head on with us, most likely resulting in significant injury or death for one or both of us.

As I began to process the reality of what I was seeing, I suddenly realized why Gabriella had seen the white dove. It was drawing us from a destructive path, attempting to keep us safe. Had she caved in to my temper tantrum and ignored the calling of the dove, we would have most certainly paid dearly, possibly with our lives. Then I began to realize why I had not seen the dove as she had. I had already fixed my mind around my personal desires, blinding myself from seeing the warning coming from the dove. If I had been there alone, I would have totally missed the call of the dove. I was so thankful at that point that Gabriella was spiritually disciplined enough to not only hear the call of the dove but to obey its call, even at the cost of angering me and enduring my griping. My anger quickly dissipated, replaced by an overwhelming feeling of guilt and selfish pride. Turning hesitantly to her, I stated, "I am so sorry for questioning you. I should have believed you as soon as you told me what you saw. My mind was fixated on the beauty of the field, and I was simply looking to take the easy way out by not having to climb this steep path."

Looking back at me with understanding, she fought a grin. "We'll store this event away in the file marked 'you owe me big time.' Then, when that day comes, and I make a fool of myself, we'll pull this one out and call it even."

"You have yourself a deal," I gladly said. "How terrible would that have been, walking into that nightmare down there?"

"Not too bad, I think, since I already spent the last hour behind another grumpy bear. I'm getting used to being around them, to be honest."

Rolling my eyes, I took her hand and began the second half of our hike, this part all downhill as we finished circling the field. Just ahead of us, I caught the quickest glimpse of a white dove sailing around the upcoming bend. I simply smiled and shook my head, being thankful for grace and second chances.

♀

The premise of this story hinges on our being in tune to the calling of the Holy Spirit. In this fast-paced world, it's all too easy to become so distracted by work, technology, entertainment and even family that we turn a deaf ear to God. By doing this, not only can we miss out on blessings that He is trying to steer us to, we can miss dire warnings that He is trying to convey to us to protect ourselves and others in our lives. Within my own family there have been amazing examples of this occurring.

The one that has always stuck out most with me occurred to my grand-mother. When my father was only a baby, he was playing with a towel tied to the doorknob as he sat on the floor of the basement, my grandmother ironing next to him. She says that she suddenly heard a voice in her head telling her to grab my father and run. Thinking this rather peculiar, she shrugged it off and continued with her ironing. Then she heard it a second time, but again, she disregarded it, thinking it was just her imagination. Finally, she heard it a third time, this time louder and with more urgency. She said she felt silly doing it, but she immediately set her iron down, grabbed my father and ran for the steps.

No sooner had she reached the steps than the basement door exploded inward and smashed into the refrigerator, followed by a huge wave of water. A flash flood had hit their town without warning, sending a wave of water crashing into houses. As she ran up the steps, the water lapped at her heels and chased her as she went. According to my grandmother, the basement door traveled directly through the spot where my father had been sitting. Had she not picked him up when she did, he would have been killed instantly from the impact of the door. As with the story, God spoke to my grandmother to protect her and my father. Because of her blind obedience to the Holy Spirit's calling, she avoided what would have been a travesty. Throughout her life, she experienced several other instances where God spoke to her and revealed critical information. Curiously, her mother was also blessed with this gift.

Another example began with my grandmother having a recurring dream for many nights over a span of years. She would dream of a brown station wagon, with an impending sense of dread attached to the dream, occurring numerous times over several years. As my father grew up, she forbade him to ride with anyone who drove a brown station wagon because she felt her dreams were given to her as a warning. When my father was eighteen, he purchased a motorcycle. One day as he was driving through an intersection, a vehicle ran a red light, sideswiping him and sending him soaring over a set of power lines. The car that struck him in the intersection was, in fact, a brown station wagon. He suffered multiple injuries, including a broken femur, a fractured pelvis on both sides that resulted in the bones overlapping each other, a smashed kidney, a torn bladder and six vertebrae cracked in two. On receiving news of my father's accident, as she was preparing to head to the hospital, she received a surprising phone call. It was from her mother.

My great-grandparents, who resided in downstate West Virginia during my childhood, were living on a farm in rural Wisconsin at the time. During this time, they did not have a phone. My great-grandmother was known to get a sick feeling anytime something would happen to my father, which I understand seemed to happen quite often. As my grandmother answered the phone, the first words she heard were, "What happened to Robert?" My great-grandmother stated that she had been feeling ill at ease about my father. When my great-grandfather arrived home, she told him about this and said she would like to go to their neighbors' house some distance away and use their phone. They had planned to travel over right after dinner, but before they even sat down to eat, their preacher arrived at their house and said that he felt for some reason that my great-grandmother was under a tremendous burden and wanted to pray with them.

On a Tuesday, as the doctors spoke with my grandmother, they informed her that they planned to operate on my father and wire his bones back together. They anticipated my father being bedridden for eleven weeks, based on the x-rays. In addition to this, they did not expect that my father would be able to walk again for at least eleven months. This news was staggering, especially for a man who had just finished his high-school career as an all-state high-school football player.

On Wednesday, my great-grandparents had eleven churches open their doors at exactly the same time and pray for my father.

On Thursday, my grandmother walked into my father's room and found him out of traction and sitting on the edge of his bed. Panicking, she called for the doctors and demanded to know why he was positioned as he was. They took her into a room and began to show her x-rays that had been taken of him that morning. The ones taken on Tuesday showed his bones displaced from each other. The ones from that morning showed the bones intact and mended. Asking how this could have happened, the doctors informed her that it was through no actions of theirs; they stated that the healing had come from above. The result: rather than walking out of the hospital eleven months later as projected, my father walked out eleven days later, fully healed.

Another example of the Holy Spirit attempting to convey a warning to my father actually occurred before his motorcycle accident. When he was seventeen, he had sustained an injury to his knee while playing high-school football. He was admitted and was scheduled to undergo surgery to the knee.

Prior to his stay, he began receiving shots in order to keep the swelling of his knee down. A week later he went in for his surgery. That evening, as he received another of the shots, he suddenly developed a reaction to it. This resulted in his heart racing, the pounding clearly visible in his chest. Then, he coded, sending the doctors racing to save him. Horrifyingly, rather than seeing a light and a tunnel, he experienced a sensation of falling backward into a black hole. As he fell, all the things that he had done in his life began flashing before his eyes. After experiencing this sensation for a period, he was suddenly brought back by the doctors, who later informed him that they had lost him twice during the ordeal. It was an eye-opening experience for him, demonstrating yet another way that the Holy Spirit speaks to us to prevent us from choosing the wrong paths along our journey on this earth.

Day 1,867

Today, Gabriella and I came to a crucial crossroads on our journey together. For several years now we have chased after the elusive stork in the attempts of gaining a baby. We have consulted many wise and respected travelers throughout our time on the road, following their advice and taking the paths they recommended to accomplish our objective. Each time we would see the stork, we would pursue it diligently, following it down each pathway in hopes of taking hold of it, yet to no avail. It would always seem to be just out of reach, like it was playing some kind of cruel game with us. Then there was the day we almost achieved our heart's desire.

We were strolling down the road chatting to each other when suddenly we spied it resting upon a tree limb. This was the closest we had ever come to it, so we began creeping up to the tree very carefully. As we climbed up toward it, adrenaline surged throughout us at the thought of finally achieving our long-awaited mission. Many days of frustration, confusion and heartache had been spent trying to achieve this goal, but to no avail. Now it was finally within our grasp. Foot by foot we moved, slowly climbing limb by limb. We had reached about fifteen feet above the ground, tied off as we were, and there he sat, about three feet from me. Slowly I reached out and got closer and closer until I was seconds away from finally capturing him. With one quick grab, I had his leg in my grip. He was caught! Looking down at Gabriella, I beamed as I held on to the bird.

But my joy was short-lived, as suddenly the tree limb I was standing on let out a horrendous snap, sending me falling instantly to the ground. In the process of falling, my unfortunate reflex was to let go of the bird and reach out for a limb. I found no limb to grab on to, and I plummeted down to the ground and landed on my back, which knocked the wind out of me. Next followed Gabriella, landing beside me and suffering the same fate because we were tied together. Gasping for breath, I looked up just in time to see the bird spread its wings, launch from the limb and take off down the trail.

As we got up and dusted ourselves off, we tried to capture our breath again, our bodies bruised and hurting from the tumble. We watched the stork fly off toward the horizon, carrying our dreams with it. Eventually, we began walking slowly down the road, having each other to lean on yet feeling alone at the same time. At that time, we began to truly comprehend the fact that we may never catch the stork. We would spy it from time to time off in the distance, and we would pursue it, only to be left with the usual result.

That brings us to the crossroad that we came to today. We began our day as usual, nothing eventful to speak of. Around noontime, we looked ahead of us as we walked and spotted something crossing the trail. As we came closer, we realized it was the stork. Instinctively, we began jogging down the path, trying to get close to it. Drawing near to it, the bird suddenly sprang from the tree and gently flew down the trail. We continued to jog after it, keeping it in view as we went and watching as it perched in another tree. Suddenly, we came to a fork in the path; the way to the right led to the stork, and a second path led to the left. As we approached the split, something made me suddenly stop. Gabriella, realizing that I had stopped, turned and asked what was wrong. I told her I wasn't sure, but that I felt I needed to. We stood there looking ahead, the stork still resting on the limb just a short distance to the right. Thoughts began pouring through my head, and I tried to figure out why I was so hesitant to continue the chase. I felt a strange sense of calm come over me, an inner peace that I had not known for so long. Before I realized it, the words just came out of my mouth. "I'm so tired of running, Gabriella."

She stood there for a second, looking quizzically at me; then her features transitioned, as if she understood what I was saying. Walking slowly back toward me, she approached silently, her eyes teary, with a look on her face that reflected a painful agreement. We stood for a time saying nothing, simply looking at the paths. The stork remained on the branch, as if daring us to follow him. Even though part of me wanted to continue the chase, the other part of me began to slowly overpower the temptation, fueled by what I felt was spiritual wisdom asking me to give up the chase. I began to pray for conformation with this decision because it was one of the toughest I would ever make.

Suddenly, as I stood staring at the stork, a second bird flew over my head and darted down the left path, coming to rest in a tree as well. Looking down the path, a warm sensation came over me, as my prayer was answered. For resting in the tree in the opposite path of the stork was the white dove. I had received my answer. Turning to Gabriella, I saw that she, too, was looking at the dove as tears ran down her cheek. She looked back at me with a fractured grin, not saying a word but closing her eyes and nodding in acceptance. I took her hand and slowly walked toward the path to the left. I turned one last time to look at the stork and found that he was looking back at me as well. I can't explain how, but he appeared to know that this was the last time our paths would ever cross. Finally, he lifted from the limb as if carrying a burden, slowly spreading his wings and gliding down the path and out of view.

I turned back to Gabriella, still holding her hand, and began to walk with her down the left path. I experienced mixed emotions, a feeling of sadness mingled with a feeling of a burden being lifted from me. Then I had a significant epiphany revealed to me. I realized for the first time that for years I had followed the stork blindly down every path, never thinking to look and see if the white dove was following him as well. I had just assumed that capturing the elusive stork was God's will, never taking the time to look for confirmation. Then I began to question myself, wondering how many wrong turns I had taken in my pursuit of the wrong white bird. The stork in itself was not bad. It was just that his path was not my path or Gabriella's path. And until this point and time, I had never fully contemplated that possibility. I realized that even something inherently good could hinder my walk with God if I put it before Him. As we began our walk down this new path, I felt closer to God than I ever had before. I do not completely understand the course He has laid out for me, but I trust that He will not lead me astray. I squeezed Gabriella's hand a little tighter and took a deep breath. We were now in uncharted territory, a land devoid of storks.

This analogy is incredibly difficult and painful to write, as it directly correlates to the personal experience my wife and I lived through while trying to have a child. When I met my wife, I learned that she had a seven-year-old son. This was not an issue for me because I had always planned to have children anyways. Throughout our marriage, the relationship between my son and me transitioned fairly well, better than I expected, to be honest, considering I was not his biological father. Shortly after we married, my wife and I began trying to have children. Despite much prayer, several years went by without success, and we began to become a little discouraged. We went to a doctor who put her on fertility medication. Another year passed without any progress. The doctor took her off the medication and considered what course of action to take next.

One day, Kim came to me with something I was beginning to think I would never see: a positive pregnancy test! We were elated and told friends and family; they, too, celebrated, knowing how long we had tried to achieve this goal. But our celebration was short-lived, as with her first ultrasound, the doctor detected a problem. By eight weeks, Kim had lost the baby. The only way I can describe the feeling of such an experience is to imagine somebody catching you off guard and punching you in the gut. It takes the wind out of you, leaving you pained and discombobulated. This is what the falling out of the tree section of the story refers to. It took quite a while to work through the hurt of such an experience, bringing to my mind a Job-like scenario. As a Christian, I believe that I was able to recover somewhat easier than a non-Christian would because I had God to put my trust in, but that is not to say that I did not go through the grieving stages like anyone else would. In the many years that have passed since, we have finally come to accept that having children was not in God's plan for us.

It is a difficult pill to swallow, as we were not seeking materialistic or selfish gains from our prayers to God. But what I had come to realize, as stated earlier, is that just because something is not wrong to ask for does not mean that it falls within God's will for our lives. We may never fully understand God's reasoning for such a thing, but we are called to respect His decisions and trust fully in Him. One day when we get to heaven, we will have the answers revealed to us, allowing us to see how and why certain struggles in our lives were used by God to accomplish His perfect plan. As much as I look forward to one day having such wisdom imparted to me, it doesn't compare to the anticipation I have for the day when I get to meet the child who would have been known on earth as Garrett or Gabriella, our unborn child currently residing in heaven.

Day 2,011

I'm journaling as I sit under the noon sun, much earlier than I usually do, due to the fact that Gabriella is feeling under the weather; thus, we halted our journey for the day. As I write, she is resting under the shade of a large oak tree, enjoying a midday nap. She has complained off and on for several weeks of feeling rather lethargic, as well as experiencing stomach cramps. Usually they have not impacted our journey too much because she would just press on through the symptoms. But today, the symptoms got the best of her, forcing her to take a break. I told her earlier today about a man not too far away from where we are that has a significant amount of medical training. We could definitely reach him by tomorrow, as long as she is feeling better. She tried arguing with me, but I finally overcame her protests and convinced her to follow my advice. So tomorrow we will make a trip to see him to try to learn what is causing her condition. I'm sure all will be fine, probably nothing more than a stomach bug running its course.

Day 2,012

The words I am writing at this time come from a heavy pen. As I stated yesterday, Gabriella and I made it to the medical man that I spoke of. We sat down and began describing her symptoms to him. I was expecting that he would listen to her and then give her some kind of medicinal concoction or diet recommendation in order to alleviate the symptoms. This did not happen. In fact, his face became drawn, his brows furrowed as he sat quietly for quite some time, deep in thought. Watching his countenance fall, my mood quickly began to take a more concerned tone. Looking at Gabriella, I realized that she was reading his face as well. He finally stood, walked over to her and asked her to lie down on a nearby cot. After lying down, he began a physical examination of her, covering her from head to toe. Then he told her that he was going to draw some blood from her and test it in order to pinpoint the true cause of her ailment. Taking the blood, he walked into a separate room and told us to wait.

The moments began to crawl, each second seeming to take an hour. Looking over at her, I could see the stress in her face. I took her hand, attempting to calm her fears but doing a poor job of it for myself. After what seemed like years, he finally returned from the other room, a grim look upon his face. As soon as Gabriella saw his expression, she burst into tears, not knowing what he was going to say but knowing that whatever it was, it could not be good. Sitting down and facing us, he reached out, grabbed her hand and looked her in the eyes. Through an attempt to *contain her sobbing, she managed to choke out the question, "Do you know what it is?" Without saying a word, he closed his eyes and nodded. Another short burst of sobbing followed, and then she asked the million-dollar question: "What is it?"*

With one simple word, he rerouted the paths we would take from that day forward, changing the course of our lives forever. The weight of the word, could it be measured, would be paralleled to a massive boulder. As he opened his mouth, the word shot forth with the force of an archer's arrow piercing the heart. "Cancer," he said his stare unflinching.

Time suddenly seemed to stand still, and a deafening silence filled the room, as no one wanted to be the next to speak. The silence was finally broken as a whimper escaped Gabriella's attempts to restrain it. I turned to look at her and saw her fighting back tears. Reaching out and embracing her, she began sobbing into my shoulder, no longer trying to hold the emotions back. I, on the other hand, rather than becoming emotional, fell into a kind of shock, actually becoming numb upon hearing the dire news. This enabled me to comfort Gabriella without falling apart at the same time. After many tears, she finally calmed down enough for me to ask what the next step was.

"She must receive surgery, immediately," he said. "The cancer is pretty significant, and I will not be able to tell how far along it is until I go in, so the sooner the better. Gabriella, I'm going to give you some medication to help you relax tonight, because I want to see you first thing in the morning as rested as possible. You will need your rest, as the surgery is going to be a very serious one. I'm not going to lie to you. There is a chance that the cancer may be too far advanced for the surgery to work. But one thing is clear, without the surgery, you will have no chance at all. Even if the surgery is a success, you will have a long, hard road ahead of you, but with the right attitude, the right amount of determination and God's grace, you can survive this. I wish I had better news for you, but these are the cold, hard facts."

Gabriella quickly sobered up, the full realization of the information starting to process through her mind. A look of resolve developed on her face, and she merely nodded in approval, saying only, "I'm ready."

This segment of the story is an actual analogy of the experience my wife Kim and I lived through. On December 9, 2011, Kim was informed by her gynecologist that a previous biopsy of a mass on her uterus was malignant. The initial belief was that she had uterine cancer. She was referred to an oncologist, which we saw Monday, December 19. As we sat in the doctor's office, he walked in and informed us that she did not have uterine cancer; she in fact had ovarian cancer. The news hit us like a sledgehammer. We were not cancer experts, but everything we had ever heard about ovarian cancer was terrifying. He told us that the surgery would take place right away. After making a quick call, he informed us that he scheduled it for Friday, December 23. The stage of the cancer could not be determined until he was able to go in and assess the situation. We were sent home to prepare for a major surgery, scheduled to take place two days before Christmas. Needless to say, we were completely caught off guard and totally blindsided by such an occurrence. Christmas came early that year, as we and our son opened presents on the evening of Tuesday, December 20. It was a bittersweet holiday, as we had so much uncertainty about what the future held in store for us. We couldn't escape the thought that this might be our last Christmas together. It's amazing how one's view of the world changes when facing eternity.

Day 2,014

Last night was one of the longest nights of my life. As we talked throughout the evening, Gabriella's emotions traveled upon a rollercoaster of ups and downs, going from despair to optimism, from optimism to fear, from fear to hope, from hope to discouragement and finally from discouragement to acceptance. The medication was a blessing, putting her to sleep within a short time and allowing her to obtain some fashion of rest for today's procedure. In some ways, I envied her, as I did not have the fortune of a restful sleep. I spent most of the night talking with God, praying, pleading, crying out, bargaining, seeking His will, trying to find comfort within the midst of a storm. I know without a shadow of a doubt that He has the power to heal any illness, but my fear rested in the possibility that it may not be His will to heal her. With this thought, I asked Him to give me strength to accept His will, as knowing it and understanding it are two completely separate things.

Now as I sit waiting for the surgery to end, I have to trust that God has everything under control, from the skill and technique of the medical man to Gabriella's physical well-being. It is a strange and uncomfortable place I find myself in, being left totally dependent on God's grace and will. Yet I know that I am not the first nor will I be the last spouse to find myself in such a crisis. And I know that Gabriella is also not the first nor will she be the last person to suffer through a terrible disease. But she is the first one in my life to do so, and she also happens to be my wife. That does not make her better or more deserving than anyone else who has ever suffered, but it does make the impact personal for me. She is not just another name or statistic; she is my other half.

⅌

After receiving the news of cancer, I didn't burst into tears or have a breakdown, I initially responded with shock, becoming numb inside. This tends to be my normal reaction when facing difficult situations. I don't tend to be an overly emotional person as far as openly expressing my emotions. In fact, to date, I don't believe Kim has ever seen me cry. I don't say that to brag or tout it as a good thing; it's just not in my nature to express that type of emotion publically. Given the struggle she was facing with the surgery, I felt obligated to be strong for her as her world was falling apart. Breaking down in front of her seemed to me a selfish act, as I didn't want to put the extra burden on her while she was trying to cope with her own grief.

I was able to keep things bottled up for a couple of days, but then a couple of nights before her surgery, I was no longer able to hold back the flood; the dam finally broke. Mentally, as a Christian, I knew that God had everything under control. I knew the Bible verses, I knew the stories where God had miraculously intervened in people's lives, I knew His power to heal, I had all the head knowledge, in fact, I was able to recall using this same information when dealing with others during times of crisis in their lives. They were such convenient tools to use, allowing me to feel like I did my duty as a Christian by providing words of scripture or spiritual insight to a hurting person, then walking away as if that solved all of their problems.

But what I didn't realize until that very night was that I had been avoiding any emotional interaction with others. The very same information I had used in the past now brought me no comfort. Mentally, I knew the facts, but they didn't help me emotionally. If someone had walked up to me that night and gave me the same advice I had given in the past, I would have responded negatively to them. The intention may have been honorable, but without realizing it I was not demonstrating true love to them. True love demands vulnerability on the part of the giver, which means not just understanding mentally what another is going through but also sharing his or her hurt with the person. As an emotionally challenged man, I did not find doing this easy.

Late that night, as Kim slept, I crossed the line from mentally understanding God to emotionally understanding God. Knowing that God knew my pain wasn't enough, I needed God to bring me comfort. For the first time in a very long time, I dropped my wall of defense and came to God as a scared and tearful child. I threw myself at His feet and pleaded for mercy. I didn't want facts, I wanted comfort. The realization of the possible outcome with her cancer sent waves of terror through me. I started envisioning life without her, and it seemed more than I could bear. Bargaining, begging, pleading and asking for His grace, I emotionally broke down in my living room. Never in my life had I ever been placed in such a circumstance. The feeling of not having control of the factors affecting my life was more than I could bear.

Amid my turmoil, an epiphany blossomed. It suddenly dawned on me that I had been working with a limited view of what it meant to be Christlike. If I were to emulate Christ, I asked myself, "How did He respond to others when they were hurting?" That is when I remembered the story of Lazarus. As the story goes, Lazarus was on his deathbed and his sisters, Mary and Martha, sent word for Jesus to come and heal him. Jesus was very close to the two women and their brother. Rather than hurry to his side, Jesus did not reach Lazarus until he had been dead in the tomb for four days. As expected, his sisters were grief stricken over the loss of their brother. When Mary reached Jesus, she fell at His feet and began weeping and saying that if He had been there, her brother would not be dead. What happened next is common knowledge. Jesus raised Lazarus from the dead. But what struck me after my own experience was what Jesus did between the time that Mary lay at His feet crying and the time He brought Lazarus back to life (*John 11:35*). *Jesus wept.*

I had read that verse numerous times in the past, but it never hit home to me until that night. Jesus knew even before He reached the two sisters that He was going to raise Lazarus from the dead. When He saw Mary crying, I always wondered why His response wasn't something more along the line of, "Why are you crying? In a couple of seconds, he is going to be living again!" In my prior level of emotional sensitivity, that would have been a suitable response from my point of view. But Jesus demonstrates true love by the fact that when He saw her crying, *"He was deeply moved in spirit and troubled,"* according to the Bible. Then the following verse states that He wept. These two words hit me like a ton of bricks. Jesus not only arrived on the scene and performed a miracle, He took the time to share in Mary's and Martha's hurting. He didn't just throw verses at them or shake His head over their lack of understanding, He cried with them. This is what true love looks like. And that night, I understood that truly for the first time.

If someone had been with me that night at three in the morning, I wouldn't have wanted them to give me opinions or facts, I would have wanted them to cry with me and share my pain. That would have meant more than anything they could have said. But even though I was physically alone that night, as I cried out, I was in fact crying at the feet of Jesus just as Mary had done. And even though I could not see it, He was weeping with me, sharing in my pain and my hurt. He wasn't just God observing one of His believers; He was a father experiencing the pain of a hurting child. By the middle of the night, I had finally succumbed to exhaustion and fell asleep, thankfully, because I had to get up early the next morning for work.

The following day was long, as I was both mentally and physically exhausted. As I drove home after work, a very peculiar thing happened. On a stretch of highway that is usually extremely busy, I found myself driving alone without another car in sight before me. I came to a stretch where, in the distance, I could see a car pulled off to the side of the road. In my entire life, I have never pulled over to help someone broken down. One reason for this is the fact that I am one of the most mechanically un-inclined people in the world. Short of changing a tire, changing the oil or jumping a battery, I don't know the first thing about cars. The second reason for this is the unfortunate fact that I have heard too many horror stories about good Samaritans being robbed or injured when trying to help supposed stranded motorists.

So as I drew near to this vehicle, I had no intention of pulling over. But as I drew closer, I noticed the motorist was a young woman appearing to be in her twenties. She was practically standing in the roadway waving her arms urgently. For some reason, this time was different. As I pulled over to the side, still with no other cars driving by, I asked her what was wrong. She stated she needed help with her tire and asked if I had a jack. Still hesitant, I parked my car and walked over to hers as she began sobbing. When I looked at her tire, I found that it was not flat. The lug nuts to the tire were gone, and the tire was twisted crookedly in place. She began to tell me about how she had recently broken up with her boyfriend, resulting in him telling her that he was going to sabotage her car. Without realizing it, she had left her place of work with the lug nuts missing on her back tire. Amazingly, she had somehow reached that point in the road, miles and miles from her work, before the tire came loose and wedged in its current position.

I quickly realized that a jack would be useless, since even if I could loosen the tire and reposition it, she still couldn't drive home without lug nuts to keep it in place. I suggested that she call for a tow truck, but she did not have a cell phone on her. As I pulled out my phone and began looking for local towing companies, she tearfully thanked me for helping her and asked if there was any way she could repay me. Still in a fog from the previous night, I simply replied, "My wife just found out she has cancer. If you want to repay me, I would appreciate your prayers for her."

To my utter surprise, she replied, "What kind of cancer?" After telling her, she informed me that she had been diagnosed with the exact same cancer as a teenager and had beaten it. In addition to this, I also found out that she was a nurse working in the same hospital as my mother-in-law. I was speechless. Before the conversation could go on much further, a police car pulled up behind us, the officer coming out to offer assistance. With him now helping her, I wished her luck, got back into my car and drove away.

As I headed home, I tried to process what had just occurred. In a sense, the day after my all-night prayer session to Him, God showed me that He was listening to me by having a cancer patient in remission flag me down on an empty road during rush hour. I realized that every case was different, and that just because she beat cancer didn't guarantee Kim the same outcome, but it was an affirmation to me that I was not alone in this life-and-death struggle. God did hear my prayer, and He let me know it. He didn't promise me how the outcome would play out, but He showed me that He was aware of my concern, that He had it under control and that I could cast this heavy burden on Him.

By the time I reached home, I was mentally and emotionally a different person. I told Kim about what had happened, and she too found significant comfort in the strange occurrence. Since that event, I've been able to maintain an inner peace throughout this ordeal. That's not to say that I haven't had periods of worry and stress, but they have been manageable, not all-consuming like that night. I have been spiritually stronger and at peace with God and His decisions. For better or worse, I know for a fact that He is in control.

⚓

My pen is shaking as I write, as I can hardly contain my excitement. The surgery was a success! The medical man came out just a couple of minutes ago and informed me that she made it through the procedure. She still has a long way to go, but he was able to remove the majority of the cancer from her. The remaining amount within her will have to be treated over time through medicinal means. There is still no guarantee that the cancer will not return or that she will make a full recovery, but I realize that I must put all my worries and concerns into God's hands now. The road ahead of us is going to be long, but at least we will travel it together for the time being.

⚓

After a three-and-a-half-hour surgery, Kim's surgeon came out and delivered the details of the operation. He stated that they had removed a large amount of ascites, which are basically fluid-containing cancer cells. They removed two large sections of her intestines, half her spleen and her omentum (which is a sheath that covers the organs); they removed tumors from her diaphragm and gave her a complete hysterectomy, all at age forty. The surgeon staged the cancer at stage 3C, almost stage 4. We were amazed that the cancer could have spread to such an extent without any signs or symptoms. Throughout that year, we had done extensive hiking, as that is our favorite pastime. We had even taken a week's vacation to Washington State in September. Now here she was having extensive surgery two days before Christmas.

My work schedule accommodated me being off for the first week, which allowed me to stay overnight at the hospital with her. She was a sad sight during that period, having an IV, a catheter and a nasogastric tube in her nose, along with the abdominal pain from the surgery. Christmas day was a surreal experience, as I never imagined spending it in a hospital room. But in its own special way, it was the greatest Christmas ever, as Kim was given the gift of life from God. The night after Christmas became a little more interesting. As I slept in a chair next to her bed, I was wakened by her at about two o'clock in the morning. She was sitting up in her bed, looking about the room, confused and asking for her mother. As I tried to comfort her, she looked at me as though she did not recognize me. Asking me who I was, I informed her that I was her husband, at which point she argued that I wasn't. She stated that I wasn't her Jimmy and then kept tearfully asking where her mom was, almost like a lost child would. I was completely taken aback. In addition to just waking up and being mentally and physically exhausted from the prior couple of days, I was at a loss. She began asking what she was doing there, and I tried to explain to her what had happened. Then I received a knife to the heart, as she tearfully asked me why I let this happen to her. I was speechless. Fighting back the tears, I continued to try and calm her down. She began reciting the Lord's Prayer aloud, going into her own little world.

Then her tone became a little less friendly. She told me that God was going to punish me for what I had done and that I was in big trouble. The next thing she said became a subject of laughter at a later point, as she informed me that her God was a big God and that He was going to squash me under His foot. I didn't have a response for that one. Then she decided that she was going to get out of bed. As I said before, she had a tube coming out of about every possible place on her body, not to mention fresh sutures all up and down her abdomen. We began a battle of wills, as she kept attempting to swing her legs out of bed and I kept preventing her from doing it. Each time I would restrain her from doing this, she would give me a dirty look and tell me to leave her alone.

Finally, at one point, a nurse came in and assisted me in calming her down. After a short period, she appeared to become drowsy once again and fell back to sleep, much to my relief. Sitting in the chair, I soon drifted back to sleep as well, only to be wakened once again about an hour later. She was frustrated once again, looking for her cell phone. She stated she was going to call her mother to come get her. At this point, it was sometime between three and four in the morning. She would not let up about the phone, so I took it upon myself to go into the bathroom and remove the battery from her phone without her knowing it. As I handed her the phone, she attempted to call and realized that she could not get it to work. I told her that the battery must be dead and that I would charge it for her, which fortunately worked. Once again, she drifted off to sleep, and I soon followed suit.

A short while later I was wakened, this time to see two nurses and a doctor at her bedside. She was still demonstrating her frustration verbally to them, arguing that she needed to get up and that she needed her mother, right now! By this point, I finally gave up on getting any further sleep that night and went to the bathroom to freshen up for the day. Eventually she fell back asleep, this time for quite a while. When she finally woke, her odd demeanor had completely disappeared. She did not remember any of the previous night's events and felt rather silly about them as I recounted them to her.

The following night, she demonstrated similar behavior, trying to get out of bed, becoming agitated, confused, not knowing where she was. Then when the morning would come, she would be back to normal. Finally we were able to find the cause of the behavior, a reaction to one of her medications. As soon as she discontinued it, there were no more incidents. Finally, on the morning of January 1, 2012, she was released from the hospital. After ten days, we were able to start the new year on home turf.

The first week home was difficult for her, as she experienced a lot of pain. Sleep did not come easy, as medication changes took a toll on her. She was scheduled to return to the hospital a week after discharge to have a port surgically placed for the chemotherapy. It was to be a same-day surgery, an in-and-out procedure. As I sat in the waiting room, the surgeon came out and informed me that, because of excessive amount of scar tissue, he was not able to insert the port normally but instead had to reopen her entire original abdominal incision to place the port and remove excess scar tissue. She wasn't coming home that day; she was admitted once again. When she woke up from her surgery and found herself in a hospital room again, I had to explain to her what had happened, which did not make her very happy. She ended up staying for another eight days, much to her disdain. During this time, it was detected that she had thrown a pulmonary embolism, which luckily did not do any damage, as it was caught in time. Finally she was able to come home, but we still had a long road ahead of us.

Day 2,028

It has been two weeks since Gabriella's surgery, and during this time, we have been granted the privilege of staying with the medical man in order for him to observe her. She has proven strong, enduring much pain and many sleepless nights. Now we must begin our journey once again, as he must press on. He has given me a very powerful elixir that I must administer to her over the next several months. It is designed to kill the remaining cancer that is in her. The medication will take a toll on her, leaving her physically weak. We have fashioned a type of dragging cot, which I will use to pull Gabriella along for most of the next several months to give her body the rest it needs to heal. To continue the journey in this fashion, we must alter our course, avoiding any hilly paths due to the weight of the cot. This means keeping to the valleys until her medication regimen is complete. I realize that the road will be rough for the both of us, but we have no other choice. We will just have to trust in God and believe that He will guide our paths. Today, the journey begins.

Day 2,074

It has been two months since Gabriella's surgery, and as suspected, the road has not been an easy one. The first couple of days on the path were the hardest. Travel was slow and not much progress was made each day. Pulling the cot with Gabriella on it was harder than I expected, limiting the amount of ground we covered each day. As the weight of the load would begin to take its toll on me, I would quickly be reminded that I still had the better end of the deal, as her pain was pretty significant. The medication that she has to take each day makes her deathly ill, sapping her strength and leaving her drained and lethargic. She must continue the regimen for three months if she is to have any chance of recovery.

As I stated last time, we are forced to follow the valleys, as I am unable to take any high roads while pulling the cot. This results in us taking a course that we did not initially have planned for our lives. The general direction is the same, but we are left to the mercy of the terrain to dictate our paths, which often means circling large hillsides rather than climbing over them, thus increasing the time needed to make progress. One of the first things I discovered about walking the valleys is that sunlight is a luxury. Often times we are winding our way through deep canyons with steep walls on either side of us. This means that for most of the day, the sun's rays do not reach us, short of the noonday sun. We often travel on cold, dark, shadowy paths that keep us hidden from the beauty of the surroundings and those around us.

Our path rarely crosses the normal paths of those we know, as they usually stick to the higher ground. But an amazing thing began occurring after we started our journey. As we would be in some of the lowest places, feeling alone, we would look up to the hills around us and see friends stepping away from their paths and winding their way down to us, sometimes to bring us a hot meal, sometimes to bring us gifts, sometimes to help me pull the cot for a while, sometimes to simply give us comfort and encouragement. Occasionally the hill would be exceptionally steep, and they would go so far as to repel, using ropes to reach us. This made the journey much easier for us to bear and much less lonely. They could have just continued on their planned courses, but instead, they took time out of their days to come to our level and share in our pain. They demonstrated that they truly understood God's love by living it out with their deeds.

Another thing began happening during our time in the valleys; we began to gain a new perspective on life. As we reflected on our travels prior to her illness, we realized that we took our comfort and ease of travel for granted. We never truly appreciated what a blessing having something as simple as your health was. By doing this, we were actually taking God for granted. It took us losing this luxury before we began thanking God for all the blessings in our life. Even in our current predicament, we began to thank God for giving us another day to walk together. Rather than focusing negatively on the health that Gabriella didn't have, we began focusing positively on the level of health she did have. We didn't let a day go by without realizing that pulling a cot was far better than walking the path alone.

This lead to a renewed maturity in our relationship as well, making our marriage even stronger than we thought possible. In the beginning, she would remind me that I had the option, should I choose, to untie our joined safety rope and climb the hills without her, as I did not have the physical limitations that she had. I realize that she was not encouraging me to do this, but rather testing these previously untested waters to see if I would be the same husband in sickness as I was in health. In response, I informed her time and time again that I had no intention of going anywhere. The immediate reason for our trial may not have been clear to me, but I have no doubt that God is guiding our paths in order to accomplish something greater in our lives. And just as with Gabriella, I know that God wants to see if my love for Him is the same in sickness as it is in health, if He is the same God to me in the valley as He is on the mountaintop. And He is. There is something to be gained in these valleys that cannot be gained on the high peaks. Knowing this is what keeps me pressing on day after day.

⁓

The valley is the perfect analogy for an experience such as cancer. During the trial, it seems that daylight is nonexistent, the warmth of day a distant memory. The journey leaves people feeling like they are trapped with steep walls on either side and no way of escape. Winding their way around mountainous obstacles, their very course is dictated by them. As Kim recovered from her surgery, her body remained weak and tired, having lost twenty pounds. On January 24, she began an aggressive chemotherapy regimen, which consisted of an abdominal chemo and an IV chemo treatment in the same week, followed by a second IV chemo treatment the following week and then a week off. She performed six rounds of chemo in this fashion. After her second round of chemo, she began experiencing the predicted hair loss. Her hair was long and dark, something she always took great pride in. Rather than watch it fall out little by little, she decided to take the plunge and have it shaved. Prior to doing this, we were able to obtain a beautiful wig that very closely resembled her natural hair. This provided some comfort to a difficult transition.

As mentioned in the story, we were blessed to have relatives, church family, friends and coworkers providing a myriad of support to us, including meals, cards, prayers, gifts, phone calls and many other offers of assistance. These people demonstrated God's love by taking time out of their very busy days and "joining us in the valley." This action is modeled after Jesus's own selfless act of leaving heaven, physically joining humankind in our own spiritual valley and walking among us to save us. To them, we are forever in debt.

During the first week of March, she was admitted to the hospital for several days due to an inability to eat stemming from lack of appetite. After coming home, she began to show improvement and slowly began putting weight on again. On May 22, she received her last chemo treatment, at which time she rang the cow bell, a tradition at the facility for last visits. Then on June 11, she began to complain of severe abdominal pain. By evening, we made a trip to the emergency room, at which time she was diagnosed with a bowel obstruction. Once again, she was admitted to the hospital and underwent emergency surgery to remove scar tissue that was blocking off her bowel. A week later, on June 18, she returned home to recuperate from yet another invasive surgery.

After her six rounds of chemotherapy, she was put on a regimen of maintenance chemotherapy, receiving one dose every three weeks. This continued for nearly a year, but then an unfortunate thing was detected. Slowly but steadily, through routine blood tests, her cancer numbers were climbing back up. She received several scans, yet nothing was detectable on them. Finally, by April 2013, the oncologists decided to act, as her numbers had reached a point that could not be ignored. She began her second regimen of true chemotherapy, receiving one treatment a week for three weeks in a row and then taking the fourth week off.

This routine continued for two months, after which time the oncologists unfortunately discovered that the cancer was no longer responding to the chemo drug being used, resulting in a rise in her cancer numbers. The oncologists made a drastic change in plan, starting her on two new, very powerful chemo drugs along with a maintenance chemo drug, all administered on the same day. This would continue once every four weeks for six months, with administration of the maintenance chemo drug every two weeks. After the first session of this new routine, we were elated to discover that her cancer numbers dropped by 209 points! As exciting as this was, we knew there was still a long way to go. By this point, we had learned to go with the flow and trust that God had us where He wanted us to be.

Before the cancer, we had begun plotting out our lives together and making plans for this and making plans for that, but we never truly took into consideration how easily our lives could be turned upside down. We came to realize that all of our strategizing and endeavors were futile and that nothing could be accomplished outside of God's sovereign will. (See *James 4:13–15.*) We came to realize that putting too much emphasis on this life was a quick road to disappointment. (See *Ecclesiastes 2:17.*) But the most important lesson we learned was the value of enduring suffering. (See *Romans 5:3–4.*)

After going through such an ordeal, we can attest to the validity of this scripture. When faced with our period of suffering, we quickly became aware that we were not equipped to handle such a crisis in our own strength. This placed us in a position where we had no one left to turn to except God. Once we turned to God, He used the period of suffering to discipline us as His children. In using the term *discipline*, I do not necessarily refer to the definition meaning to punish, although this type of discipline is sometimes used by God, such as when Samson lost his eyesight. The type of discipline I'm referring to is the kind a coach would apply to an athlete. The purpose of this kind is to push the athlete past his or her comfort zone in order to attain a higher level of readiness or to develop perseverance.

As people develop perseverance through discipline, their priorities begin to parallel those of the One administering the discipline. As their priorities come into line with God's, this begins a transformation of their character, or who they are when no one is looking. This sets the stage for the final transformation. As people's characters become more in line with God, they are able to see their lives and their struggles through a spiritual lens rather than a worldly lens. This spiritual lens brings the focus of their lives and priorities to heavenly aspirations rather than earthly aspirations; the result is hope—hope for a new body in exchange for this ever-aging one; hope for eternal treasures to replace these moth-eaten and rust-covered ones; hope for an end to suffering, initially in their own situation but ultimately for all who suffer; hope for reunion with loved ones who have left this world; but most of all, hope for the coming of their Savior and an eternity praising Him.

Day 2,207

As I write this journal entry, I do so with a heavy heart, as this will be my final journal entry ever. In order for you to understand what I am talking about, I must explain the last several hours and all that has transpired.

Earlier this morning, Gabriella and I were walking down the path, reminiscing about days gone by and having a couple of laughs. As we rounded a bend, I suddenly got the strangest feeling of déjà vu, feeling like I had walked this path before, even though I knew that was impossible. Gabriella, still laughing about the time I had found myself stuck in a tree, decided to sit along the side of the road and take a rest. Looking ahead, I noticed that to the left of our path was a very steep hillside. The hillside and the path curved around the bend, the trees to the right of the path blocking my view.

As I stared at the path, above my head flew a flash of white. It was the dove. I watched as it flew down the path a short distance and landed on a branch. Despite the many times I had seen it, it never ceased to leave me in awe when it would appear. But this time, it did something I had never seen it do before. As it sprang forth from the limb, it landed on the path. I was perplexed. In all my time on this side of the river, I had never once seen it do that. It began hopping down the trail and then paused for a moment, just long enough to look back in my direction as if to see if I was following. Then it continued around the bend and out of sight.

Looking back at Gabriella, I saw that she was still sitting along the side of the road, digging through her backpack. Deciding to further investigate, I began walking down the path to where the dove had last been seen. After going about sixty feet, I reached a point in the bend where I could see the part of the path that had been obscured by the trees. As I looked around the corner, I could see that the path ran a short distance farther and then came to a dead end against the sheer hillside. The feeling came back stronger—déjà vu once again.

Resting at the very end of the path stood the dove, staring at me. For a minute or two, we simply stood staring at each other. I had the feeling that it wanted to tell me something, if it had been able. As I stood looking intently at it, I suddenly felt a strange sensation course through me. As I looked around me, everything began moving. We were in the middle of an earthquake! It became difficult to maintain my balance, as the ground was shaking so hard.

My attention was suddenly drawn back to the path as I heard a scream come from Gabriella. I turned to run back to her, but I was immediately halted as large boulders began raining down from the hillside to my right. Jumping back to avoid being smashed, I landed on the ground and watched as the path between Gabriella and me became completely blocked by an impenetrable wall of rock. Then, on the opposite side of the path, the ground completely gave way, taking with it all trees as well, leaving a large gaping hole in the ground that seemed to have no bottom to it.

It was then that I realized why I had experienced such a feeling of déjà vu; this was exactly how I had last seen Clarence before he passed on. Looking out ahead of me as the dust began to settle, I saw a large void, probably thirty feet across to the other side. To my right was the wall of rock that had come down. Behind me stood the steep hillside, probably one hundred feet high if I had to guess; to my left was the dead end. There was only one major difference now: it wasn't a dead end anymore. During the earthquake, an opening had appeared in the stone wall, appearing dark and foreboding.

The path I stood on was about ten feet wide at its farthest point. As I studied the path running toward the cave opening, I found something fascinating. The white dove remained standing in the exact same place where it had been standing before the earthquake, just as if nothing had even happened. I was dumbfounded.

Looking across the open void, I could see Gabriella standing on the other side staring at me. I could tell she was scared by the look on her face. Panicked, she began yelling over to me, "Garrett! Garrett! Are you all right?"

"Yes!" I replied. "I'm all right. I somehow dodged the landslide, luckily. Are you all right?" I hollered back.

"Yes!" she answered, the sound of her voice obviously indicating that she was shaken.

I watched her as she began assessing the situation, looking at the rockslide, then at the great void between us, realizing that there was no way for me to get to her. In a panic, she called out again, "How are you going to get out from there?"

As she said those words, I began to notice some movement from the edge of my path. Looking to my right, I noticed that the edge of the narrow path on which I stood was slowly crumbling, falling into the bottomless void before me. Looking back up, I saw that Gabriella noticed this as well. Scampering around, I watched as she desperately searched for some means to save me, but ultimately in vain. Looking to my left, my eyes fell upon the dove once again. He sat intently, solemnly, gazing back at me. Then slowly, I watched Him turn to the entrance of the cave, fly up and rest on it, once again facing me.

It was then at that exact moment that my eyes became opened to the reality of the situation before me: I was about to die. Throughout my whole life, I had contemplated this exact scenario, wondering how I would feel and how I would handle it. And now as I stood facing it, strangely enough, I had a peace come over me that I had never expected. A feeling of acceptance and understanding washed over me like an ocean wave. I looked back over to Gabriella, still panic-stricken and completely frantic at this point.

Just then, another large section of the path fell into the dark void, sending me closer to the cave as I avoided falling into the vast hole before me. Once again, Gabriella screamed out, "Garrett! What are we going to do?"

Without saying a word, I simply looked back at her. Through all our days of being married together, we had gained the ability to read each other's body language. In some ways, our body language spoke volumes more than we did verbal. Slowly, I looked to my left again and then back at her. In a sudden flash of realization, her face expressed the dire truth that her mind had just come to understand.

"No! Garrett, no!" she screamed at the top of her lungs through her tears. "Oh God, no!" she cried out. She fell to her knees and wept into her hands. "You can't leave me like this, Garrett! You can't go!"

She continued sobbing profusely, and my heart broke for her. "It's all right, Gabriella. Please don't cry. It's going to be all right." The words were hard for me to utter, as my heart was dying a thousand deaths watching her suffer as she was. At that moment, I was a conflicted man. On one hand, I realized what was about to happen, and strangely I found myself at peace with that reality. But, on the other hand, as I watched my other half writhing in pain across a vast span, I just wanted to sweep her up in my arms, comfort her and make her tears stop. But I knew I couldn't do it. As I stood thinking about it, even if we had been given another fifty years together, at some point and time we would have found ourselves in this exact same situation. One of us would be standing before the entrance of a cave, and one of us would be standing helpless on the other side of the gulf. And even with another fifty years under our belt, it wouldn't be any less painful.

"I can't walk this path alone, Garrett! How am I supposed to go on from here? Please don't leave me alone, Garrett; please don't leave me alone!" She continued to sob out of control.

"Gabriella, I wish we could walk another ten thousand miles together on this earth. I would do so if given the chance. But that's not the course God has planned for us. I thank God that He brought you into my life. I thank God for every minute, every mile and every step we spent together. The truth of the matter is that there would never be enough time for us down here, no matter how long we lived. If I had another year, it would only be that much more difficult for me to say good-bye after it passed.

"I love you, Gabriella, more than you will ever know. And I hate to have to leave you alone on this difficult path. But you will not be alone. God will be with you, and He will protect you every step of the way. And you will find the strength to carry on, and you will continue to grow in the Lord, and you will continue to lead others to Christ. And then that day will come, however the circumstances transpire, and you will find yourself as I am right now. And in that moment, you will walk into that dark cave, and that darkness will be replaced with light. And standing within the light, the first person you will see will be me, waiting for you

with open arms. And we will have new bodies, as we trade in these old and tired ones for eternal ones. And there will be no more tears, no more pain, no more cancer, no more uphill climbs, no more heartache, no more chasing storks and no more death. We will spend eternity together with Jesus, and we will never have to say good-bye to each other again."

Gabriella seemed to process the words I spoke, and the intensity of her crying seemed to subside a little. Looking back at me, she replied, "I love you too," between her heart-wrenching sobs. Then painstakingly, she attempted to muster a smile, although doing so seemed to take every ounce of energy she had. She reached her hand out toward me; I, in turn, did the same.

Once again, a section of the path collapsed into the dark abyss, leaving only a small ledge on which I could stand. Smiling back at her, I said, "My time here's almost up. I'm so sorry to have to leave you this way, but please stay strong for me! And never forget that I'm nuts for you, no jOAK!" This final statement produced a chuckle from her, which was worth more than gold to me. With that, I placed my hand over my heart as I looked at her and then blew her a kiss. Smiling at me, she placed her hand over her heart and blew me a kiss in return. I then turned toward the cave and began walking. Just as I entered the mouth of it, I heard Gabriella scream one last time, "I love you too, Garrett! No jOAK!"

As I now stand at the very edge of the darkness, I prepare to take the final steps into this unknown territory. Yet even though I cannot see what lies just ahead of me, I will put into action the same faith that has carried me all these miles to this very point. I know that God's promises are true and that just past this temporary darkness waits the light of His glory. With a heavy heart, I now take leave of Gabriella and entrust her to God. I have fought the good fight. I have finished the race. I have kept the faith. Now there is in store for me the crown of righteousness, which the Lord, the righteous Judge, will award to me on that day...(2 Timothy 4:7–8).

Day 1

Hello, my name is Gabriella. That name should be familiar to any who have read this journal. I am overcome with grief as I make this first entry, as just yesterday my best friend and husband, Garrett, passed on to glory to be with the Lord. You may ask how I came to obtain his diary. That is a valid question indeed.

The details regarding what transpired were covered by Garrett in is his last entry. As I watched him walk through the cave entrance, the remaining fragment of ledge on which he was standing collapsed and disappeared into the void. Then, just after entering the cave, I noticed the most amazing thing occur. Exploding forth from its mouth was the most brilliant light, which caused me to hold my breath in utter amazement; then, from above the entrance flew a white dove, the same one I had seen quite often on my journeys, and I watched as He flew through the light and into the cave. Then, within seconds, He flew back out, only this time He was carrying something with His feet. It was this journal.

As He came to rest just several feet from me, He laid the book on the ground and stood on it. He stared at me and, as crazy as it sounds, seemed to appear sympathetic for me because He dipped His head and looked at the ground. His presence seemed to bring my crying to a temporary halt, and I felt a sense of peace come over me from Him. Then after several moments, He sprang up and flew over the void and back into the cave. Several seconds after this, the fantastic light began to dim until eventually it was no longer visible. Moments later, a rumbling noise could be heard coming from the cave, followed by an explosion of rock and dust bursting forth from the entrance. Then, all was quiet.

I can remember Garrett telling me about how he had a similar experience with his good friend Clarence as he passed on from this world to join the angels. Now that Garrett has followed him, I don't know how I'm going to make it without him. I feel like someone has just cut off half of my body. Needless to say, sleep did not come easy last night because my crying has nearly been nonstop. When I woke this morning, I prepared to begin the journey once again, only this time alone. Why God would take Garrett when it feels like I need him the most is unclear to me. If I were to simply follow my emotions at this point and time, I would be afraid to see the paths I would choose. But despite this pain and despite the lack of understanding for God's timing, I'm going to choose to count on God to help me finish my course. Looking beyond the emotions and the tears, I know this is the path I must take.

As I pull my Guide Book out of my pack, I bow my head for a quick prayer to God, wiping a falling tear from my cheek. Opening my eyes, I stand and step onto the path. Clutching the Guide Book, I close my eyes once again and then open them to see that the Guide Book has now taken the form of a walking staff. This is what I desperately need at this exact moment: something trustworthy to lean on.

With staff in hand, I take my first steps down the path without Garrett. In a strange way, I feel like he is walking beside me still, which for a moment makes me smile. Looking ahead, I see a bend to the right in the road. Then out of the corner of my eye, I see a flash of white travel around the bend and out of sight, causing me to stop for a moment. It is the white dove, leading the way for me. As I stare ahead, a warm breeze begins to blow, and I become lost in the beauty of the rustling leaves in the trees. Then a strange sensation comes upon me, startling me at first, until I realize what it is. A limb from a tree, blown by the wind, begins to gently pat me on the back, almost as if it is trying to comfort me. I breathe in deep and exhale and then look up toward the sky and simply say, "Thank you."

I begin my journey again with the aid of my staff, one step at a time. As another gentle breeze passes through the trees, I hold out my hand to feel it blow against my skin, and feeling a tear stream down my cheek, I think to myself, **"Weeping may remain for a night, but rejoicing comes in the morning"** (**Psalm 30:5**).

EPILOGUE

... **a**nd thus ends the tale of Garrett. I apologize to those readers who had anticipated a happy ending. Granted, Garrett dying is far from happy, but what I had hoped to achieve by this choice is to remind the reader of the fact that life doesn't always give us a happy ending, at least from our limited worldly perspective.

Just a short time ago while driving alone in my car, I was hit with an epiphany that made a significant impact on me. I then shared it with my wife, and we began discussing it in further detail, allowing us to gain a greater perspective regarding her ongoing battle with cancer. The epiphany was relatively simple and came down to this point: "When did God ever promise us that we would live to see old age?"

I know this question may sound strange at first, but I ask you to really think about this for a second. On one hand, we know for a fact that lives are cut short on a daily basis. Any day of the year, we can turn on the television and hear about babies, children, teens and young adults losing their lives in tragic accidents, horrendous natural disasters or disease-related deaths. We even reach a point where we have become almost desensitized by such news because it occurs so regularly. Yet when we find ourselves, a dear loved one or a close friend facing death's door at an early age, we suddenly fall into a state of shock, often times lashing out at God in anger over the news.

This brings me back to my question: "When were we ever guaranteed to reach old age?" As this revelation occurred to me, I began to realize that I had fallen into the same trap for years as well. This brought me to my next realization, whose truth was even harder hitting: "It is this very way of thinking that robs us of our contentment throughout our lives." Ouch. But honestly think about it. By expecting God to grant us seventy, eighty or ninety years on this earth, we are in fact living with an entitlement mentality. Once again, I have to ask, "Where in the Bible did God ever promise this?" The answer is nowhere.

After much soul-searching, I came to realize that with this faulty attitude, we will never know true contentment in this life or truly love God the way we should. This is because our correct attitude should be this: "Whatever years I have been given up to this point are a gift from God. I am not guaranteed another day beyond this one. If the Lord chooses to take me home before tomorrow comes, then I will praise Him in heaven, but if He sees fit to give me another day here on earth, then I will praise Him from down here until He calls me home." This is how we find true contentment.

Unfortunately, for so many of us, our prayers to God are more like these:

* Why would you allow me to go through this?
* What kind of God are you to take my child away from me?
* How could a loving God take a wife away from her husband and a mother away from her kids at such a young age?
* I'm too young to die!
* There must not be a God since my prayers for a healing have not been answered.

When we look at these statements, we begin to see a distressing pattern unfolding: the fact that our love for God is contingent on what He can do for us rather than who He is and what He has done for us. Just as the bride and groom are asked to vow during their wedding ceremony, "in sickness and in health, for richer or for poorer," we are called to the same oath regarding our relationship with God. Will we cherish Him in health, but not in sickness? Will we love Him when richer, but not when poorer?

If we go through life believing that we are entitled to live to an old age, we will toil away the years God has given us, fretting about what may happen to us. Instead, we should see each and every day as a gift from God, starting with the premise that we do not deserve anything to begin with and then thanking God for whatever time we are given by Him. With this mind-set, we become free from the fear of death and can truly live life the way it was intended. We can learn to love God unconditionally and completely, not contingent on how our life fares or on what He can do for us. When faced with death, we can pray to Him and seek His will, knowing one of two things will result: either He will hear our prayer for healing and answer it, or He will not bring about physical healing as we had hoped, thus leaving us with the knowledge that His will was still done. Either way, He is still God, and He calls the shots.

We are not called to always understand His ways, but we are called to always accept them through faith. We are not called to always like the way events unfold in our lives, but we are called to love God and those around us regardless of what happens. Once we reach this mind-set, we can truly learn to live each day to its fullest, to love God as He deserves to be loved and to accept our fate in humility rather than in selfishness.

At the story's end, we find Gabriella taking over the journal after Garrett's passing. I felt the need to end it this way to emphasize the fact that as one person's story comes to an end, another's is just beginning. As Garrett's story closed, Gabriella's story as a widow walking the narrow road alone began, starting a new chapter in her life. We, as Christians, must face this reality as well, the reality that the one thing we can always count on in this world is change. Sometimes this change is positive, such as with a wedding, a birth, a graduation, a new career, a promotion or even a new ministry. Yet other times the change is negative, such as losing a job, losing a home, falling into financial hardship, facing criminal charges, breaking up a relationship or even what Gabriella faced, the death of a spouse. With all change, we must put our faith in God that He will guide us on the right paths and that He will never give us more than we can handle, even when our mind is telling us otherwise.

So in closing, to the Christian readers, I have to ask—what does your journal look like? How does it read? How did you describe your initial bridge-crossing experience? Who in your journal played the role of Clarence? Have you spent more time off the path than on it? Are there many chapters that mention the white dove leading you? Are you familiar with the *Guide Book*? Do you routinely take advantage of its transformational properties? What are your thoughts as you look across the river to the Southern Lands? Do you ever miss living there? How heavy is your backpack that you carry? Do the hills on this side of the river ever wear you down? Have you any experience with pitfalls as you travel? Are you generally content with the food along the path, or do you find yourself drawn to the food off the path? How many strangers have you encountered along the paths that have helped you during times of need? How many strangers have you been able to help along the path? Which side of the path do you find more difficult to steer away from, the left or the right? Have you had to travel any valleys on your trip? Has anyone close to you ever had a cave experience? Are you prepared for your own cave experience?

And to those who continue to reside in the Southern Lands, I offer an invitation to experience the other side of the river. I know the walking there is easy, and it is heavily occupied with those you are comfortable with, but living there is like living on a floodplain. When the waters begin to rise, they bring to ruin all that is found in their path. Deep within you is a still, small voice, and it is calling you to come to the river. Throw your burdens over the edge and tell God you are ready to walk the narrow path. The walking will be harder, without a doubt, but the payoff that lies at the end of the trail will make it all worth it. Just pray with a humble heart for Jesus to forgive you for your sins and acknowledge Him as your Savior and Lord, vowing to Him that you will live this day forward as His child and you will call Him Father. Then look to the river and find your bridge waiting for you. Cross over it and leave the Southern Lands behind you, never looking back. Take your *Guide Book* in hand and use it as you navigate your journey. Then one day, you will find yourself at your journey's end; you will lay down your staff, relieve yourself of your backpack, trade in your hiking shoes and receive your eternal reward: your narrow road exchanged for streets of gold!

ADDENDUM

After I completed this book in December 2013, Kim bravely continued her fight against the cancer. She worked her way through every chemotherapy regimen that was available, including an experimental one that reached FDA approval earlier than expected. She continued to work full time at her job throughout the first three years, despite constant chemotherapy treatments, surgeries and a daunting commute every day. I constantly tried to get her to stop working or at least decrease her hours out of concern for her health, but she refused to quit. She stated that she was afraid that if she stopped working, she would have too much time on her hands to just sit and dwell on her situation. In hindsight, I guess I kind of understand.

But in November 2014, her health took a turn for the worse, forcing her to stop working at the law firm where she had been employed for twenty-five years. Between November 2014 and May 2015, she underwent two surgeries: one for a bowel obstruction caused by a crowding tumor and one to insert a colostomy bag. Needless to say, she was not happy about the fact that she had to have a colostomy bag, but as with everything else, she accepted it with grace.

By mid-May 2015, it became apparent that the chemotherapy treatments were no longer working and, in fact, were only causing her more pain and decreased quality of life. After speaking with her oncologist, the three of us sadly came to the agreement that she would be placed on hospice. This was a huge step for us both, as we were forced to totally submit to God and trust in His will for her moving forward.

She transferred into a hospice facility for about eight days in order to get her pain under control. She was discharged home the Thursday before Memorial Day weekend. She and I took what we knew would be our last weekend getaway together, staying in a cabin near Gettysburg, Pennsylvania, that we had frequented for years. This trip was also the first time she had reached the point where she needed to use a wheelchair. As I sat next to her on a small beach area surrounding a lake near the cabin, it was the most bittersweet moment of my life. There we sat on a beautiful, sunny day, surrounded by laughing children and people having fun; yet at the same time as I looked at her, I felt like I was watching sand fall through an hourglass, knowing our time together on this earth could be measured in moments.

By the time the weekend ended, she found herself back in the hospice facility for another couple of days in order to get her pain back under control. On May 30, she returned home for thirty-two days and slept in a hospital bed in our living room. During that period, her physical and mental condition deteriorated rapidly, resulting in her sleeping nearly twenty hours a day by the end.

On July 6, around 10:00 p.m., she was readmitted to the hospice facility. I sat next to her bed that evening and spoke with her until she fell asleep. That was the last time she was ever conscious. On July 12, 2016, at 5:14 a.m., she breathed her last breath on this earth and took her first breath in heaven.

There will come a day when I too shall breathe my last breath on this earth, and when that day comes, as I open my eyes and take my first breath in heaven, my prayer is that I will see three people standing before me: Jesus, Kim and my unborn child. And I hope that the three of them are ready to hike, because we'll have a lot to catch up on. But I guess that's what eternity is for.

The
path of
life leads
upward for
the wise to keep
him from going down
to the grave. Proverbs 15:24

KIM & JAMES PATTERSON

KIM AND JAMES ON A HIKING TRAIL

KIM WITH HER FIRST PET

KIM WITH INLAWS, ROBERT AND EVON PATTERSON

KIM WITH SON, JUSTIN

KIM DURING EARLY DAYS OF CHEMOTHERAPY

KIM ON OUR FINAL MEMORIAL DAY WEEKEND TRIP,
1 WEEK INTO HOSPICE

FRIENDS PROVIDING COMFORT FROM OUR CHURCH,
KELLY GOODLIN, CASSIE DIRENZO (PASTOR'S WIFE),
BECKY PROVENZANO

KIM AND JAMES' FINAL PICTURE TOGETHER

ABOUT THE AUTHOR

James Patterson spent his life helping people both through illness and in their walks with Christ. Patterson spent four years as a hospital corpsman in the US Navy before working as a licensed practical nurse for three years. He now works as a physical therapist assistant. Patterson's religious undertakings include serving as a church's teen youth director, an adult Sunday school teacher, and an occasional speaker at churches. He lives in Pennsylvania as a father and widower.

32437555R00151

Made in the USA
Middletown, DE
04 June 2016